Note

The events and conversations memorialized in this book are real and have been largely reconstructed from audio recordings, charging instruments, trial transcripts, police reports, and Charles's personal recollections, all of which were communicated to authorities in his role as an undercover informant. Although not all of the individuals depicted in these accounts were convicted of the misdeeds alleged, dozens received lengthy prison sentences in connection with these investigations, others pled guilty to lesser offenses, a few were acquitted, and some testified against their own.

The names and identifying characteristics of a few individuals depicted in this book, including law enforcement agents who remain undercover, have been changed.

Acknowledgments

This book is dedicated to the men and women in law enforcement, the ATF and the San Bernardino County Sheriff's Department. Special thanks goes to Koz and S.K., you are my heroes. Thank you JD, Gringo, and Bobby, the true stars of Operation Black Diamond. A sincere thank-you also goes out to Carr, Ciccone, Britt Imes, the United States Attorney's Office, and the cover teams of both operations, without whose support these investigations would have surely failed.

And thanks, Roger, for having an open ear to my sordid past. Kerrie, thank you for being such a great writer and a good listener. Last, and most of all, without the love and support of my wife and my Lord Jesus Christ, I would never have made it. Thank you.

—Charles Falco

Special gratitude is extended to the San Bernardino County Sheriff's Department and to those deputies, who shall remain nameless, for your important contributions. Thank you to my editor, Rob Kirkpatrick, for his encouragement and faith in my abilities; to my agent, Jill Marsal, who campaigns tirelessly in my best interest; and to my children, who have always been my only light. A nod goes to my writer friends Kim and Linda, who endured endless pages of fight scenes with humor and grace. And thank you Sergei and all those men and women in law enforcement (and those who work with law enforcement) who, every day, sacrifice their souls to give us all a safer future.

—Kerrie Droban

Maybe there is a beast . . . maybe it's only us.

—William Golding, *Lord of the Flies*

PART I

Operation 22 Green

It is not the strongest of the species that survives,
nor the most intelligent . . .
It is the one that is the most adaptable to change.
—ATTRIBUTED TO CHARLES DARWIN

1

Getting Inside

Police found the man's body spread-eagled facedown in bloody gravel. He looked grizzled, early forties, a tweaker the *Daily Press* later identified as James Gavin (aka Little Jimmy), a man gunned down "in the wrong place at the wrong time." One surviving victim, a woman with lazy eyes and skinny shadows, recounted how two strange men opened fire in her living room. One bullet pierced Little Jimmy's back and penetrated his heart as he fled into the street. Blood spurted from the hole in her own arm and formed dark mosaics on the tile.

Everything happened like flash film, according to the woman, quick hot bursts on a white screen. Sounds amplified, loud bangs, muffled screams, the front door slammed shut like a cough in deep summer. The intended victim had curiously left minutes before the intruders stormed the house. He said he felt "spooked" and set up for a drug rip.

No one guessed the gangland murder had the Vagos' signature.

No one knew anything about the killer.

No one except me, and technically, I didn't exist.

Eight months earlier, November 2003,
Victor Valley Chapter

San Bernardino County, California, with its thinly populated deserts and high mountains, was home to the Vagos Motorcycle Club, an outlaw biker gang composed mostly of ex-military personnel, known as "violent predators" and dubbed the "largest urban terrorist" organization in the United States by San Bernardino County DA Michael A. Ramos. Intelligence sources warned that the Vagos, known as "the Green Nation," posed an "extreme threat" to law enforcement. Members had purportedly infiltrated public safety agencies, operating as moles, securing sworn and nonsworn positions, and working undercover to obstruct and dismantle police investigations.

"Can you get inside?" Detective Samantha Kiles* of the San Bernardino Sheriff's Department (SBSD) challenged me one chilly morning before Thanksgiving 2003. She sat across from me in a room in the department's Criminal Intelligence Division and warmed her hands on her coffee mug. A petite blonde with an affable smile, Kiles disarmed. Trim and fit, she looked every bit a marathon runner. Fiercely determined, she watched me with the steady gaze of a predator sizing up her prey. At six foot three I towered over Kiles even seated. I had no experience with the biker subculture, had never ridden or owned a Harley. Moreover, I didn't look like a biker. When I smuggled narcotics for the Bulgarian mob, I blended in as a businessman, clean-cut, sharply dressed, no tattoos. But I faced a minimum sentence of twenty-two years in prison for conspiracy to distribute

---

* Pseudonym.

and manufacture a hundred pounds of methamphetamine, so it was in my best interest to cooperate. And I had already been betrayed by my so-called "loyal" minions.

"You grew up here." Kiles took a sip. True. And I had already proved my reliability as a confidential informant (CI) for the U.S. Customs and Drug Enforcement Administration (DEA). Newly released from pretrial house arrest, I now had mobility to work more complex cases, not just drug deals or cartels but gangs. I had voiced as much to my "handler" at the DEA, and he had connected me to Kiles.

"I know skinheads," I said and named gangs where I could easily blend in as a Caucasian male. But more than any other group, Kiles advised, the Vagos terrorized Southern California.

My poverty-stricken childhood as a white sore in a Hispanic barrio flashed in my mind's eye. Freedom had one exit and I took it: I became a drug dealer, my life consumed by smuggling large quantities of cocaine from South America to Europe. Money motivated me and I had talent. At the time I justified my activities with my own felonious code of ethics—at least I wasn't a snitch or a child rapist. And as the drug market evolved from cocaine to methamphetamine, I became a cook, earning half a million dollars a year. As I shuffled from room to room in my spacious mansion with its white walls and fancy leather furniture, I struggled to save the illusion even as my addiction ravaged me. Money blew around me, smacked into the ceiling fans, fluttered into the street like confetti. My expensive cars disappeared, repossessed. My wife left. Sweat drenched me. I paced the halls, slammed each door shut, worried that the shadow people might find me. Without electricity, my house became an inferno.

Foil covered my windows, blocking the sunlight. My life continued without definition, hour after hour of endless monotony. I closed my eyes and hoped no one saw me. Pounding at my front door, loud, crisp shouts: *Police. Open up.* I raced to the nearest bathroom. On my knees, hands shaking, I flushed drugs down the toilet. Water splashed onto my cheeks. My head clouded with noise. Black-clad bodies crashed through my bathroom door, their raid jackets announcing in bold white letters LOS ANGELES COUNTY SHERIFF SWAT TEAM. MP5 machine guns targeted my chest and red laser beams framed my heart, yet I felt sudden relief.

Other federal agencies had launched several unsuccessful investigations into the Vagos. Four or five times the size of the Hells Angels in Southern California, the gang's violence was legion, and law enforcement had become increasingly alarmed as the Vagos' penchant for brutal and unprovoked assaults, firearms trafficking, distribution and sale of dangerous narcotics, extortion, loan-sharking, and murder spread from the biker scene into the general population. Like rats, the gang members lived deep in the city's sewers, foul and deadly. But the government had no interest in pest control; they needed extermination.

"What do I have to do?" I folded my arms across my chest, pumped for the assignment. Kiles briefed me on the Vagos' history and growth: The club formed in the 1960s in San Bernardino City and spanned twenty-four chapters in Southern California, Arizona, Hawaii, Nevada, Oregon, and Utah with ten chapters in Mexico (Baja California, Jalisco, and Mexico City). The gang, originally called the Psychos, chose as its insignia Loki, the Norse god of mischief, riding a motorcycle. The gang had no official enemy, no incentive to declare war on rivals like the Hells Angels or Mongols. So-called fence riders, their power derived from their unpredictability and terror campaigns. The club subscribed to the philosophy that it was better to be feared than revered. They were the mafia on wheels but without the pretense of respectability or legitimacy. The Vagos never hid their brutality; they flaunted it. And whether their bravado derived from sheer machismo, raw animal instinct, or jockeying for position in the drug economy, their acts left a staggering body count.

"Get inside, gather intelligence on the gang, identify the club's leaders, purchase drugs from them, and collect as many illegal firearms as you can," Kiles said and recited a list of bars the Vagos frequented within a forty-mile radius of my apartment. Members would not be difficult to spot, she continued. Outlaw biker gangs proudly flew their "cuts," denim or leather sleeveless vests adorned with coded patches that signified a member's criminal and sexual achievements. They *wanted* the public to know they were outlaws, so-called one percenters who represented a minority of motorcycle enthusiasts responsible for committing 99 percent of all crime.*

"Look for officers." Kiles drained her coffee, but when I said I had no clue what officers were, she simplified: "the green patch." Full-patch members wore a bottom rocker that announced CALIFORNIA and a top arc that displayed VAGOS. The triangular center patch reinforced the "V" of Vagos and depicted Loki. The name Vagos, though sounding vaguely Hispanic, actually stemmed from the word "vagabond"—moving around—and its membership was 70 percent white (the leadership, however, was Hispanic).

"After that, you'll have to improvise."

My "pay" for my risk was time, not money. If I didn't want to spend the rest of my life behind bars, I would have to produce results. Twenty-two years tightened like a noose around my neck. I had no plan, no bike, and no government protection. I had never felt more alone.

※

At first, I took Kiles's lead and hung out at armpits like the Motherlode, hoping to eavesdrop on conversations with bikers as I shot pool and drank beer with patrons. The Vagos' drinking cheer, "Viva Los Vagos and butt fuck the rest," thundered through the place. Graffiti on the walls was a strange combination of reality and fantasy, from Grand Theft Auto gaming—a fictional Hispanic street gang in Los Angeles at war with a fictional Grove Street gang. I watched members slam back shots. Stress coursed through me like an electric current. I lived in a dingy apartment thirty miles from the county line with my pit bull, Hercules. Each night I drove in the chilly darkness from my home to the bar, then back home, often stumbling in

---

* The term "one percenter" became a symbol and now appears on the stitched appliqué patches worn by OMG (outlaw motorcycle gang) members.

after three in the morning, dehydrated, hungry, sleep deprived, and anxious about beginning the charade again hours later.

After two weeks of nothing, I formulated a plan.

The Motherlode, situated in Hesperia, smelled rank, a mixture of beer, piss, and puke. Harleys lined the perimeter. Music pulsed like a frantic heartbeat. Dimly lit, hazy from cigarette smoke, cramped with pool tables, a jukebox, and green-tinted walls (in honor of the Vagos), the place buzzed with an undercurrent of violence. Several full-patch Vagos huddled together, beers in hand. The bartender, a rough-looking troll of a woman, slid a cold Bud across the counter toward me with hands that resembled slabs of meat. Green fluorescent lights flickered above the bar. Paraphernalia advertising Vagos' parties (we called them "runs") littered one corner. Conversation punctuated the noise like grunts.

My attention focused on an attractive brunette draped around a worn denim-clad biker who looked like something recovered from the trash. Dressed in black jeans, shirtless, with tattoos covering every inch of his arms and a green swastika tattoo across his protruding belly. A grisly handlebar mustache framed his mouth. A green bandanna covered his tightly cropped hair. The number 22 was displayed prominently on his left arm, for the twenty-second letter of the alphabet: "V" for Vagos. The woman glanced at me, and her expression lacked the haunted, vacant look of an addict. Color washed her cheeks. She had glossy hair and teeth. I wanted to rescue her. *What was she doing with him?*

"That's Vinny's old lady," a tweaker (meth addict) next to me volunteered over the noise. The woman offered a startling contrast. She was clearly a misfit among misfits, strangely protected as the property of Vinny. No random bikers pawed her or passed her around their laps, unlike the tweaker, a waiflike bleached blonde, who fluttered in the shadows like a fly, landing randomly on bikers who cruelly swatted her away. I snapped my fingers at the troll bartender. I had found opportunity: women.

"Can I buy you a beer?"

My heart raced as I approached Vinny's table. He frowned menacingly at me and left the chilly bottle sweating next to him. He resembled a bull—stocky, spun tight, and ready to charge the gate at the first sound of gunfire. Young, maybe midthirties, he had the hardened look of tough leather. I eased the tension between us through flattery, told him I admired the Vagos, especially after one had defended me in jail. Vinny bought the lie and drained his beer. His girlfriend also approved. She smiled at me and introduced me to her pals at the table: Bandit, Cornfed, Spoon, Truck. They formed a green blur of patches. We exchanged few words. Mostly we stared at each other. The woman smiled. I smiled at her. Truck spread over two seats. I struggled for an opening, something that might connect us. It was a little like being at a table with large blow-up dolls.

Then action broke the awkward silence. Vinny scowled and motioned to a patron seated at the bar. The letters "IE" (for Inland Empire in the Riverside–San Bernardino area) were prominent on the back of his neck. Clearly an outsider. Vinny's face flushed and he stood without a word, curled his hand into a fist, and slammed it into the man's temple. The startled gang member fell backward, grabbed his head, stumbled outside with his wife in tow, and climbed into his white Suburban. The sound of tires peeling made my heart race. And then the scene outside played in slow motion as the Suburban plowed through the Vagos' motorcycles, knocking over Vinny's in the process.

The kickstand gouged the asphalt. *Game on.* Just like that, my first meaningful night of Vagos infiltration was over before it even began. As bikes hit the pavement, Vagos emptied the bar like so many roaches and chased the Suburban into the street. Truck puffed to the curb and jotted down the license plate. Sweat poured from his temple.

"We'll find out where he lives." He slipped the note into his pocket. Undeterred by the cops' presence, he added, "We'll take care of business." Instinctively I knew what that meant. The Vagos planned to hunt down the gang member, drag him to a desolate place, and show him the meaning of respect. No exchange of insurance information or beating. The Vagos, if they found their victim, likely intended to stomp the driver, demolish his Suburban, smash the headlights, kick in the car doors, break the windows, and gut the engine. There would be no "victim" and no police report, no prosecution. Fear of retaliation by club members would silence him.

Later, sitting on the edge of my bed, Hercules' head on my knee, I reported the threat to Kiles but knew even as I did that there was little hope her department could stop the certain violence. The victim would become part of the human debris, another nameless figure in a terror war without rules. I realized then that I didn't want just to *report* intelligence to Kiles. I wanted to make a dent, to get inside the Vagos' organization, befriend the leadership, *be* a Vago.

But how did I do that without a bike, protection, or money?

After the incident at the Motherlode, the troll banned the Vagos from her bar. Vinny regrouped at Hustlers, a dive thirty miles from my apartment. The place resembled a sweaty cave. Smoke lingered in the air and cast a ghostly glow over the members' faces as they huddled over beer and discussed their next motorcycle run. Their goal was always to "black out" police surveillance and to party uninhibited in deserted areas. But even serious discussion yielded to distraction, to Terrible, a neo-Nazi lowrider and longtime hang-around for the Victorville Vagos chapter. He personified violence: chiseled features, tattooed .22 on his neck, pierced forehead, and two protruding flesh devil horns. He had already consumed five beers in the span of an hour when he boasted that his brother, Robbery, had shot a man in the face. The confession sputtered out of him like a defective spark. My recorder clicked inside my jockstrap. I had removed the cup and tucked the device into the flap between my legs. My underwear secured it in place, and unless someone grabbed me in the crotch, I was fairly sure I was safe from detection.

Terrible gave me a swift lesson in payback. "A guy owed him money. He fell asleep behind the wheel, wrecked his car, and spent two months in the hospital in back traction." His laugh strangled out of him as if he were unused to talking. I nodded. *Payback.* Terrible twitched beside me, growing increasingly agitated by the sudden lull in the conversation, the irregular gaps. He seemed unaware that his story about his brother began in the middle, as if we had met before, as if I had asked, as if I knew that Terrible once belonged to a family. Lost in a drug fog, his world rushed at him in fragments, bits and pieces of speech, flashes of memory, wide desolate spaces that left him confused and panicked. He struggled to make sense of things that made no sense at all.

Maybe it was tension that propelled him, maybe a need to restore order to his chaos that made him spring without warning from his stool, ball his hands into fists, and move like a wrecking ball through the bar, targeting any patron who looked at him sideways. His improvisational style had a cartoonish flair as he knocked bodies to the floor and slipped in rancid grease and broken glass. Warm beer spilled over my hands. My first test: Would I jump in or back off? Either way, I was screwed. If I punched too hard and hurt someone, I might gain the approval of the Vagos but the reprimand of the sheriff's department. Not that I had a noose, really. I wasn't bound by government strictures, but I had to stay clean, participate carefully, and weigh the pros and cons of being too much a gentleman. The government wanted measured success: arrests, kilos of dope, useful intelligence. But bait, like me, required patience.

I was on the hook, in swift white water, waiting to be eaten.

I swung. A patron rode Terrible's back like a growth, his hands circling Terrible's throat. I punched the man off. He hit the floor, staggered at the impact, caught his breath, and rebounded. I played fair, not mean, conscious that eyes watched me, judged me, and assessed my allegiance. And after several rounds of punch, wait, punch, wait, an invisible bell chimed and the boxing match ended. The back of my hand swelled red and glossy. Blood trickled through slits in my victim's eyes as he crawled away in defeat. For what seemed like several moments, I heard nothing but heavy breathing. Then, like a stampede, full-patch members scrambled to the doors ready to continue the fight in the street.

Terrible swatted me on the back, looking relieved. He snapped his fingers at the bartender, "Beer for the hang-around." Just like that, I had advanced in rank, relegated one level above women and dogs. Like the Mafia, the Vagos and other OMGs had their circle of criminal followers called "prospects" and "hang-arounds," mob associates willing and ready to carry out the gang's dirty work, using the club as a conduit for criminal enterprises. Terrible made me his official chauffeur, grateful that someone else lacked the quintessential biker accessory, a motorcycle.

➤✕

Days later, the Vagos reserved a bar in the middle of nowhere and planned their next run. The destination, always a secret among members to keep cops guessing, had more hype than delivery. In the end, surveillance always knew the Vagos' locations. In fact, most law enforcement made a production of videotaping the gang, snapping their photos, recording intelligence. When we arrived at the bar, a crumbling shell of a structure against a black, empty landscape, the members straddled chairs and stools in the mostly blank space and looked at each other with glazed eyes. No one drank. Cops might be stationed along the stretch of dirt road, hidden in the sandy ditches, waiting to initiate arrests for drunk driving.

General paranoia settled in. And boredom led to recklessness: women.

They flickered in the dark like dying bulbs, some partially nude, others barely dressed. Without rules or limits, men pawed them randomly, pinched a butt cheek, twisted a nipple, and sampled them as if they were snacks on the table. In a corner, Vagos climbed one after the other onto the pool table, straddled another nameless body. I saw legs quivering like slippery white meat. I was in trouble. It was one thing to knock the wind out of some unsuspecting victim, knowing the man might be sore for a few days, might bruise, but otherwise recover. It was another thing entirely to watch the brutalization of women or, worse, to be forced to participate. When the human auction began, I bolted for the bathroom.

The foul-smelling urinals nearly made me gag. The walls, smeared with excrement and marked by graffiti, formed a tiny refuge. I splashed cold water on my face, afraid the bowl might breed bacteria. My reflection in the rusty mirror distorted. Dark circles surrounded my eyes. The emotional drain of being two people had taken its toll: I was no monster, no sociopath, nothing remotely like the Vagos I pretended to admire. Behind my mask of calm, I imploded, suddenly unsure whether I could really do this, become a bona fide member of an outlaw motorcycle gang. With no gun, no backup, and no relief, I had nothing but raw instinct to guide me.

Would that be enough?

I expected they would test me: Would I fight, do drugs, do women, do crimes, kill for the club? When I returned to the table, the members focused on a more pressing goal, red wings: cunnilingus with a menstruating woman. Surrounded by former Marines from both the Victor Valley and Victorville chapters of the Vagos, Rhino, the sergeant at arms, a stocky tank of a man with massive sleeved arms like loaves of bread and gauges in both ears, and Twist, his young sidekick and a hardened sociopath, selected their target. The woman, a club groupie, volunteered to be the prize, probably hoping afterward to advance in rank to "property" of or "old lady" of a full-patch member.

She had a dirty beauty: I'd seen her earlier, flat against the wall, humped by three Vagos in succession. Her expression stoic, eyes closed, not enjoying the degradation but not protesting either. They mounted her like animals, oblivious of others in the bar, to their public environment. They grunted, covered her face with their large claw hands, and relieved themselves as mindlessly as if they were taking a piss. Her tangled blond hair fell across their shoulders.

Red wings had a protocol, at least two full-patch witnesses. Rhino and Lizard volunteered for the job and I tagged along as a guard, not because I wanted to watch three men pin a poor woman's head to the toilet rim and spread her legs wide, but because I needed to know she would be safe. Thin and pale, she looked as if she might blow away. Twist tugged her into the girls' bathroom, a smelly black hole-in-the-wall with two stalls. The toilet bowls, peppered with caked urine, dried feces, and rust streaks, protruded from exposed pipes.

The air stank of rot and stale water. Twist ordered the woman to strip. Lizard, a fifty-five-year-old drug addict, wore a crazed expression that made him look as if he were still lost in an LSD trip. He shut the door in my face. I waited in the sweaty dark listening for jeers, cries, banging. But I heard nothing, as if the room swallowed them, transported them to a dark unspeakable place. When they emerged minutes later, Twist spat several times into his bandanna, wiped his mouth with the back of his hand. Lizard and Rhino slapped him approvingly on the back. The bathroom door creaked closed. I peeked inside, saw a shape curled at the base of the toilet, and heard a faint sniffle.

Lizard lurked in the shadows, watching me, testing me, waiting for me to do something out of character, to react as anyone with a conscience would. But I didn't. Instead I watched the woman struggle, the floor beneath her chest gritty with broken glass. Slivers of beer bottles winked like dark ice in the urinal. She crawled to the door where I stood, her jeans balled at her ankles, her torn panties stained with blood.

I pressed into the wall, resisted the urge to help her up, knowing that if I showed any compassion, any human residue, I would be finished, my cover blown.

2

Punch-Drunk

The Vagos needed to fight the way others needed a drug fix. It didn't matter their target or their purpose; winning or losing, the act brought relief. My nights blended together in a fog of full nelsons and curled fists, my face rammed into the concrete floor until my teeth sliced open the flesh in my cheek, my eye swelled shut, and my boots left blood prints on the tile. Police never intervened because no victims called them. Amid the grunting and noise and hysterical shouting, I carefully punched until the violence became seamless, ordinary, and expected. Punch. Deflect. Punch. Deflect. My life existed in flashes, light in the after-midnight blackness. Any fear I had hardened with each mutual combat. And as sharp pain jolted through my right shoulder and my head thundered, I developed rapport.

So much, in fact, that Terrible invited me to the Victor Valley chapter's eighth anniversary party at the Screaming Chicken Saloon in Devore, an unincorporated area of San Bernardino County sandwiched between two freeways on Route 66. The bar, a renovated gas station from the 1940s, served only beer and wine, no hard liquor. Dust coated the inside; the bartenders looked weathered, like fixtures from another era in need of a good wash. Dollar bills fluttered on the walls. A mounted bike fender jutted from the bar next to the neon "V" twin beer sign. More than two hundred Vagos crammed into the hot space and mingled with members of other chapters and support clubs. The bar expanded onto an outside patio complete with a horseshoes game area. Weapons and chains blurred around me. The stench of beer and urine assaulted my nostrils. Pink flyers advertising a breast cancer fund-raiser littered the floor and stuck to the bottom of my boot. Women strutted around in bikinis.

Some Vagos still wore their helmets, reminiscent of World War II storm troopers. Rows of bikes adorned with Valkyrie-like wings on the handlebars, mostly black, bronze, silver, red, and blue, lined the perimeter of the bar. Life for the one percenter focused on motorcycles and the cannibalization of stolen or junked bike parts. Terrible squeezed through the bodies and headed my way with a mug of cool beer. He seemed particularly charged. Words tumbled out of him in rapid succession. He spoke of payback for drug dealers who had purchased goods with counterfeit bills, human hunts he initiated on behalf of the Vagos to collect outstanding debts, assaults he'd committed, and the mangled faces and eye sockets he'd transformed into bloody pulp. I turned up the volume on my recorder.

Terrible made me nervous not just because he looked demonic but also because he fought without provocation, forgot threads of stories, ended conversations midsentence, and, when he grew too stressed, punched his "shadow people." But he presented opportunity, a way in to key players like Twist, a Vago from the Victor Valley chapter, and Rhino, the sergeant at arms of the Victorville chapter, who both emerged from the dark portals in the Screaming Chicken, toting bags of white powder and small-caliber pistols tucked into their front pockets. Mentally, I checked off their sleeved arms, massive strides, and the large gauges in Rhino's lobes. Both penetrated me with flat, blank stares. I imagined they had suffered camouflaged childhoods, subjected to emotional poverty, drenched in television violence while their working-class parents struggled to put food on the table. I *knew* them, people like them. Conversation seemed futile. Neither was interested in discussing anything he didn't initiate. And it didn't matter anyway. Talking might only provoke them to punch. Besides, I was there to observe, record, and manipulate, not to fix them.

I didn't know it that night, but I had just met two of the Vagos' most violent killers.

⋙

By early January 2004, the San Bernardino Sheriff's Department Criminal Intelligence Division contacted Special Agent John Carr of the Van Nuys office of the Bureau of Alcohol, Tobacco, Firearms and Explosives to inquire whether they might be able to use me in a more productive capacity. Carr and Special Agent Darrin "Koz" Kozlowski met with the DEA and me at the SBSD Intel office. Carr already had an informant working a Riverside County investigation into the Vagos. ATF and DEA reached an agreement and ATF signed me up. My handler would be the legendary Koz, a federal undercover agent who had infiltrated the Vagos in 1997 and attained the rank of full-patched member.

He had used a CI like me to make the initial introduction into the gang, but only a month later, his investigation turned lethal. Koz's CI had a fatal motorcycle accident on Hollywood Boulevard. The Vagos obtained the accident report from the LAPD and learned that the motorcycle's vehicle identification number identified it as government issued. The Vagos interrogated the CI's wife, demanding to know why her husband had crashed a federal bike. The wife, threatened with the slaughter of her family, revealed the CI's identity and disclosed that he had worked as an ATF informant. At the same time, she disclosed to the Vagos Koz's business card that marked him as a federal agent. The Vagos made it their mission to eliminate Koz. As the ATF scrambled to end the investigation in 1998, the

Vagos learned Koz's undercover address, terrorized him, and threatened to kill him. Eventually the ATF assigned members of its Special Response Team, armed with assault rifles, to stake out Koz's home. The Vagos backed off but Koz, undeterred, resumed undercover work.

Now, as Koz shook my hand, he laughed easily and warned, "You do realize this is all improvisation?" He carefully explained my mission—to work deep cover in Operation 22 Green. My goal: Target the Vagos under the federal VICAR statute (Violent Crime in Aid of Racketeering) and identify the club's international officers as well as the officers for each chapter.

"What's your rank?"

"My rank?"

"What do you do for the Vagos?"

"Hang around with them?"

"Do you even know what that means?" A flicker of doubt flashed across Koz's face as he explained the club's rank-and-file structure: The goal of every hang-around was to advance to prospect and eventually to full-patch. The real talent assumed leadership roles: president, vice president, secretary, treasurer, sergeant at arms. A gift of brute force might qualify a person for the club's elite enforcement unit; the guy could be a hit man or a fixer. Every outlaw club had such talent, Koz explained: the SS for the Outlaws, the Filthy Few or Death Squad for the Hells Angels, the Black T-Shirt Squad for the Pagans, and the Nomad Chapter for the Bandidos.

"The Vagos are different," Koz warned. "They prefer discretion."

They wouldn't be as easy to identify. And they would be impossible to infiltrate without a bike.

"We'll work on that," Koz assured me.

❊

Meanwhile, the Vagos' next planned run occurred at Lake Havasu in Arizona, located on the Colorado River sixty miles south of Bullhead City. The desert lake, surrounded by red ocher mountains and cliff walls, was actually a Colorado River reservoir created when the Parker Dam was completed in 1938. Home to the famed London Bridge and English Village of shops and restaurants, the quaint resort town attracted a dangerous mix of college students and outlaws. Palm trees and lakeshore contrasted with hard-edged partying. The Havasu run was a uniquely Vago event and coincided with the Laughlin run.

Still without a motorcycle, I rode in the RV with members of the Victorville chapter. We towed the bikes behind us. At least the RV provided some shelter from the blazing heat, temperatures that could soar over one hundred degrees. The Hells Angels claimed Arizona and a large portion of the West Coast, but the club had not yet absorbed the Vagos, who dominated Southern California. Lake Havasu represented a significant territorial goal; presence mattered more than strategy. But as a mere hang-around, I had little access to any important conversations. Instead I spent long hours fetching beer and cigarettes for members, inflating, deflating, and inflating again Head Butt's rubber bed, and providing instant entertainment. After a while, "Down on the ground, twenty-two push-ups," took its toll. Exhausted and dehydrated and surrounded by crank-fueled bikers and prospects who blew meth in my face, I considered if prison might be a relief.

The Vagos had commandeered an entire hotel, spilling into the parking lot with makeshift tents. Terrible, who just weeks before the run had been dubbed an "official Vago prospect," melted in the heat. I shadowed him, hoping to learn what prospecting entailed, though the distinction between our two roles was marginal. I enjoyed slightly more sleep and could drink beer without permission. I dropped hints when I could that I had purchased a bike, a prize I knew would instantly elevate me in the members' eyes and make me eligible for promotion. Head Butt especially perked up at the announcement. He didn't need to know that it would be weeks before the ATF could wade through the bureaucratic red tape to deliver my bike.

For days I grabbed any space I could—patches of exposed tile, a curb, a couch, even a wall, and attempted restless sleep. Foot traffic jostled me awake; elevated voices and sounds of sex rumbled through the RV and outside. Snippets of conversation floated my way—drug and gun trafficking, brewing trouble with the Hells Angels—but I could never actively listen. Instead I blended into the gray walls, up before dawn, my world a fuzzy distortion. Terrible guarded the camper, looking like some kind of lake creature—devil horns, slitted eyes, ink markings, an addict who could survive days without sleep or food, a model soldier motivated by a warped sense of mission and duty. He emitted a kind of dangerous energy that left me unsettled and tense. And as much as I hated the thought of spending more time with him, he could introduce me to key players.

By day three of the run, just as the sun dipped over the lake and I had fetched my twenty-second beer and Terrible, looking wilted and sleep deprived, had danced on one leg for the last hour, Psycho, the chapter's president, announced Head Butt's advancement. We crammed inside the RV, members and prospects, and watched as Psycho handed Head Butt his center patch. He gave him fifteen minutes to sew it on his cut. Terrible reached into his fanny pack and produced a needle and thread. Psycho offered up his old motorcycle.

≈

In the days following the Havasu run, Terrible invited me to the meth house he shared with Rhino and Twist. The cramped space teemed with half-naked women hovering in the doorframes like racks of ribs, waiting to trade sex for drugs. Bodies moaned against the wall, near bowls of meth propped on the floor, on the bald couch dusted with drug residue, and under the Nazi flag, the dark swastika cutting bladed shadows across the ceiling. Foil on the windows blocked the sunlight. The stench of wet stone and beer filled my nostrils. My eyes burned in the drug fog. AK-47s propped in plain view by the door; pit bulls lazed on the floor. Flies buzzed in their ears. Dog crap clumped near the drugs. Twist grunted at me and lit a glass pipe, his .380 caliber pistol in his belt.

I hugged the wall, listening to skin slapping, sucking sounds, and chatter like rare species of birds. In the semidarkness, Rhino's shadow loomed large as he absently fondled a woman's breasts, his Buck knife winking from his waist. He collected women the way some people collect weapons. His old lady in the corner looked like a stain. Pass-arounds lined up for his attention, rail thin with sunken eyes. They waited for him in the hallway, in the bedroom, on the couch, on the floor. Rhino's girlfriend seemed unfazed. If I didn't want to spend many more mindless nights watching bodies flop around me in a drug-induced fog, I needed to make my move.

Nerves shot through me. Fear sharpened my edge.

"I've seen you before." Rhino nodded at me. Neither of us extended his hand. I would have committed my first affront had I initiated conversation with a full-patch as a mere hang-around.

"I'm getting my bike in a month. I've already paid for it," I volunteered, and a strange stillness hung between us. Rhino's bloodshot eyes penetrated mine, and for what seemed like several torturous seconds, neither of us blinked.

Then, as if I'd passed some invisible test, he announced, "I'd like to sponsor you."

My tongue felt thick against the roof of my mouth. "I'd be honored." Just like that. I was in. Maybe I looked too excited, too relieved, because a shadow crossed Rhino's face and he lowered his voice, "Don't ever make me look stupid."

⋙⋘

Terrible enlightened me later. "Stupid people," he had heard, errant prospects, suspected informants, were dragged into the high desert, beaten, duct-taped, and shot execution-style. I promised not to be "stupid." But becoming an official prospect, however, required a club vote at the next Church meeting. As a hang-around, I had already acquired a cursory education in the Vagos' basic club hierarchy, codes, and Church protocol. The club masked criminal activities behind its bylaws and constitution as well as its perverse interpretation of biblical laws. Club meetings, for instance, reserved for members only, were known as Church. At these gatherings, full-patch Vagos took care of business.

◈

A week later on a cool Sunday evening, Psycho held Church in his RV parked in his driveway. Rhino, Spoon, Powder, Sonny, and Chains disappeared inside with several other members to discuss my fate. I grabbed a corner curb, sifted gravel through my fingers, and reflected on my week. My days so far had blended into each other, hours and hours of boredom, beer, pool, and mindless banter, waiting for opportunity, introduction, something to advance the investigation. And now Terrible paced beside me, a hard-core gangster who would snap my neck in an instant if he knew my real identity.

A door banged open. Psycho, framed in the harsh glare of the RV's porch bulb, waved me inside. The cramped space smelled of plastic and stale smoke. The camper, likely worth several hundred thousand dollars, served as a symbol of Psycho's success in the drug world; trappings gave him the illusion of power. But I knew his haunted look too well: The paranoia that seized him in the dark made him perpetually cautious and restless and empty.

Several members dressed in green headbands and dirty cuts formed a semicircle around me. Machinelike soldiers, well trained, armed, and leached of emotion.

"So you want to be a prospect?" Psycho folded his arms across his chest, looking more like a Marine sergeant than a criminal. Sounds of crickets cut through the tension.

"More than anything." My heart pounded.

"You know what that means?" But before I could answer, he leaned close and whispered, "You'll be a slave, on call for any Vago twenty-four/ seven. You could be asked to do anything." His tone implied business— sacrifice, prison, even death for the club.

"And if I decide one day I don't like you, I could order you run down in the street."

I nodded. I knew Psycho meant it; I had heard rumors of kidnapping and torture committed in other chapters.

"If we have to go to war"—Psycho paused, caught the eyes of the others—"you'd be expected to fight. You'd be expected to kill." I said nothing, but my heart hammered in my chest.

Psycho handed me my bottom rocker. "Sew it on your cuts when you get one."

✁

Later that night, my hands shook on the steering wheel as I drove to The Slapshot Bar, where Spoon and other members had some "advice" for their new prospect. I couldn't believe it. Barely four months into the investigation and I was accepted, no questions asked. I felt like I'd lost my virginity. I had no bike, no vest, nothing but raw promise. No one asked me to complete an application; no one checked my criminal credentials. Unlike undercover government operatives who formed fake identities, bogus arrest records, credit reports, vehicle registration, and work history, I actually had a legitimate criminal background, though for now I would have to play a fake real criminal.

Spoon ordered a beer and smoothed his long goatee; it skimmed his belly. A curtain of black hair draped around his shoulders. A bandanna hid the top of his bald head. In the dim green glow, Spoon recited the Prospect Song and made me repeat it.

> I'm a Vago prospect, it's plain for all to see,
> I wish they'd hurry up and give me my patch
> so everyone will quit fucking with me.

He gave me a notebook and a pencil, told me I should write it down and be prepared. I felt like a Boy Scout. He gave me a list of essentials, items I should carry in my "Prospect Survival Kit," things like condoms, Tylenol, a sewing kit (in case a prospect suddenly patched over), tampons (to plug up blood from a bullet wound), shoelaces, lightbulbs, and Vicodin. Spoon ordered another beer, and the evening stretched well into the wee hours of the morning.

※

At dawn, I drove Terrible home. Exhausted but wired, I vaguely registered that in three hours I would have to report to Napa Auto Parts and begin my other job. Lizard and his entourage drove a few paces in front of us. Movement in the backseat distracted me as Lizard adjusted, wiggled, and exposed his bare ass in the rear window. *What the hell was he doing?* Of all the members I had met, Lizard seemed the most touched, the most out there, perpetually lost in an LSD flashback. In the "real world," he probably would have been institutionalized, officially labeled "insane," and heavily medicated, but the Vagos considered him eccentric and not at all sociopathic. They wouldn't conceive of excising him for age or illness. And I quickly learned there were degrees of crazy; among gangsters, Lizard wore a perfect mask, blending with darkness, unable to see what swirled around him. It didn't matter that he was lost . . . they *all* were. It didn't matter that Lizard was sick . . . they *all* were, all of them misfits among misfits trying hard to maintain some semblance of order amid dysfunction.

Terrible opened the window. Wind rushed in. Lizard tossed something into the street; it landed with a splat. Spots slapped my windshield, brown and runny, like . . .

"Shit." Terrible cupped a hand over his mouth and quickly rolled up his window. "That motherfucker threw his shit at us." It took me a moment to process Terrible's insight—not crazy or eccentric, but strangely, oddly appropriate.

※

Finally, I stumbled into bed, pausing long enough to stuff my head with earplugs. It had proved too draining to travel the forty miles from Upland to Victorville three or four times a week to hang out with the Vagos. So I secured a cheap apartment in Old Town Victorville, a Hispanic barrio close to the Vagos' watering holes. But I had barely dozed off when I heard *bam bam bam* on my steel security door. Less than two months earlier, pretrial services had paid me impromptu visits. I never shook off the fear of night visitors.

Irritated, I tossed off my sheets, pulled on my shirt. Hercules zipped full speed the length of my apartment, barking maniacally at shadows and headlights. I glanced into the dark street expecting to see police Maglites and red flashing wigwags. Nothing. Stress zipped through me. I padded to the back door, cracked it open. Eerie silence unnerved me.

Hercules whimpered as I climbed back into bed. But sleep eluded me. *Something was out there, I just couldn't see it.* For the next two hours I listened to my heart thump. My alarm flashed at me, 6:30 A.M. I fumbled into my work clothes and opened my front door. Uniforms huddled in the street. One officer knelt and drew chalk circles through bloodstains on the pavement.

"What happened?" I managed. Relief shot through me. *This wasn't about me.* Having lived so long as a criminal, it was hard to remember I was a good guy now.

"You tell me." Sarcasm tugged at the officer's upper lip.

"I didn't see anything." But I knew the officer didn't believe me.

"Of course you didn't." The officer pointed to the slugs in my door-frame. "Some kid got shot in the ass."

Then I realized. What I had thought was pounding had actually been gunfire.

3

Prospecting

My first month of prospecting differed little from my few weeks of hanging around the club except that now my initiation was round-the-clock and it became harder for me to move between my day job and my real world. The words "no," "downtime," and "in a minute" did not exist in the Vagos' vocabulary. As Rhino's slave, I fetched him lottery tickets and Taco Bell sometimes two and three times a night, at two in the morning on the opposite side of town, and sometimes he changed his order upon delivery. He wanted soft tacos *without* salsa, burritos *without* black beans, refried rice *on the side.* I returned the food, exchanged the orders, and did it all without complaint.

I lost my name, answered to "Prospect," and scooped fresh dog poop from Twist's living room floor. I stifled gags when offered half-eaten pizza and cleaned bikes over and over. When I didn't do it *right*, I did it again. I watched Rhino drift in and out of a crank-fueled stupor, willing my legs to stand, propping my worn, exhausted body against the wall, next to the AK-47s.

In the evenings, after barhopping, I reported the weapons and dope I saw in plain view to Koz: the body armor, brass knuckles, and hooded effigy suspended from a hook on Rhino's bathroom door, roped at the throat with a noose. And then one afternoon Twist surprised me. He called me up and in hushed tones told me about Rhino's impromptu visit from a San Bernardino sheriff's deputy.

"He was looking for Dominic, a Mexican drug dealer wanted for parole violations," Twist said. "Rhino told him he wasn't there." The deputy muscled inside anyway.

"The place was loaded," Twist reported. "Rifles, dope, knives . . . the dude told us to clean up our shit. We were about to be hit hard."

In fact, unbeknownst to me, the ATF had planned to raid Rhino's place. Corruption in the police force was nothing new. Still, I never understood veteran deputies who informed on their own or mixed with the criminals they aimed to arrest. The lines blurred, and apart from dirty cops, the Vagos, too, reportedly had moles inside, women who took jobs as dispatchers or administrative assistants, who had access to records and conversation. If Rhino had police informants leaking him information, what if his cop friends knew about me?

I lived in a state of veiled paranoia, mentally retracing my steps each night: *Had I done anything to make them suspicious? Had I flinched? Had I said the wrong thing?* Now I needed to prove my loyalty not only to Koz but to the Vagos as well. I vowed to be the best prospect the Vagos had ever seen. I hung out in bars until wee hours of morning, belted out lyrics from Madonna's "Like a Virgin," and participated in forced drinking contests, at times downing five shots in succession.

Head Butt, in particular, relished my new position and wasted little opportunity to test my resolve. He engaged me in games of pool, whacked me hard in the shins with his stick, and laughed cruelly as I winced. I knew how to play, but Head Butt invented his own rules. If I shot too well, he accused me of "disrespecting him"; if I scratched, I needed to be "corrected."

When I recovered from his impromptu strikes with the pool stick, he punched me several times in the head—*pow, pow, pow*—like a windup toy, deriving pleasure from my torture. I felt like an amateur boxer preparing each night for his next match with no time to recover, no time to anticipate. Except for the rare moments I fed my dog and reported to Koz, I served at Rhino's whim, accompanying him on human hunts to recover drug debts and confiscate motorcycles. Most escapades turned out to be false starts, lots of buildup and anticipation followed by ultimate letdown. We arrived at suspects' doors, debated our entry, waffled, left, returned moments later, and eventually knocked on the front door. Rhino functioned like a cartoon villain, the threat of bodily harm spewing above his head in a giant bubble cloud until the victims paid up.

One night Rhino broke the monotony. He was slumped half dazed on his couch draped on either side by women he had swapped for sex. Propped against a far wall, my eyes smarting from smoke, I watched like a voyeur in some carnival freak show, the only one standing still in the center of a merry-go-round. Then, as if awakened suddenly, Rhino tore his lips from his latest conquest, snapped his fingers, and a shadow emerged from the bedroom. Big Guy, whom Rhino had introduced to me as his designated "gun source," appeared in the darkness and produced a shiny Beretta .25 caliber pistol. He was a stubby man with baggy eyes and a hooked nose. Rhino grunted his approval, peeled the woman from his arms, dropped her to the floor, and nearly stepped on her head. It was then that I noticed she had no legs. She had stumps, a slim torso, and a muted face. I vaguely wondered if the Vagos had a patch for that kind of conquest: missing wings?

Rhino stroked the barrel of the gun and announced, "We're taking a road trip. Bullhead City."

I knew better than to ask for details. Still, a chill coursed through me. What was in Bullhead City, an armpit nearly two hundred miles away on the Colorado River in Mohave County, Arizona? And what did Rhino plan to do with the gun? He ordered me to store the Beretta in the trunk of my car and "separate the magazine and ammo" in case cops pulled us over. Then Rhino mounted his motorcycle, high as a kite, his hands shaking, and started the throttle.

"I can't see shit at night," he said and sped into the darkness. I followed close behind him. Bikes, as a rule, had one speed—fast, sixty-five in a residential zone, over one hundred miles per hour on the freeway and plenty of fishtailing. But this was worse, flying down miles of dark, empty desert road.

After a few minutes, Rhino pulled over. "I'm tired, man," he said and handed me his keys.

Now was not the time to announce I had ridden dirt bikes only as a youth and still waited for my government ride. I slid onto the warm leather seat, flashed Rhino a weak smile, and watched him climb into my car. As I maneuvered the bike back onto the pitch-black road, inhaled exhaust, and burned motorcycle oil, I prayed that no other motorists had ventured out this morning. Wind tore my face. I had poor depth perception as a result of astigmatism in my right eye. I needed glasses. My heart thundered in my chest. The most danger I ever faced was death by motorcycle. Rhino swerved behind me. Gold headlights traveled too close to my back tire. My arms ached from gripping the bike handles, and I mentally repeated, *Avoid pavement. Avoid road rash. Do not peel skin back to the bone.*

A thousand mental tragedies replayed in my imagination as gravel and rock rattled my frame. Fear, like a cold ball, knocked at my conscience. *What if something happened to the motorcycle—a piston seized, a head cracked, a tire blew? What if I capsized and broke an arm or a leg?*

Inside Bullhead City's limits, Rhino flashed his lights at me. I pulled over and he ordered me to remove the Beretta from the trunk of my car and hand it to him. My legs felt like rubber as I hit the fob. Rhino's face, slicked with sweat, looked like it might burst. Unease itched up my spine as Rhino loaded his gun and mumbled something about payback and surprise. His old lady lived in Bullhead City; he suspected her of cheating on him and he intended to "take care of business."

As I slipped into my car and started the engine, nausea overcame me.

My nerves taut, I dialed Koz and reported my midnight excursion, hoping Rhino's bike might break down.

＞＜

"We've been at this for six hours." My voice cracked with fatigue. It was two o'clock in the morning. A light drizzle splashed my windshield. Terrible agitated in the passenger seat, his eyes overbright and glassy. I knew they saw nothing, like looking through thick ice. If there was life inside them, it was hidden beneath a cold, frozen shell.

We drove down wet streets, the scene skipping like a scratched film. I parked, idled the engine, waited as Terrible huddled with shadows in the doorway, in side alleys, on the curb, satisfying his fix. Once I had lived like him. That, more than the boredom and fatigue, was the worst part about being with Terrible, seeing my past in his present. He had lost what made him human, his dignity. Without that, he tumbled down a dark hole where he lived in arteries of hard, packed black dirt, wasted and lost. It was the big lie perpetuated over and over through dope, club, code. The promise of being transformed left those who followed empty and scared.

Koz loaned me $3,000 cash in government funds. The bills crumpled in my front pocket. Terrible had assured me several hours earlier when I bought him a burger at Jack in the Box that he knew a big meth supplier named Rancid.

"Where is he?" I pressed, the hamburger settling in my stomach like a rock.

"Late."

"Or not coming?"

"He'll be here." Terrible fidgeted. I knew he operated on impulsive opportunity. Plans changed at a moment's notice. If Terrible scored another deal along the way and was too high to "work," he'd cancel the buy.

And then Rancid pulled into the driveway. He slammed his truck door shut and ushered us inside his dilapidated house. Mangy hair framed Rancid's wet eyes and he smelled like fertilizer. The airy rooms, stripped bare, had no furniture, no fixtures. Wires snaked from grooves in the ceiling.

"I just sold the place." Rancid shrugged as if registering my suspicions. "I'm moving to Arizona." Maybe he was. Maybe he wasn't. He was a drug dealer. They were all nomads. We followed him into the kitchen, where he produced a quarter pound of meth and a scale from a canvas bank bag. He flashed his cigarette lighter over the fine white powder. Then he asked us for a favor: "My old lady is getting death threats from her ex-boyfriend. Can you guys fuck him up?"

"You want us to kill him?" Terrible needed qualification.

Rancid bristled at the suggestion. "*Scare* him." He weighed the meth.

And while the two plotted suitable payback, I handed Rancid a wad of cash, my adrenaline raging. Experience didn't matter. I'd negotiated hundreds of drug deals, each one charged with a different energy. Paranoia caused people to snap. At any given moment the dealer could renege, get spooked, pull out a gun and pop off a bullet.

Terrible asked for his cut in dope.

"I can't do that." I shook my head and handed him $200 cash. Reluctantly, Terrible stuffed the bills into his jacket, then reached across the counter and pinched a gram of meth from the open baggie. Now I would have to explain to Koz why some of the evidence was missing.

It was time to take Terrible home before he craved more and dragged me from house to house as his chauffeur. While my mind raced with exit strategies, I turned the key in the ignition and listened as metal scraped against metal.

"Dead battery?" I couldn't believe it. I had borrowed my girlfriend's car. I had a quarter pound of meth in the front seat. Stuck was not an option.

I panicked. "Dude, we can't stay here. The cops could roll up on us."

"I'll be back," Terrible lied, and his teeth chattered as he stepped outside. *Of course he wasn't coming back. Like hell would he risk being caught in possession of meth.* Rain fell, hypnotic and steady. Within seconds he was soaked. His clothes clung to him like a second skin. He sloshed to the house, and when the door opened, Terrible slipped into filtered light and disappeared. I needed a jump.

"Can you coast down the hill?" Kiles suggested over the line.

And I put the car in neutral and rolled to my rescue.

※

My 1992 government-issued black Harley, the same bike Koz had used three years earlier when he infiltrated the Warlocks in Northern Virginia, finally arrived minus a turn signal. I parked it in my living room and practiced riding it to the grocery store, the gym, winding through back alleys, my hands firmly gripped on the handlebars. I rode it in the rain, on slick streets, in the cold when temperatures bit my cheeks. I wanted to be *prepared*. Not possible.

※

About ten of us met at a local gas station near the freeway the morning of my first mandatory run to Tijuana, Mexico. The border town, situated just three hours south of San Bernardino County, boasted a dusty pub and endless strip clubs. As warm sun beat down on the rows of chrome and steel parked like cattle near the pumps, I worried about the ride, not the destination. We traveled like a black swarm, our bikes so close we grazed each other's knees, clipped side mirrors, and inhaled exhaust. The experience, reminiscent of stock car racing, left me breathless and anxious as I split traffic and roared ninety-five miles an hour down the freeway. My hands shook so badly they tingled. When we finally arrived in the dusty Mexican town that smelled distinctly of goat, we recovered in a Tijuana pub, a dive on Avenida Revolución, sandwiched between tin sheds that brimmed with handcrafted artifacts, jewelry, fine leathers, and perfumes. Tourists found us amusing, a novelty they photographed and tucked inside their purses.

But the more they flashed their cameras at us, the more agitated Psycho became. Cords in his neck bunched. And by his fifth beer, I volunteered to retrieve the film.

"Sorry, ma'am, you can't take our pictures." I towered over a slim woman in a floppy flower hat and large white sunglasses. Her jaw slacked in surprise. Her silver bangles clinked as she erased each shot. Satisfied that the evidence had been deleted, Psycho spent the next eight hours exploring strip clubs. He dragged me along for good measure. I began to wonder what I was doing, as one club resembled the next, each pole dancer more vapid than the last. And as the sun dipped below the horizon, Sonny handed me my helmet.

"You all right?" He reminded me of a skinny Clint Eastwood, chiseled features, wrinkles cut deep around his eyes. He wore three Buck knives on his hip and drove a truck. But his real source of income was drug dealing. And he was a major target of the ATF's investigation.

"You and me." Sonny winked. "We're always the last to leave. I'm always looking out for you."

I liked Sonny. He seemed displaced somehow, caught up in a world he never meant to inhabit. But he discovered he had talent; he was well liked, respected. It was hard to leave that persona, to return to ordinary.

➤←

Barely one month into prospecting, Psycho announced he needed a bodyguard. His old lady had split on him, and he now had renewed interest in barhopping. Naturally I volunteered for the position, more than eager to leave behind Rhino's meth house and increase my accessibility to the president. But my first night at Mickey McGees nearly proved to be my last in the investigation.

The place buzzed with patrons. Some Hells Angels supporters proudly wore their 81 T-shirts. Two in particular circled the pool table, immense, shaped like squares, stuffed into too-tight jeans and shirts that rode their bellies. One displayed a frosted beard that tickled his chest. The other wore a shiny skullcap. Psycho slammed back his third shot and grew increasingly agitated at their mere presence. He spit at the floor. Head Butt and Rhino watched, like predators crouched low in the grass, picking up the supporters' foul scent.

Heavy metal crunched my nerves. The assault began with a glare, a steadfast look that penetrated Psycho like a bullet. He bolted from his stool and I mirrored his movement, my shoulders towering above his head. Then, without further provocation, Psycho lunged, his fist striking Bearded One's chin dead center. The force slammed the man into the pool table, and I heard a resounding crack. Baldy sprung into action, but before he could strike Psycho, I blocked his blow and knocked him to his knees. I grabbed him from behind, feeling sick inside, not wanting to really hurt the man but needing to *pretend*. As an ATF informant, I wasn't supposed to initiate fights, but as Psycho's prospect, as his bodyguard, I had no choice.

I pummeled the Bearded One loosely, drawing just enough blood to look impressive. Meanwhile, Baldy recovered, his face a bloody mask. Head Butt and Rhino attacked him. Each punch hit like percussion. Screams, thuds, and shattering glass mixed with tinny metal. I dragged the Bearded One toward the exit, holding him from behind, hoping to punch him into the street before Psycho and the others finished him off with guns or knives. Adrenaline shot through me. I needed to get him out of there. The Bearded One, drenched in blood and sweat, wiggled in my grip. He scratched my arms, swung wildly at my head, his fists punching air. At the exit, I practically threw him into the empty street. He scrambled to his feet and bounded away like a wounded gorilla and I knew he wouldn't return. Behind me, the bar looked like a windstorm had tunneled through: chairs and bottles strewn across the floor, pool balls scattered. Glass shards glittered in Head Butt's hair as he wrestled Baldy to the floor and Rhino stomped the man's head, his kicks so fierce he left an angry gash above Baldy's eye. As Baldy struggled to his feet, Rhino swung and knocked him unconscious. *I could explain a fight; I couldn't explain a kill.*

Blood oozed from my knuckles. Sweat pooled from Rhino's armpits and slicked his forehead. He panted. Still amped from the fight, he paced near the body ready for Baldy to suddenly awake and resume the struggle. But Baldy was down for the count, his face streaked with blood. Rhino squatted next to the man, checked for a pulse, and then, as if disgusted that Baldy still breathed, kicked him hard in the ribs.

I retreated to the toilets, my heart racing. So far no one had called the cops. The bar transformed into a bloody mess. I stood over the urinals feeling nauseous, shaking. Then the door opened and Psycho entered. He grinned at me, walked over to the urinal, unzipped his pants, and peed. I had a wire in my jockstrap; suddenly it felt too large.

Psycho boxed the air, turned to me, and said, "Nice work, Quick Draw."

⚡

"I know who you really are." Joanna's voice quivered. My head throbbed from last night's beating. I glanced at the digital clock on the nightstand. The gold numbers flashed 6:00 A.M. I had been asleep for only four hours. My girlfriend's back faced me. Sun lit up her hair. Black waves rolled across the computer screen. Slowly, I pulled the covers from my legs. This couldn't be good.

"What do you mean?" My heart pounded in my chest, and it began to finally register that maybe it hadn't been such a great idea to acquire a girlfriend after all.

"You're a cop, aren't you?" She swiveled around to face me. Her accusation hit me like a punch to the gut. But before I could manage an answer, she clicked the space bar. The letter I had drafted to my father-in-law a few weeks earlier flashed on the screen, a cruel reminder that deep cover had its casualties. I had hoped to reconcile with my estranged wife by confessing my latest role to her pastor father. Emotion had made me careless. I had left tracks. *Shit.*

"You talk about infiltrating a gang for the ATF." Joanna's brow arched.

"Come on, now." I swallowed, hoping I sounded incredulous.

Joanna glared at me, arms folded across her chest. I had known her only two weeks. She was friendly with Psycho's ex-girlfriend. I was in really deep trouble. A quiet waif with luminous eyes, she asked too many questions.

"I told you, I'm going to paralegal school."

She cocked her head sideways.

"It was just an assignment." Nerves shot through me. "The letter referenced a court case."

The thick vein in her temple stopped beating. The lines around her eyes smoothed. But it wasn't until she dressed that morning, slung her purse over her shoulder, and left the apartment that I exhaled. I clicked the dead bolt, leaned my head against the heavy door, and dreaded the fallout. I knew Joanna would gossip. And soon Psycho would ask questions.

Undercover operatives steered clear of the club's so-called fringe benefits. They circulated stories among their biker peers about bedding multiple girlfriends in different counties, none of whom knew about the others. Why invite confrontation? they insisted. But morality had nothing to do with the agents' fake discretion. Worried about future prosecutions and compromising the integrity of the investigation, they never wanted to be accused at trial of inappropriately touching a club president's old lady or hitting on another member's property.

But as an informant, I had fewer restrictions. Or so I thought. And although I knew there would be some risk involved in acquiring a girlfriend, Joanna surprised me. And now I had a problem: If I suddenly dumped her, she would get suspicious. If I kept her, she might keep digging. I decided to take a risk. I kept her.

4

The Confession

Psycho's eleven-year-old girl snapped her fingers at me.

"Prospect." She sucked a lollipop and pointed to a protruding nail in the deck I had just sealed. Sweat stained my armpits. My head throbbed. And as much as I wanted to ignore her, Psycho was her father and I had been a club prospect for only three months. As a mere probationary member, my job was to obey Psycho even if his commands filtered through his bratty kid. She blinked at me, flipped her dark braids behind her shoulders, and skimmed her bare heel over the rusty head.

"Careful," she whispered. "Someone could get hurt."

I grabbed a hammer and glanced across the yard. Psycho huddled on a cube of brown grass near his aboveground swimming pool and conducted club business. Joined by Powder, his vice president, Sonny, his sergeant at arms, and another full-patch, Spoon, Psycho planned to patch in Tony "the Barber" and Knuckles (so named when his knuckles were blown off his right hand after he grabbed the barrel of a gun pointed at his head), friends he had known for years but who had never prospected. Terrible stood guard a few feet away.

Psycho's girl tapped her foot impatiently. Sun dipped over the horizon and cut a thin red line through the sky. Tony and Knuckles' ceremony lasted a mere two minutes as Psycho handed them their colors and shook their hands. The president summoned Terrible into their circle, and the two spoke in hushed tones. Psycho's expression turned dark as if a shade had been drawn over his face.

His little girl tugged on my vest. "What do you want?" I swatted her hand away.

Terrible marched to my rescue. "Quick Draw, let's go for a ride."

We climbed into my beater Ford Explorer parked on the street. Terrible slid into the passenger seat and lit a cigarette. His hands shook. He cracked open the window, flicked ash into the street. We rode in silence for several minutes and then Terrible wagged the butt of his cigarette at me. "I'm going to tell you some shit." His pronouncement thundered in my chest like foreboding. Terrible averted his gaze, stared into the black street. "There was a murder last night . . ." His words resounded like gunshot inside the car. Confessing to a gangland-style shooting was every informant's dream, and it was fast becoming my nightmare. Drug rip. I had no recorder. Terrible rattled off the coconspirators—Sonny, Rhino, Twist, the club's enforcer and his rogues. *Shit. Shit. Shit.* I wanted him to slow down, to stop talking altogether until I could get him on tape.

"Sonny planned the whole thing." Terrible threw the sergeant at arms under the bus. Sonny never showed up. But Rhino and Twist, keen on opportunities, stormed the supplier's drug house and surprised the few dopers inside. Thoughts raced in my head as Terrible spilled more details: He had planned the robbery with Sonny, but he hadn't participated, afraid he might be recognized by the intended target. *Stop talking.*

"No one was supposed to die," Terrible added with a hint of regret. Shot in the back, the victim stumbled into the street, leaving a blood trail and silent witnesses. Worse, Rhino and Twist, in their haste to leave the scene, left deep tire marks.

"A fucking calling card." Terrible flicked his cigarette out the window. Silence hung in the air between us and I forgot to breathe.

"We need to clean up his shit," he said matter-of-factly, almost forgetting the reason he had asked me to drive him in the first place.

I drove to Twist's house in Apple Valley, and a cold realization hit me: Twist could not be linked in any way to the Vagos. Murder attracted heat and unwanted attention. Psycho had ordered Terrible to remove any Vagos paraphernalia, including the murder weapon. I parked down the street and shut off the engine. Darkness cloaked us. Dutifully, I helped Terrible remove duffel bags from Twist's empty house, stuffed with club colors, banners, flags, swastikas, and handmade wood carvings engraved with Vagos' insignia.

And the first chance I got, I called Koz.

"Can you get it on tape?" he asked.

My heart hammered against my chest. Surrounded by dark shapes clad in denim and dirty patches of heat, I had never felt more alone. As an informant, I had no backup, no surveillance team, no one to hear the bullet penetrate my skull if things soured. Without Twist's confession, the government had nothing but a body in the street. Only I knew the players involved. But technically I didn't exist. I was deep cover in the most violent biker gang in California. How was I going to entice a killer who barely knew me to confess?

I secured a recorder and spent the night awake.

⚡

Twist's car lay in pieces in his driveway. The dashboard in the dirt, seat cushions piled one on top of the other, radio parts scattered in the rocks. He probably thinks his car is bugged, I thought. Shattered glass crunched under my feet. I peered through the screen door; a white haze filled the entrance. Lumps formed on the floor. Flies buzzed in my ear. I knocked, and instantly a hand shot through an opening in the wall above me and pointed a .22 at my head.

"Jesus, Twist," I said, trying not to implode.

"What do you want?" he barked. I could hear water shut off. Twist had punched a hole in his bathroom wall so that he could watch the street as he showered. He poked a wet head through the makeshift opening and grinned. "Sorry, man."

He nodded to the door. "Come on in." In the thick drug fog, two women smoked meth on the couch. Barely dressed in panties and bras, they blew circles in my face and stared at me with dull cow's eyes. I waded through trash, discarded pizza boxes, overturned ashtrays, drug paraphernalia, and rat droppings and grabbed an edge of cushion.

"Want some?" One giggled. I still craved the drug, though I had been clean for nearly two years. The smell lingered in the air, seductive as candy.

Adrenaline pumped through me and fired my heart into overdrive. My recorder stuck to my skin like a brand. No way would Twist confess to anything with the women present. They were stoned out of their minds. My eyes watered and I struggled to breathe. I wanted to leave. Undercover work was largely improvisation. Federal agents received some "training" in psychological manipulation, when and how to use electronic equipment, what warning signs triggered danger, how to protect against the legal concept of entrapment, and when to ingest drugs to survive. But as an informant, I had no formal instruction. I relied on raw instinct. I had a simple plan—to visit Twist on my lunch hour, make sure his "stuff" had been removed, and hope Twist would offer up a morsel. I hadn't counted on houseguests.

"No, thanks, I'm working," I managed. It was a good excuse. Serving as Psycho's prospect had some benefits. The club president expected me to be sober for construction projects.

Twist snapped a towel at me and gave me a big clumsy hug. He'd been up all night juicing and God knows what else. He talked like he was pumped full of thiopental sodium. I cringed as Twist nestled between the women and settled in for a long afternoon. With his .380 caliber pistol in his lap and his AK-47 assault rifle propped against the bedroom door, Twist smoked and bragged about the arsenal he had stashed in his closet. After two hours of inane banter, I stood to leave.

Twist walked me to my car and I casually invited him out for a beer, though I knew he would never come. He lived as a recluse, content to get high alone in his dark cave, too paranoid and skittish to trust his own reaction with strangers. I had one last shot. "Everything cool or what?"

His hooded eyes skimmed mine. In the stark sun his skin had a white glaze.

"You know about that?" He shifted, his hands clenching and unclenching.

"I hear parts of parts." My heart pounded in my head. I was scared shitless. Twist was a psychopath.

"What do you know?"

"Some bad shit happened." I hoped my voice didn't vibrate.

"But they have no fucking clue who did it." Twist laughed. He folded his arms across his chest. A muscle in his jaw ticked. He studied me as if I were an insect he considered eating.

"Did you guys leave any shit out there?" I gambled. Dust blew over my boots.

"Nothing." Twist looked past me into the street. "Nothing whatsoever. We wore gloves, long sleeves, shades. Brother, it wasn't my first rodeo, you know what I mean?" He winked at me. Then, incredibly, he enacted the scene, formed his fingers into a gun, spun around, and said, "I operate like a machine when I'm doing business." He held his fingers close to my temple and whispered in my ear, "Poof."

"Just one shot?" My throat scratched. I hoped to hell the recorder was picking up his hushed tones and that he admitted details only the cops knew.

"Yeah." He paused. "I shot him once. It went through his heart and hit his girlfriend in the arm."

"Nice." I nodded, and in that moment I could have walked, delivered the recorded confession to the ATF, and declared the investigation over. Not only had I confirmed for the government that the Vagos trafficked in drugs and illegal weapons; I also had established they were involved in committing homicides, the violent trademark of motorcycle gangs. I swelled with a sense of duty, of serving society. My role was no longer about self-preservation, it was about justice.

⫯⫯

In the days following the murder, Rhino disappeared, only to reemerge two weeks later with the desperate plea, "Hide me." Panic laced his voice, and when I hesitated he elaborated. Initially, Rhino fled to his mother's place, thinking it was a safe harbor, but when homicide detectives knocked on her door hoping to question him about Twist's movements, Rhino sped for the nearest exit: me. To him, I probably looked safe—no surveillance, no dopers, no obvious tip-offs. At two o'clock in the morning, my girlfriend sat alert on the edge of my bed, picked at loose skin on her thumb, and watched Rhino pace, pull the shades down, and immerse us all in gloomy shadow. I hoped I hadn't made a mistake keeping her around.

Rhino studied me intently. Hours ticked by in the darkness. None of us spoke. Acutely aware that I had temporarily lost my connection to Koz and to the outside world, I needed a plan. My apartment wasn't wired. The ATF thought I didn't have enough night visitors to make the exercise worthwhile. Who knew I would harbor a coconspirator to murder? Occasionally, I flipped on my recorder, hoping Rhino might slip and leak a confession. But he never did. A gangster's code dictated that important conversations happened in the street or en route inside a car where there was less chance to record. The decision to record involved considerable risk. Intuition guided me. If a situation didn't *feel* right, I listened. But mostly I hid the device inside my jockstrap.

"Would he come in?" Koz asked.

"You mean give us Twist?"

"If we offered him a deal?"

No way. Too risky. Rhino might balk at the suggestion to betray his own. His refusal could compromise the entire investigation.

"Let's take a drive." Rhino's eyes narrowed to slits. It was early morning. "Take me to the 7-Eleven." He had arranged to meet a girl there and shack up with her for a while. Outside, he hesitated on the curb, shoved his hands into his pockets, and glanced over his shoulder, down the empty alley. A pigeon skimmed the rooftop above us. Rhino slipped into the passenger side of my Ford Explorer. My mind raced as I hit the gas pedal and switched on the recorder.

"Twist says he's a professional," I opened, hoping I could incite Rhino to talk.

Rhino stared straight ahead and balled his hands into fists.

"He panicked, dog." Words tumbled out of him. "It wasn't supposed to be like that. It was supposed to be a setup. But one of them decided to keep the money. You know how tweakers are, dude."

I nodded.

"Fucking Twist didn't want to leave."

Instead he left deep tire tracks at the crime scene.

"I didn't see no reason to cap that dude." Rhino sniffed. "If Twist was acting like a machine, how come we didn't get the money?" He looked at me finally, his expression stone. "It wasn't focused shit. *I* was the only focused one. Fucking son of a bitch used my gun."

✂

"I could hide the gun for you."

Twist studied me with interest, shoved his hands in his pockets, and stared at the fat moon above us. We stood outside near the dark street. He shifted positions. A flicker of doubt skittered across his face and he shook his head. "No need."

My heart slammed into my chest. The recorder hummed in my crotch, no doubt picking up the crunch of gravel. Rhino had been the perfect decoy. While he prowled my apartment, fearful of police, Twist had carefully disposed of Rhino's Jennings pearl-handled gun with the scratched-off serial number. Without physical evidence, prosecutors had nothing.

But discretion wasn't Twist's strong suit. He bragged about the murder, reenacted his role, insisted he was a "machine," and several months later homicide detectives arrested him. When they executed a search warrant of Twist's home, they found one small revolver, several newspaper articles about the murder, and various Vagos indicia. Even caged, Twist could not be contained. He demanded a speedy trial, blabbed to his cell mate that his case should be fast-tracked—after all, he *was* a killer. And he insisted he acted alone. No one, other than me, knew of Rhino's involvement.

But homicide prosecutions could languish for years, and with a weak government case—no physical evidence and a jailhouse confession to an incarcerated inmate—Koz worried that a premature trial without the benefit of my recording could compromise ATF's larger investigation and result in Twist's acquittal. The ATF could not risk a government loss, much less my exposure.

"Drop the case," Koz said to the lead detective. "Let him go."

5

Shadowboxing

"We know you're a cop." Bubba, a skinny muscle with a blond goatee, challenged me one night as I stood guard outside Church. He had never officially prospected for the Vagos. Psycho had known him for years and simply gave him his colors. Sleeved with tattoos, bald, and fiercely empty, his tone provoked something feral in me and I leaned close, tapped my finger to his chest, and promised one day to "stab him in the heart" if he ever insulted me again with his "cop nonsense."

Bubba sucked in his breath and I waited for the inevitable beating. A prospect never spoke like that to a full-patch. Other members milled nearby, watching the interplay with interest. Rain lingered in the air. Lightning lit up our faces. Bubba's chiseled features twitched slightly as he processed my threat. Adrenaline shot through me. Heat flushed my face. I had learned to treat the Vagos like animals and never show fear. They would sense that in me like a vibration and pounce.

Bubba's dull eyes sparked suddenly and he bellowed a laugh, smacked me playfully on the shoulder, and walked into the street.

Rhino, perhaps pretending to be sympathetic, bear-hugged me and grabbed my crotch. He had never before touched me below the belt. His gesture startled me, knocked the wind from my lungs. Only moments before, I had left my recorder in the car. I had worn it in my jockstrap every day except this one. A small warning echoed in the back of my head. Some might call it intuition, others damn luck. I liked to think of the voice as divine intervention. But it saved my life. Rhino's hand held fast to my crotch and relief skittered across his face. In that single gesture he telegraphed his lingering doubt about me. I would have gone down in a blaze of bullets, dropped right there on the pavement with no chance to recover, no chance for a rescue. No one would ever know what happened. Rhino removed his hand. A wry smile lifted the corners of his mouth. I was safe for now.

But maybe it was time to get rid of Joanna?

***

From a purely investigative standpoint, prospecting had some perks, including participation in the Vagos' drug trade. As a probationary pledge, I was fungible. Not every OMG allowed its prospects to buy and sell drugs, but the Vagos had a looser code. Psycho ordered me to handle a "large-scale" drug buy from an associate with whom he had formerly done business, a guy named Casper who was a high-ranking member of the Nazi Low Riders, a racist criminal organization. He expected to receive thirty pounds of marijuana and entrusted me with $10,000 cash. Psycho had a prior commitment with the Canadian cartel. He needed me to "hold the drugs" for him until he returned. And, in case of a police bust, he preferred I take the rap.

"Stay at my place," Psycho added almost as an afterthought.

It didn't take much to convince Koz that the drug buy would not only boost my credibility with the Vagos but also afford me unfettered access to the president's quarters. Psycho never supplied me with any particulars. I knew only that he regularly smuggled large quantities of marijuana from Canada to California and earned enough money from his various transactions to afford three tattoo shops, a luxurious RV, and a spacious property.

Koz supplied me with a camera. Psycho's house resembled an armory. And as I prepared to guard his residence, I snapped photos of weapons on his nightstand, a Ruger P89 9mm semiautomatic pistol, a Taurus .380, a shotgun mounted on the wall next to several wrapped long guns in Psycho's bedroom closet. On the floor, bales of marijuana lay wrapped in one-pound quantities. An SKS assault rifle leaned against the bathroom door.

"I don't trust anyone," Psycho explained before he left, and warned me about rogues, real "outlaws" like Dollar, a former Vago who was too reckless with his drug consumption. He was a "control problem."

"You know what happens to people like him?" Psycho said, and I knew Dollar's story was meant to warn me. He ordered me to "kidnap him" and drag him to Psycho's Crossroads Tattoo shop for a lesson in "respect." Over the next few days, until Psycho returned, I pretended to hunt for Dollar and Wicked and Little Man, hoping Psycho would soon lose interest.

⋯

I expected him to designate me as his drug courier and trust me enough to drive to Washington State, collect pounds of marijuana, and haul the dope back to California several times a month, but the logistics involved made the ATF's head spin. Koz couldn't guarantee he could get me permission to cross state lines.

Instead, Psycho's contact, Casper, sold me weed. More than any other drug dealer, Casper unnerved me. He had an army of loyal followers ready to do his bidding. At a menacing six foot three and 250 pounds, Casper wore his hair long, had a mustache and goatee, and approached drug dealing like a hunt.

"I'm not comfortable with this," I confided to Koz.

"Why?"

"He might rob and kill me," I said.

"If he opens fire, I'll shoot him."

"You'd be too late. I'd be dead already." I laughed.

"Maybe I could hide in your closet?" Koz offered. *Not a good idea. Drug dealers notoriously looked in closets. If Casper decided to peek, we'd both be dead.*

"How about I just watch the house, wait outside for you, and if anything happens . . ."

But no scenario Koz suggested had any practical play. Backup crews were great in theory, but unless the drug dealer enjoyed slow torture, gunfire was too quick. In the end I met Casper inside, in a back room, hidden from the street. He brought along his brother, Fat Bastard, for good measure. Now I had two people to worry about. No one spoke. We didn't have to. Fat Bastard spread on a puffy chair, his body lost in extra skin, looking like a forest troll who'd just swallowed the village children.

Each time I returned to Psycho with the forty or fifty pounds of marijuana, he placed the drugs in the trunk of Bubba's Ford Contour just in case he was raided by police.

➤✖

Meanwhile Bubba continued to negotiate cocaine buys, and after several deals in the back of his tattoo shop he introduced me to the club's meth source, a Vago who regularly offered up "samples" at Church meetings. The source gave me the name of his supplier, a multiple convicted felon named JB. And soon I identified the Vagos' intricate web of dealers. On any given day, I huddled with Bubba in back rooms in his tattoo shop, exchanged cash, then waited for further instructions in parking lots. The meth source slipped me notes, cryptic codes: "11th & Main, Rite-Aid, JB," along with a phone number. With my nerves shot, my head pounding, I dialed the number on the torn paper. A disembodied voice instructed me to travel south to a seedy residence on Muscatel in Hesperia. I pulled into a dark driveway and shut off the engine; my boots crunched across the gravel. Acutely aware of the eleven grams of cocaine stashed in my pocket that I had not yet had time to deliver to Koz, I knocked on the door. No lights inside. Ten o'clock at night. A dog barked. Wind tickled my cheeks.

A child cracked open the door. The boy, barefoot, dressed in a stained T-shirt and underwear, motioned me inside. Shadows darted across the room. Mattresses strewn on the floor contained lumps curled on top. In the dark, I heard a female voice and the yelp of another child. JB emerged, grunted his greeting. He looked disheveled, rumpled like old clothes. He wore a .45 caliber pistol on his hip. Tattoos snaked his arms and neck, and around his wrist he wore the image of a barbed-wire bracelet. The child clung to JB's leg; his hollow, haunted eyes watched as I handed JB the cash. He handed me two plastic baggies.

As I maneuvered my car through the back streets, my hands shook. My head pounded. Exhausted, I still had to meet Koz and deliver the dope. Around one o'clock in the morning I dragged myself into bed. But just as I dozed off, my phone shrilled.

"Psycho needs cigarettes," Rhino barked. "There's a shop he likes in Sacramento."

❦

The next afternoon, in blazing sun, I did push-ups in Lizard's garage. My arms burned after the first dozen. Dust and sweat stung my eyes. Conversations buzzed around me, but I saw nothing but boots. They formed a semicircle, closed in on me, and mentally I cursed Psycho and his choice of entertainment. Four months of prospecting, of being Psycho's slave, had resulted in calculated abuse and midnight runs that made my legs and butt feel like rubber.

As I lowered my arms for number twenty-two, Psycho tossed a piece of cloth at me.

He laughed. "You have fifteen minutes to sew that on." Just like that. I had my colors. No fanfare. No celebration. When I started the investigation, I hoped to advance in rank, to achieve full-patch status, but I always expected the promotion to follow a dangerous test, a rite of passage that involved some criminal exploit or degrading act. My heart racing, I stopped the push-ups, scrambled to get my Prospect Kit, and fumbled for the needle. Fifteen minutes to sew it on. The others watched intently as I threaded the needle. My fingers shook. I stabbed my thumb a couple of times. Drops of blood trickled down my hand. I slipped on my cuts and proudly displayed them to the others.

"What do you think?" Cheers and whoops erupted from the group as they slapped me on the back, shook my hand, and enveloped me with bear hugs. A car door slammed. Sonny, late as usual, marched across the driveway, his face flushed red beneath his handlebar mustache.

"It's fucking crooked," he barked and ripped the patch off my cuts.

He slapped the cloth in my hand, a smile dulled in the back of his eye. "Do it again."

✕

Later that night, at Mickey McGees, the Vagos celebrated my promotion. The Irish bar dazzled with energy, and I felt like a celebrity surrounded by bodyguards and groupies. Patrons, caught up in the partying, congratulated me, slapped me on the back, firmly shook my hand, bought me beer. Scantily clad pass-arounds draped their arms around my shoulders, sat in my lap, attentive as windup dolls. Psycho kissed me on the cheek, hugged me, both of us drunk with accomplishment. I could now advance the investigation; he could grow his chapter. *Win-win.*

We spilled into the parking lot, the crowd inside frenzied and hot. I downed my fourth beer, dizzy with relief. Psycho sat on the tailgate of his truck and shared stories of his initiation; I pretended to care, to listen as a brother, but in truth I didn't care. I was tired, my head throbbed, and I craved an ending. It was Halloween night all over again. I had had enough candy. It was time to remove my mask, sweaty and stinking of rubber, crawl into my body, and sleep.

But movement near the exit sign caught my attention. A kid, maybe twenty-two, stumbled a few yards from Psycho. He looked clean-cut, dangerously polished. Psycho noticed him, too, the way an animal picks up a scent. Mentally I kicked the kid home. *Move on.* But he walked toward Psycho, slurring his insults, looking directly at him. Then he hurled his varsity frame at the president, and I swung, propelled by instinct, by club motto, *Protect protect protect.* My fist collided with the kid's front teeth, the impact so forceful I knocked them in half. Porcelain veneers embedded in my knuckles and punctured my hand. The kid fell to the pavement, scrambled to his feet, and through a lisp apologized to Psycho for his stupidity.

Meanwhile, blood trickled from my hand and I vaguely registered the dull pain.

"Nice shot." Psycho laughed and summoned me inside Mickey McGees for a round of gratitude. As the night wore on and the bar thinned, my hand throbbed. When I finally stumbled home and flopped on my girlfriend's couch, it had doubled in size. It looked deformed, like a borrowed limb from a monster. A yellow glaze coated my dreams. Bugs pricked my skin from the inside, trapped in a sticky goo. And by morning, my fever raged to 103 degrees. A puffy red line snaked from my hand to my elbow.

"Staph infection," a nurse diagnosed me later and threaded an IV into my arm. Antiseptic and bleach made me nauseous; the emergency room was so white I squinted.

"Something bit him," my girlfriend confirmed, her voice sounding distorted.

"Human. Animal?"

Maybe a little of both?

➤✦◄

As a prospect I had attended any Church meeting that involved discussion and preparation for war. Now that I was a full-patch, I could do more than listen. The Vagos' latest battle was to occur at their annual run over New Years at the Gold Strike and Nevada Landing casinos. Terry the Tramp, the Vagos' national president, had sanctioned a war with the Vagos' rival, the Sons of Hell. He had commissioned other Vago chapters in the area, specifically Hemet in the San Jacinto Valley in Riverside County, to assist the Victor Valley chapter. Anyone who refused to fight was given the option to leave voluntarily at the next Church meeting or suffer "physical punishment" for his cowardice. No one left. Even those who were not felons or decent sharpshooters like Spoon, our chapter's sergeant at arms, were expected to participate at least as "lookouts." The plan, Psycho explained, was to blast the Sons of Hell "all at once to make a statement" and then pull their patches and steal their bikes.

"Watch yourselves." Psycho lowered his voice, "We have a leak."* Psycho elaborated that the "fucking police" had apparently questioned several Vagos during a routine traffic stop. One cop let slip that his department had "received an anonymous tip." Vagos were headed to the Mission Bar. My mind flipped cartwheels. *Who warned the police about the impending massacre?* Hammer's face swirled into focus. The former Vago turned snitch had once sold explosives and firearms to club members. No one suspected he had a double agenda. Spoon promptly posted Hammer's photograph on the Web site whosarat.com. But publicly outing an informant wasn't enough for Psycho. I knew what they did to snitches. I was fairly sure I didn't want to be the leak.

"A lot of brothers are riding on that motherfucker," he said. "If you see him, kill him."

✖

War with the Sons of Hell was postponed.

"Did you hear about Sonny?" Rhino's voice cracked through the line.

"No," I said. Morning seeped through my blinds. Hercules opened one eye. I had overslept and he'd left me a gift.

"He was killed last night in a motorcycle accident." Rhino wheezed

---

* The leak involved an informant named George who had attempted to infiltrate the Vagos in a case out of Riverside County.

and he seemed genuinely upset, like maybe he had feelings. But sadness transferred to fear as he ranted that Sonny's death must have been intentional, payback for his involvement in the botched home invasion and murder Twist committed. My head ached. Sonny, Victorville's largest methamphetamine dealer, supplied the club with significant drug revenue. He would have been a major player in the investigation. His death represented a setback.

"A great loss," Psycho honored Sonny later at Church. Condolences soon turned to business. "Several people still owe him money. It's going to be our job to collect." He nominated Rhino for the task.

Bubba, who had stayed in the background, suddenly stumbled forward, looking more disheveled than usual, and cautioned Psycho about speaking openly, considering "there was the business of the informant." But Psycho dismissed Bubba's paranoia and confided in me later about Sonny's methamphetamine source, an 18th Street gang member named Sticky Fingers, who supplied meth to Sonny and Truck.

"I'm thinking of asking him to take over Sonny's business. What do you think?"

Someone had to be Sonny's successor. And while the Vagos shoveled dirt over Sonny's casket and family members shed genuine tears for his passing, Sticky Fingers hovered in the crowd, waiting for the appropriate pause before inserting himself into the sentence. I needed a new target, a new way in to the drug trade. *Two steps forward. One step back. That was the undercover dance.*

❈

As a full-patch I had access to more than drugs. Now I could participate in gun buys. I had seen Psycho's arsenal of sawed-off shotguns, assault rifles, and machine guns. Powder, the chapter's vice president, offered to sell me a stolen automatic weapon. Simply, he needed the money. Koz supplied me with cash, and the next morning, armed with my recorder, Powder drove from Barstow. He had a rental in Hesperia, a dive he used mostly for storage. Bullets pocked the windows. The front door creaked open, missing a hinge. Powder ushered me inside. Dull afternoon light cast long shadows over broken and discarded toys scattered across the carpet. Barbie dolls with missing heads, metal tractors, Erector Sets, baseball bats, gloves stretched palms up gripping plastic balls.

"We had a toy fund-raiser," Powder mumbled. Pale and skinny, he disappeared into a side room. A cold draft scratched my face.

"What happened to the good ones?" I asked, accidentally crushing a Barbie's head. The notion that motorcycle gangs had any interest in charities or children was perverse. They needed money to fund their drug and arms deals. And they fit into the real world the way sociopaths blended, by mimicking human emotion and wearing acceptable masks, by pretending to care about children's causes.

"We kept those." Powder slung his AK-47 over his shoulder. He blinked at me, his pale blue eyes framed by white lashes. He resembled a human negative, underdeveloped. "The rest we can sell for dope."

I nodded to the weapon. "Is it hot?"

"I'm not worried." Powder winked. "I have a contact in the department who runs interference."

"He's checked the serial number?"

"I stole it from a guy I worked for in Silver Lakes." My recorder picked up his confession; he was a prohibited possessor with a hot assault rifle. "I have a stash at my place. The rest my mother keeps." I made a mental note to find those guns next.

"Does it work?"

"Absolutely," he said in earnest for the tape. I slipped ATF cash into Powder's hand and sealed his fate. A cannibalized bike lay in pieces near the toys.

"It's a rebuild." Powder shrugged as he counted the bills.

"Where'd you get it?" I pretended to be impressed. Really, I just wanted another confession.

"My friend reported it stolen to his insurance company so he could collect the money. I'm trying to get after-market cases and frames to put it back together."

"I could help you with that," I lied.

⚍

Later that night, an off-duty San Bernardino County sheriff's deputy drank with us at the Motherlode. The Vagos forced the owner to keep the place open after hours. We parked our motorcycles inside the bar, most of us too drunk to risk the ride home. And, too, we didn't want them stolen. As dawn seeped through the cracked windows, the deputy's face smarted from alcohol. Even seated, he was an imposing figure, with a large belly and early gray at the temples. Married to a woman who worked in the sheriff's office, he talked bitterly about his years in law enforcement, his low pay and impossible schedule. I nursed my third beer and watched him guardedly. Amid black and chrome, dirty denim, and rows of empty bottles, I listened for verbal cues, words that signaled betrayal. But the Vagos seemed amused by the deputy's conflicted loyalty. More than a threat, they considered him useful.

"Steer clear of him," Koz warned me. "He might dig up something on you."

As the deputy stumbled home in bright sun to put on his uniform, I puzzled over his choices. We were opposites, each of us dressed in costume hoping to disguise his true identity.

6

The Murder Unit

Ten o'clock Saturday night and my head was spinning. Flushed with fever, I had a raging migraine and already too much Tylenol. But sleep was not an option, and flu a weak excuse. Psycho planned a birthday celebration for Head Butt's brother, the chapter's newest hang-around. He expected me to be at Mickey McGees in twenty minutes. My hands shook as I laced up my boots. My face ached from the night before. Yellow tint shined beneath my right eye. My lower lip was swollen and my knuckles were split. My dog hid in my sheets. My girlfriend slept soundly. I still needed to do something about her, but at least for now she had promised to quit snooping.

Loud music pulsed from inside Mickey McGees, a smoky, standing-room-only Irish bar that attracted a dangerous mix of bikers and yuppies. A security camera scanned the rows of motorcycles stacked in the parking lot. More recorders were tucked into ceiling nooks inside the bar. But all the monitoring proved no deterrence. The Vagos routinely pulled out the videos and shredded them. No witnesses. Several unmarked cars from San Bernardino's gang unit dotted the dark streets in response to the random violence that had erupted just three weeks prior in another high desert bar between Victor Valley Vagos and local patrons. Those bikers, released on $50,000 bail, faced aggravated assault charges for the brutal beating of a student with a pool cue. Their arrests made local news but had little, if any, chilling effect on the club's activities.

Bandit and Psycho, well into their second round, stomped and clapped as a prospect, Rodney Rust, a musician by trade, belted out karaoke. He looked pissed. Lyrics morphed on the screen. I had no strength to walk the distance to the bathroom. My reflection in the chrome mirror was pasty white. Shapes moved behind me; pool sticks clacked against felt; balls swished into pockets. I nursed a beer, the urge to pee so strong my bladder hurt. Psycho, tired of Rust's croaking, pounded on the table and ordered the prospect to the ground. "Knuckle push-ups." Bandit joined in Psycho's chant. My only thought was peeing. But just as I considered wading through the crowd, a short-cropped clean-cut pool player brushed Rust's elbow. The prospect bristled at the contact.

"This is a Vagos table," Rust snarled, dribbling his beer on the kid's Rockports. We were in trouble. I wanted to yell to the patron, *Run, get the hell out while you can!* But instead I quietly sipped my beer. Meanwhile, the patron looked perplexed, like he hadn't heard Rust over the din of heavy percussion. He shrugged, positioned his pool stick on the table, and prepared to strike. Rust swung; pure reckless abandon cracked the kid's jaw and jerked his head backward. Screams erupted nearby. Hang-arounds rushed from the darkness like wolves on a rabbit. Bandit, too, leapt from his barstool. Beer sloshed over his hand as he grabbed the kid's hair and smashed his face into the pool table. As an active Marine stationed in Barstow, Bandit had managed so far to straddle both his gang and military lifestyles. As long as he committed no crimes; being a gang member apparently qualified only as an extracurricular activity. Red streaks blotched the green felt. The kid's burly friend swung his stick at Psycho, and I knew that was the beginning of the end. Bandit rushed to defend Psycho, transforming the scene into a tangle of tendons, muscles, and veins, corded and wet under a cube of white light. Bandit wasn't going to stop; relief came with each blow as he smacked his fist into thin, hollow ribs. Meanwhile, hang-around Joe picked up a stool, lifted it high above his head, and prepared to smash it into the first kid's face. Joe's whole body shook until he blurred around the edges.

"Stop!" I blocked the blow.

The kid writhed on the floor, clutching his head, blood oozing between his fingers. Patrons scattered into the far corners, slipping on pool balls and beer. Glass broke. Bottles smashed. Shards glittered on the floor. Jagged bits crushed between exposed wooden planks. People bolted for the exit. No police stormed inside. Joe tossed the stool against the wall and struck a woman in the head. Unflinching, he let out a low whistle, and Vagos bounded from the shadows, dragged the bloody kid by his limbs toward the exit, his sweaty body tinged yellow, as if dipped in wax. In the parking lot, his beating continued. Steel-toed boots pummeled his temple, and still the police waited for backup. Panicked, I pleaded with Joe, Eric, Walter, and Rust to stop, painfully aware that if I didn't do something the kid would die.

"Get the fuck inside."

And as if stunned back into consciousness, Joe suddenly stopped. The kid curled on the pavement. He coughed up blood and several teeth. *Where were the fucking cops?* I hoped they had staked the perimeter and had called for reinforcements. A strange stillness defined the moment between retreat and risk. Would the Vagos grab their guns and shoot their witness point-blank like a boar they'd tracked in a hunt? As we waited inside the now empty bar, my body shook with tension. Would they accept that I had stopped the beating because of the cops? Would they question my loyalty to the club because I had intervened? Joe was agitated. His boots crunched over shards of glass. The kid's friend had already bolted. Bloody prints tracked his movements to the exit.

This was it. No doubt he had gone to the police or the hospital. We all sensed it like trapped animals. But no one moved to leave. We were like sitting ducks. A bald bulb suspended from a ceiling cord spotlighted our faces. I steadied myself on a stool, needing so badly to pee. The kid moaned outside. At least he was still alive.

Then, as if a camera flashed, cops, dressed in green raid jackets and Kevlar vests, stormed the bar. White lettering across their chests announced SAN BERNARDINO COUNTY SHERRIFF'S DEPARTMENT and HIGHWAY PATROL gang units. Barks, smoke, and commotion followed as police pinned my hands behind my back, cuffed me, led me outside into blinding white light, and shoved me into the back of an unmarked car. Psycho followed, his expression grim. Neither of us spoke. We suspected that the cops had a recording device planted somewhere inside the car. My knees hit my chest. A mesh cage separated our plastic bench from the front seat. Pain shot through my bladder. Psycho watched me intently. Joe and the others climbed into different cars. We traveled in tandem to the San Bernardino West Valley Detention Center—"Gladiator School"—one of the most violent facilities in the country.

7

Pulp Fiction

> Your asses would be dead as fucking fried chicken, but you happen to
> pull this shit while I'm in a transitional period, so I don't wanna kill
> you, I wanna help you.
> —JULES, *PULP FICTION*

My head spun with the image of the kid on the pavement. If he didn't die, he would suffer for months drugged and numb from his injuries, fearful of leaving his house, worried about gang retaliation. All for what? So strangers could flex some muscle and prove their allegiance to a biker club? Across from me, Psycho dozed, jerking with the bus's movements, and I marveled that he could sleep at all. Vagos were criminals always; they didn't have downtime or conscience or moments where they lived any kind of normal. Undercover operatives debriefed, had hours, sometimes even days where they decompressed, but not bikers, not me. Safety dictated that I pretend to cherish the Life and not just the criminal enterprise.

I had committed no assault. I knew I would be released. I was okay.

"California Penal Code 186.22, the STEP Act," Koz explained to me later. This was the Street Terrorism Enforcement and Prevention Act, which adds time to sentences for being a gang member.

I cradled the phone between my shoulder and ear and squeezed my eyes shut; fever pounded in my head as Koz elaborated, and I heard only snippets of his plan: "Best to proceed as normal . . . no one but Sergeant Bentson knows who you are." Bentson was head of the San Bernardino gang unit. Local law enforcement couldn't be trusted with the knowledge of a federal investigation; in fact, the ATF already knew of four San Bernardino sheriff's deputies who regularly supplied sensitive information to the Vagos. Koz and I agreed to inform the U.S. Attorney's Office about my arrest and instruct them to keep me incarcerated in the state judicial system until it became "absolutely necessary" to intervene with the local District Attorney's Office.

The judge set our bail at $50,000 each. Psycho looked smug; he planned to be gone the next morning. He had "people" on the outside with cash.

Meanwhile, deputies hustled us into a holding cell. The walls smelled of wet stone. My palms sweated on the steel bars. Psycho crouched low; his toes—the only body parts without ink—were exposed through the jail-issued sandals. They looked unnatural, sickly white like the underbelly of a fish. He mumbled something about scraping off his Vago tattoos and denying any affiliation with the gang.

Familiar claustrophobia enveloped me. We had been dropped in a cage with no skylight. Shock and hurt slid behind Rust's eyes as he absorbed Psycho's betrayal. I couldn't believe that Psycho had renounced his own leadership either, but I used his weakness to my advantage. All color drained from Joe's face. Hang-around Walter clenched and unclenched his fists. Puffy bags framed his pale eyes. His expression cold and distant, broken already by a system meant to break people like him.

Deputies targeted Walter, Joe's half brother, and pegged him as a Vago. Because he was already on parole, they placed him with the Aryan Brotherhood, where he received lockdown in a super-maximum-security unit. Survival instincts kicked in. My emotions shut down, and although I knew my fate was temporary, that knowledge didn't erase my apprehension.

At least for now I was a gangster and a felon and, according to the jail's classification system, I belonged in the "Murder Unit."

This newer facility was an octagon-shaped jail containing a single guard tower surrounded by six steel tanks, thirty-six cells two levels deep. Each housed seventy killers awaiting sentencing. A glass-front panel allowed deputies access into each coffinlike containment. We were shuffled inside, segregated by race in our cells. The F tank, dubbed the "fag unit" by inmates, held the transvestites and homosexuals. Psycho and Bandit shuffled apart to different tanks opposite mine; I squeezed into the C tank with six other whites and several Hispanics and blacks. Deputies led Joe, Rust, and Walter to different units and I lost sight of them.

Each tank served as a microcosm of society, a cultural pocket that dictated rank and protocol. And though the guards controlled by force and dissent, real manipulation existed inside among the inmates. I never got used to eyes watching me or the constant noise: moans, screams, toilets flushing, chains rattling, batons smacking against glass. We pissed, shit, slept in front of someone. But the dehumanization began with the clothes, shapeless orange scrubs made of thin cotton. Tough killers reduced to convention and sameness. The strong survived; the weak shriveled with fear. *I could do this for one night.* Warm air constricted me, like a noose around my throat.

The normal process was to post bail.

➤❈

The next morning, Psycho and I, chained together, attended our bail hearing. We opted for the physical experience of the courtroom rather than a video-screen prompt and a borrowed public defender. The court considered the Vagos, more than any other organized gang, an extreme public threat and ordered a full SWAT team to guard the perimeter and interior of the courthouse. At least twelve armed deputies lined the jury box. And while the show of force may have served as protection for the judge and spectators, it also had an unfortunate consequence—it inflated the Vagos' "terroristlike" persona.

Psycho, confident that his release was imminent, assured me the club would loan me 10 percent toward my $50,000 bail. Koz promised to pay the rest in a week. Warm air filtered through the ducts inside the courtroom; a hint of peroxide skimmed my nostrils. Long rectangular windows sealed out sunlight. A young prosecutor, maybe no more than thirty, clicked across the floor. She huddled at the bench with defense counsel, her face animated, blond head shaking side to side.

This couldn't be good.

She insisted $50,000 was too low, that the Vagos ran a "terror campaign" and their "brutality knew no limits." The judge agreed, increased our bail to $500,000, and ended the verbal ping-pong.

"I could go to the DA right now," Koz assured me as soon as I could reach a phone.

"No." I was adamant. "That would just invite suspicion. Let's wait." None of the witnesses had mentioned my involvement in the fight. I figured the DA would either reduce my bond or drop my charges altogether based on lack of evidence.

"We can't post your bail."

"I know."

And while we formulated a plan that would keep me safe, protect my cover, and preserve the integrity of the investigation, I returned to the Murder Unit.

✖

Once a week, cellies in each tank enjoyed an hour outside in the concrete yard, unless the lone deputy "forgot" or confused the rotation. If that happened, an entire cell could suffer a week without exercise. The space consisted of four walls and a shaded bulb to simulate a colorless outdoor sky. Mostly the yard offered a chance to stretch. Some races clustered together for a fierce game of handball, the sound of balls bouncing on concrete eerily similar to fists hitting bone.

The Murder Unit was run by two disinterested deputies. They announced day-to-day routines with whistles that signified meals, yard, lights-out. But really, the Aryan Brotherhood, a white supremacist prison gang, controlled the "Woods" (their moniker for whites) throughout the complex. Each race ruled its own: the Mexican Mafia, housed in another unit entirely, dictated the rules for the Hispanics in the Murder Unit. The Bloods and Crips ruled the blacks, and so forth.

Each tank, equipped with an open bathroom and a so-called dayroom where meals occurred, offered the illusion of humanity. But in fact the "amenities" created opportunity for abuse. Once the steel doors of our cells buzzed open for meals and we funneled to one of the fifteen tables, the deputies' attention diverted.

※

I shared a cell with Jan, a tall Mormon who resembled an SS guard, with pale skin, a tuft of blond hair cropped close to the scalp, and cold reptilian eyes. He had been in the Murder Unit since his eighteenth birthday two years earlier.

"I stabbed my girlfriend's mother in the throat thirty-three times," he volunteered matter-of-factly by way of introduction. "I'm a virgin."

Already my first few minutes in the cell seemed too long.

Jan prattled on about his tortured childhood, his parents who kicked him out, his girlfriend's mother who had "tried to give him a blow job" in the parking lot of a grocery strip mall until she "got what she deserved."

"Fucking bitch." He spat, then leaned forward, elbows on his knees. "'Why, Jan? Why, Jan?'" he mimicked, reliving the mother's last pleas. Next he described in chilling detail the spurting blood from the cuts in her neck, how she "burped, farted, burped, farted" until she expired. Jan shuddered, then closed his eyes at the memory as if the whole retelling somehow aroused him.

"When I get out of here"—his eyes fluttered open—"I'm going to be a serial killer."

8

The Rep

Our cell's steel doors buzzed open and we scrambled into the dayroom, lined up along the perimeter like soldiers waiting for inspection. A large black deputy surveyed us, made sure our shirts were tucked in and that we all wore orange shoes with matching socks. He couldn't care less if we looked alike, only that we followed orders. Unarmed, he wore an ill-fitting brown uniform. Angry lines etched into his face. He scanned a disheveled Hispanic inmate in bare feet with disdain.

"He's lucky that motherfucker doesn't launch him face-first into concrete," Jan whispered to me later as we ate. "He's done it before. He handcuffs dudes from behind, hogties their ankles, and launches them into the air like missiles."

And when they lay in pools of blood, I was certain there would be no infirmary, no stitches, and no recovery. The inmates made sense of their world through order and structure, codes of conduct that united them against a common enemy—the deputies—and perpetuated an us-versus-them mentality. But really, we were not so different. The deputies, too, operated in a quasi-military structured institution, their prime focus punishment of individuals who did not live up to certain standards, who disobeyed rules, or who foolishly believed they might be human or even valuable as anything other than part of a larger machine. With the uniform came a mask, a role that allowed them to dehumanize those outside their world. *Not so different from the Vagos.* The cuts, the bike, the tattoos—all encouraged a persona that led to increased aggression, strength in conformity.

✄

I learned the rules quickly. Each tank designated a Rep responsible for "checking" inmate misconduct. The Key Holder, selected by the Aryan Brotherhood who controlled the entire prison, monitored the Rep; so-called Bullets enforced the Rep's orders. The rank-and-file structure mirrored the Vagos except that in the tank the stakes were much higher.

My first meal arrived, a tasteless sticky clump of carrots drizzled with white sauce that reminded me of snot. I vowed my next meal would be M&M's from the commissary. At the Rep's signal, we shuffled to our places. Each race sat together at one of the fifteen tables. Narrow spaces separated them. The Rep controlled when we ate, when we sat, when we left the table. The system functioned through obedience and precision, a simple hand gesture, a nod of the head. No room for error, for lapse or accident. No one spoke. Eating was a drill, necessary soldier fuel. The Woods ate together. No one left the table until everyone finished eating. A lone Wood was vulnerable to attack.

I sat across from a tall, angular inmate with feminine hands. He lowered his eyes and reached across the table for the salt. His sleeve grazed my plate. Like a spark, the room ignited. The Rep snapped his fingers and Bullets grabbed the offender by the elbows and dragged him to a cell located behind the stairwell and hidden from the deputies' view.

Although there were only six of us Woods in the entire mix of seventy inmates, no race interfered with another's discipline. If races crossed, the results could start a prison riot. The Rep's job was to enforce. Ours had a rap sheet for kidnapping, torture, and murder with a hammer. Short and stocky, he spoke little. A long scar cut into the base of his neck. A circle of inmates formed around the Bullets as they checked the inmate, punching him in rapid succession in the chest and stomach for thirty seconds like a military drill. Without protest, the beaten inmate doubled over, stumbled back to his table, and resumed eating.

I spent the next hour circling laps around the fifty-by-fifty-foot tank just to pass the time until I returned to my cell, to Jan and his ramblings about death and torture. Day blended into night and I slept little. Exhaustion wore on me like a heavy coat. All around me inmates slowly rotted, pressed together, slipping in blood and sweat, soon to be serving life sentences. Theirs was no kind of life. And yet, most wanted to be there, took comfort in rules, in structure, a world within a world, none of it real. Deputies existed like fixtures in the tower, lightbulbs that flickered on and off and faded to black.

I had been in the Murder Unit only one day, but already it felt like months.

⌘

By day two, the Rep had designated Jan and me as the tank Bullets.

"You're as big as a house," Jan explained. "And a gang member."

"What's *your* excuse?"

"I'm tall."

That was pretty close to the truth. Our size made us eligible.

⌘

Hours filled with mini assaults and "exercise." My laps around the dayroom relieved stress. I blocked time by counting. Soon, I had company, a small pale creature with bulbous eyes and large hairy feet. He rarely spoke and reminded me of a Hobbit. He kept pace beside me, breathing heavily as if the exertion gave him asthma. Then an apple sailed past our heads and splattered against the nearby wall. Juice dribbled onto the concrete. I stopped walking, startled by the juxtaposition.

"That's Mexican Hitler." The Hobbit nodded to the Hispanic deputy with cinched pants, a black strip of mustache, and polished boots. The deputy scavenged through the cells kicking errant bananas, stray oranges, and bruised plums. He smashed the fruit into wall phones so that the receiver became sticky and attracted bugs.

"He hates it when we hoard fruit." The Hobbit shrugged as if this behavior were completely normal.

>≈<

Apart from Mexican Hitler, the deputies left me alone. My only experience with abuse came in the form of deliberate neglect. I had never fully recovered from the flu and my fever raged intermittently, making me clammy and weak and dizzy. I worried that my asthma inhaler would run out. Without a prescription refill, soon I could literally take my last breath. The deputies ignored my requests, "lost" my paperwork, or "misplaced" the forms beneath piles of bureaucratic files. Other inmates contracted viral infections, vomited, and fainted at regular intervals, and they never got relief.

"You have to practically be dead before they'll do anything for you in here," Jan said.

>≈<

By the end of the week, the deputies transported our Rep to his preliminary hearing. As he shuffled to his place on the chain, we all spotted the deputy's error. He had mistakenly hooked the Rep next to a convicted child molester. Panic skittered across the inmate's face. He knew his fate already. Prison code dictated that wolves devoured rabbits. Survival required adaptation. Child molesters were excluded; no one protected them. The F tank offered the illusion of separation. But now on the chain, in the presence of a wolf, the child molester became prey. Head bowed, hands limp, breath heavy, the inmate stumbled, as if drunk, eyes glazed and watery.

The Rep had no choice. As the tank bully, he had to strike or risk retribution from his own kind. He recoiled from the inmate as if the child molester had a foul odor. Silence hung heavy around us. If the child molester returned from court unscathed, Bullets would "roll" the Rep out, beat him to a pulp, demand that he "ring the bell" to summon a deputy, and insist on suicide. The Rep might spend time in isolation, crouched in darkness until deputies transferred him to another unit. But if the child molester never returned, the Rep might still do time in solitary.

At least he would preserve his dignity.

Secret sexual encounters happened during church services, the only place where prisoners were permitted to mingle with inmates from the F tank. But while some prayed and others confessed their sins, transvestites and gays disappeared into the communal restrooms.

><

"You know what happens to stretchers in here?" Jan enlightened me later that night.

"Nothing good," I acknowledged, darkness pressing in on me like a mask.

Jan wagged a finger at me and said, "If anyone put his pecker in me, I'd force him upstairs and toss him over the railing."

He spoke the truth. Sex offenders were "disposed of" in the Murder Unit, forced by fellow inmates to crawl on their hands and knees to the top level of the tanks and free-fall onto hard concrete.

"Sometimes when it's really quiet, I'll hear the thud of a body."

9

King of the Killers

Without a Rep to control our tank, we had to rely on the Key Holder, a prospective Aryan Brotherhood member housed in the next unit, to "check" inmate violations. We couldn't see him through the steel doors, but his voice thundered through the cracks. He had loyal spies. Failure to follow the Key Holder's orders had deadly consequences. As we lined up at our tables, one Hispanic inmate stood across from me, arms folded across his chest, jaw jutted in defiance. Though dark skinned, he insisted he was white because he *spoke* white. And in truth, it was easier to be white in the Murder Unit simply because the Woods had fewer numbers and fewer opportunities to mess up.

But more than rejecting his own race, the Hispanic/white inmate renounced his allegiance to Southsiders (aka Serrano), a group for which he still wore the tattoo on his back. The inmate had disrespected both races; he needed more than correction.

The Southsiders Rep planned to jump him. He issued orders to each Hispanic in the tank to punch the inmate at least once in the head. The

Woods, too, were expected to participate. But without a Rep, someone had to take control. I banged on the steel door in the dayroom. "Get me the Key Holder," I said. Within minutes, a deep disembodied voice ordered a beating. At my command, Bullets emerged from the corners and ushered the Hispanic/white inmate into a cell behind the stairs, a blind spot where deputies had no visual access. The cell doors opened with an old-fashioned key and often just stayed open.

The inmate protested mildly, whined that the rules were "stupid," that he could be white if he wanted to be white. Who were *we* to decide? *Maybe he had a point?* Several Hispanics pummeled the inmate with sharp blows to his stomach. Wired and frenzied, they followed their punches with kicks to the head. Blood flew from the inmate's nose onto their orange shoes. He rolled onto his side, moaned, sputtered, and clutched his head. He rocked in the fetal position, his hair sticky with sweat and blood, his back slapping the concrete wall behind him. Anger exploded in the inmates' faces.

"Get up," one ordered. But the Hispanic/white inmate refused. Another kicked him in the back of his head, and I heard a loud crack. A small crowd formed around the perimeter of the open cell. The beating had become a spectator sport. The Woods each took a swing at the slumped-over inmate. I worried that the man might die. He caved inward with each blow to his ribs. Blood oozed from his eyes. He struggled to stand and glared at me with dark wet eyes. I extended my hand. He gave it a weak shake. The Southside Rep shook the inmate's hand, too.

"It's cool," he said. And just like that, order was restored to the tank.

Later, we learned that the inmate actually had mental issues; he was slow. Maybe he really thought he was white after all?

><

"I should be the new Rep," Jan announced later as we lay in the dark listening to the clank of metal and drip of water. "I've been in this hole the longest."

"You should apply." I encouraged him, knowing our tank needed a replacement Rep. No one else jockeyed for the job. The Rep typically incurred additional charges. He had to commit or supervise assaults or risk being killed. Jan had two years in the tank, and a flash temper and brute force that matched his frame. Perfect.

But the Key Holder had other ideas. He nominated me.

"*You?*" Jan bristled. He paced our small cell, chewed the inside of his lower lip, and made a sucking sound that grated on my nerves. "What makes you so special?"

I lay back on the cot, clasped my arms behind my head, and closed my eyes, but Jan's voice droned on as he recounted his crime: *virgin, blow job, stabbed thirty-three times.*

"When I get out of here, I'm going to be a serial killer," Jan repeated.

By now I'd had enough of Jan and his career aspirations. "Listen to me." I sat up, swung my legs over the cot, and rubbed my hands through my hair.

"What's the matter with you?" Jan stopped pacing. A spider crawled across his foot and in a flash he snatched it between his fingers and dangled it upside down by its legs.

"You're not ever getting out," I promised, my voice a tight whisper.

"What do you know about it?" His pale eyes pinned me in the dark, unsettling and cold like the steady gaze of a fly.

"You murdered a woman, brutally." I restated the obvious.

"She deserved it." Jan crushed the spider between his fingers and its bulbous belly burst.

"If you brag to me one more time about wanting to be a serial killer, I'm going to kill you."

><

As the designated Rep, I checked people every three days. Mostly the violations involved words exchanged between the races, jeers or insults mouthed through the glass. I also reviewed new arrivals' papers to make sure they

had been classified correctly. I paced, wired by lack of sleep and heightened awareness, knowing if I missed an affront, if a check went unpun-
ished, my inaction could spark a prison riot. I had some perks—my own
table in the dayroom, extra food.

I was king of the killers.

Each morning I led the Woods in mandatory exercise—four hundred
push-ups, two hundred sit-ups—like a general preparing his soldiers for
war. Actually, it helped me pass the time. And meanwhile, twenty feet across
from us in the dayroom, the Hispanics chanted their own battle cry: "Big,
Bad Sous" (Serranos Southern California Mexicans). I gave geriatrics and
inmates suffering from drug withdrawals a pass. Once the steel doors buzzed
open, each inmate had two minutes to scramble to his place in line and
drop to the floor for push-ups.

But there were always inmates who refused. One Wood in particular
perpetually missed his workouts. The steel doors to his cell buzzed shut
after two minutes and he stared at me through the glass, a wry smile plas-
tered on his face. Maybe he was testing me? When his cell door reopened
two hours later, I hovered in the entrance, arms folded, weary of the game.

"You know the rules."

"What if I don't like the rules?"

"I'm going to have to check you," I said, and I knew he was in trouble.
Independent thinking had no place in the tank, no place in a gang, no
place in the real world. I felt sorry for him. He was part of a cycle; he challenged, I disciplined, and if I detoured, someone else would discipline *me*.
War operated in the same fashion. Good, decent people could not exist in
this environment. It was the natural order of things.

The inmate lowered his head, nodded, and accepted his punishment.
"When?"

"Tomorrow. After lunch."

The next day the inmate surrendered to his fate behind the stairs.
Woods punched him for thirty seconds in the stomach.

A few days later, the same inmate did it again. As the steel doors buzzed shut, he remained asleep, curled on his side, back to the dayroom. Again, I ordered the Bullets to beat him.

"I can't stay in here much longer," I advised Koz over the phone. "It's just a matter of time before I get more charges."

"We can pull you out right now," Koz said.

I stalled. "Let me get to the preliminary hearing." There was no rush, not really. The ATF wasn't paying me for my services. I didn't cost them any money being incarcerated. In fact, Koz confided to me once that I was "the cheapest" investigation his agency had ever funded. Had I been a government agent, my stint in jail would have ended far sooner.

The same Wood emerged flushed and sweaty from beneath the stairs after his third beating in two days and, undeterred, committed yet *another* violation. He shoveled in a few bites of runny mush, then pushed his plate aside and left the table before the others finished eating.

I scraped back my chair and blocked his exit. "What's the matter with you?"

The inmate, tall and skinny, with a zipper tattoo across his skull, sucked in his breath and shrugged. "These rules are stupid."

The other Woods at the table watched me intently, their plastic forks paused midbite. Instinct propelled me and I head-butted the inmate hard, split open the thin flesh on his scalp and tore the length of one eyebrow. Stunned, the inmate fell backward. A whimper escaped his lips. My heart raced. I hadn't meant to attack in the open, in front of the blacks and Hispanics, in plain view of the deputies. But my impulsive act produced the effect I wanted. The inmate grabbed his forehead. Blood seeped through cracks between his fingers. Other inmates quickly dispersed, all of us mindful that at any given moment a deputy could enter and we would all be in trouble.

"Go back to your cell and stay there for a couple of days," I ordered. Both of us knew better than to report the other. My head throbbed from the assault. I was sure the inmate needed stitches, but that wasn't going to happen. He held a rag to his head and shuffled into his cell. With one eye swollen shut he glared at me through the other, blinked back blood, and nodded. We understood the unspoken rules.

✺

Two days later, the black deputy eyed the damaged Wood suspiciously. The inmate's face looked bruised and shiny, his eye still swollen shut.

"What happened to you?" the deputy sneered and stood inches from his face. My own head still throbbed from the gash in my forehead.

"I fell down the stairs." The inmate played the game.

"Sure you did." The deputy glanced down the line at all of us, looking for cracks in our expressions for signs of slippage. We all stood stoic, eyes straight ahead, the code of silence in full force.

✺

A few days later a Hispanic inmate who called himself Beast motioned me over, said he wanted to speak in private. "I know what you are," he whispered, his accent thick.

I knew what he was, too, a triple murderer. I had read about Beast in the local paper before my incarceration. He was a drug dealer who had gunned down several of his cousin's "problems" in the confines of his own garage. Unfortunately, Beast had also inadvertently shot and killed his cousin. His pronouncement jolted me, but there was no way he could know who I really was.

He looked at me with small flat eyes and asked simply, "What do I have to do to be a Vago?" I couldn't believe it. Beast actually wanted to prospect. He wanted me to sponsor him. I couldn't imagine how I would accomplish that given the confines of the Murder Unit, but it would play well with the Vagos, especially since Psycho had lost control of his tank and had renounced his own gang. *He* had not been asked to be the Rep.

"Vinny." I cupped the phone to my ear later in the dayroom. He now served as the vice president of the Victorville chapter, the second oldest chapter in the Vagos' history and the birthplace of the Hells Angels' first chapter. "Beast says he wants to be a Vago prospect."

"*That* motherfucker is in there with you? He's hard-core." Vinny deferred to me, and I suddenly realized the clout I had with the club. I sponsored Beast. But I couldn't really order him around, not the way a true Vago prospect would be ordered to serve. That would only incite a race riot. Beast had to remain a predator for his own survival. Still, Beast enjoyed the idea of being my prospect. I had a natural rapport with him, having grown up in a Hispanic barrio. Plus, Beast and I had drug dealing in common. The Woods and Hispanics were considered allies against the blacks. Having a prospect slave like Beast at my command bolstered my image in the eyes of my fellow Woods as well as the Vagos. Practically, I knew there was no chance Beast would ever emerge on the outside. He faced a triple life sentence and would likely rot in prison.

The night Beast became my official prospect, a riot erupted in the tank next to mine. The commotion began, as all fights did in the Murder Unit, over race. A black inmate disrespected a Hispanic, and the Hispanics, forced to retaliate, attacked with fists and makeshift shanks, knives carved out of toothbrushes, razor blades melted into pens. Dark stripped away the inmates' toughness, left them raw and exposed. Sounds morphed into wails, pained anguish, yelps, cries that wrenched through steel. Latches opened, and through the small portal deputies hurled grenades into the cell. They contained tiny rubber balls that smacked the skin like bullets, traveling at speeds of four hundred miles an hour.

"Like being hit with a baseball bat," Jan described. The dayroom filled with smoke. My eyes smarted. I watched an inmate get struck in the ass, fall to his knees, and sob from the pain.

"This happens sometimes," Jan breathed, his face too close to mine, through the portal. His lips were chapped and a small row of pimples formed around the edges. "Fucking animals."

And it struck me that brutality was human, that each of us had savage impulses we contained and civilized rules we aimed to follow to redirect our primal instincts into productive tasks. A person's desire to kill, for instance, could be channeled into a desire to hunt. Slaughtering a deer or a pig was acceptable if the animal provided nourishment. But killing for thrill was just plain murder. In here, in these cells, inmates concerned only with their own base desires became unable to see each other as human beings. The more beatings they endured, the easier it became for them to harm and kill each other. Mistreatment facilitated the process of dehumanization. It was only a matter of time before they turned on one another.

>≪≪

By my third week as Rep I had upgraded to commissary food, M&M's and ramen noodles. As I checked each new arrival's paperwork to make sure he had been properly classified in his tank, I noticed a lump curled on a mattress "boat" in the dayroom. We had no cells available. Twist slept knees to his chest on a bald pad in the middle of the floor. His skin had a bluish tint and he looked like he suffered from drug withdrawal. What were the odds that Twist would be thrown into my tank?

I tapped on my cell window to get his attention. "Hey, dude."

He opened one hooded eye and shuddered.

"Want some M&M's?" I waved the bag at him.

His lips curled into a crooked smile and he shook his head.

"What are you in here for?" I hoped it wasn't for another murder. Koz had ensured that Twist's original charges had been dropped; still, I knew eventually I would have to testify against Twist. That fact never bothered me. I always knew my job. The line between gangster and hero never blurred. I had no love for Twist or what he represented. Prison was just a revolving door for damaged people like him. The Vagos, like any outlaw gang, backed their own because they loved to fight; loyalty, brotherhood, code had nothing to do with it. Respect was just another word for fear.

Members bragged they could always count on their Vago brothers to bail them out. But it was all illusion; it was all bullshit.

"Felon in possession," Twist mumbled, and he spent the next two days asleep.

※

And then I heard about Bernard, a Mexican drug dealer housed in a nearby federal facility, who faced twenty-five years minimum in prison. Thanks to me. His case circulated in the papers. It was a case I had worked before ever infiltrating the Vagos. His trial loomed in the weeks ahead. I planned to testify against Bernard. But as long as I remained in the Murder Unit, my identity could be revealed, my cover blown, my life taken. It wouldn't take long before he learned through pretrial discovery my information, my exact cell and unit, my affiliation with the Vagos. And Bernard wouldn't need a contract hit.

I shivered in the dark, listening intently to chains rattle metal. A large clock in the deputies' tower ticked the hours. Nearly midnight, and I sensed Bernard's presence like an amputated limb. He knew I was in the Murder Unit. Paranoia settled in. I imagined the Hispanics emptying their cells, blowing into mine like a harsh wind, knocking my head into the wall, carving me up with their knives. Worry chipped at my resolve. Each time the cells opened, I anticipated the deadly assault, helpless to stop it but determined to end my days fighting.

"He'll kill me if he finds out I'm in here," I told Koz. "He's tight with the Mexican Mafia." He never became a member of that prison gang, easily one of the most brutal and ruthless in existence. Bernard didn't need to join La eMe; he was a millionaire drug dealer who didn't want to spend the rest of his life in prison. If he wanted me dead, he only needed to name his price. And there was no way I would ever testify against a Mexican Mafia member.

"The prosecutor wants to interview you for Bernard's case," Koz said.

I absorbed the news with dread. "If I'm singled out and the only one taken from my cell, I'll just attract suspicion."

"What do you suggest?"

I hesitated, knew my only option. "Put me in the hole."

The next day, Kiles made sure fifteen of us Reps moved cells. By relocating all of us at once, she ensured my safety. I would not be singled out. I would not arouse suspicion. Beast grunted a sincere good-bye, mumbled something about seeing me soon, on the outside. Hard-core gangsters hugged me in succession. They wrapped clumsy arms around my shoulders, some knuckle-punched my fist, even Jan looked genuinely sad. I felt like a celebrity walking the gauntlet, shaking hands, making false promises, hoping to see them each again. The inmates parted the way for me like I was Moses leaving my people.

I went to solitary confinement.

10

Solitary

In the hole, light had its own claustrophobia, heavy and still like lake water but without the quiet. No windows, no blanket, and no fresh air. Chilly concrete walls entombed me. A mattress in the corner vomited cubes of foam. My toes curled with cold. In the next cells, Black Bubba's government rants exploded in my head. Hollow and loud, he shouted at shadows and imagined rats that clicked through the pipes. Fear gnawed at me: *What if my rescue never came? What if I were simply forgotten? After all, I didn't exist.* I curled on the hard floor with my feet touching the wall. Pain shot through my belly, my last meal a distant memory. The steel door sealed me inside like suction.

The first few hours I spent sleepless, straining against the light, waiting for my eyes to adjust to the brightness. But they never did. *This* was madness: locked down for twenty-three hours a day in a cell the size of a closet. No human contact. Disembodied voices. Boredom tore at my conscience; everywhere was whiteness and dead space. Solitary, designed to house the "worst of the worst" or the mentally ill, only warehoused problems.

Paranoia gripped me and I experienced druglike visions. I imagined myself behind glass in an incubator, spotlighted, watched by people I couldn't
see. I saw bodies stacked rows on rows still alive in a mass grave waiting
for release. I felt my mind shutting down. Numbness. I couldn't complete
a whole thought. I saw partial faces, friends', Bernard's. They flashed around
me like fragments from a strobe. I heard voices that melted together into
white noise, difficult to make out any words. Thick tones of my father,
guttural grunts of the guards, empty sounds of the other inmates. Bubba's
screams next to me. His voice echoed through the vents, boomed down
the skinny hall where a shower splashed cold water on my face, stiffened
my hair, and made me shiver.

"How long have I been in here?" I asked Koz after the deputy hustled
me back into my hole. I never learned his first name; he went by Atkins.
But they changed all the time; sometimes the black deputy came, sometimes Mexican Hitler. They barely spoke, and as far as I could tell they had
little other human interaction. They lived in silence like animals, like the
inmates they supervised. They shared an office in the fishbowl, a colorless
room, a box within a box.

They never saw sunlight either. Maybe they had a family on the outside, maybe they saw them just long enough to watch them sleep. Deep
lines etched into their faces, stress brought on by living in a tomb, isolated
from human contact. They looked at me with an emptiness that made me
shudder.

"It's only been three days," Koz assured me on the telephone. Sweat
drenched my shirt. I had heard of inmates who had never suffered any
mental illness suddenly developing symptoms of psychosis. Solitary was the
prison's solution to gang violence. Inmates could be locked down for days,
even weeks, at a time until they renounced their affiliations. But what officials failed to realize was that gangs in prison actually served a purpose:
status, respect, even a sense of community. Isolating gang members in the
hole only made them angry.

I paced; the exercise increased circulation in my legs. When panic made me dizzy, I moved faster. This is what I imagined being buried alive must feel like. I had seen programs on television about skiers lost in snow-drifts or avalanches, knowing their fate but desperate to claw their way out only to meet more snow, more whiteness, more cold. It didn't matter that my situation was temporary; within hours I thought about death.

Then I heard the click of the lock, the bolt slide back. Sharp light filtered through a wedge in the open door.

"You have visitors," the deputy said.

⋙⋘

Kiles drove Koz and me to the U.S. Attorney's Office in downtown Los Angeles after she checked me out of Solitary like a library book. The assistant U.S. attorney (AUSA) prosecuting Bernard for drug conspiracy charges wanted me to identify the particular jewelry store inside the Diamond Mart where Bernard had purchased a precious necklace. Now that Bernard had resurfaced after three years as a fugitive, his federal case resumed. And the AUSA, learning of my recent arrest, wanted me to testify against Bernard *in my jail clothes.*

"The jury will wonder about [Charles's] status." She revealed her igno-rance about my safety. After all, if I testified in jail clothes, Bernard would know I was in custody on *other* charges.

"Make sure she knows I didn't assault anyone," I urged Koz, worried that she might revoke my federal release conditions if she believed I had committed a crime while out on bail. I had learned to trust no one, not even prosecutors. Every department had its moles, dirty cops, biker infor-mants, overzealous defense attorneys, careless prosecutors who might let it slip that I worked undercover.

But I had no choice. We told her.

⋙⋘

Sunlight and fresh air assaulted my senses through the open car windows. My first exposure to the outside world in two months and I felt reborn:

Traffic signals flashed primary colors, ocean spray tickled my nostrils, the honk of a horn jolted me, smells of rubber on asphalt—*freedom*. I had fantasized about this moment, envisioned burgers and fries in my cave like a mirage.

"Any special requests?" Koz laughed.

"In-N-Out Burger," I blurted.

I hadn't showered in days. Jail covered my orange scrubs like a sweetly rotten intimacy. I smelled like spoiled fruit. My skin had a sickly glaze. My reflection in the rearview mirror made me shudder. I looked like a negative partly developed, unnaturally white. I squinted at the harsh sun. Sharp pain pressed against my belly. Koz ordered my food at the drive-through. The young cashier with the paper cap recoiled at the sight of me. I snatched the bag from him and inhaled my burger. I probably could have swallowed ten, as the patty practically dropped into my stomach like a half-dollar coin.

After my quick lunch, Kiles pulled into a No Parking zone on a narrow street in downtown LA. Guards lined the perimeter of the Diamond stores, but none noticed me as I strolled down the street in my slip-on canvas shoes, dressed in my orange jail garb with SAN BERNARDINO COUNTY JAIL prominently displayed across my chest. I was a curiosity, a Thing. People couldn't process me; visually I didn't make sense with the backdrop. I suddenly understood why crime victims had trouble describing their assailant. The brain rejected what it could not understand. I took my time identifying the jewelry store. The fresh breeze, the street sounds, the smell of baked bread from the shop on the corner all amplified. Deprivation made me notice details, the shiny studs on a woman's boots, a mohair purse, the flutter of a skirt.

✂

The AUSA, a smartly dressed woman in her early fifties, smiled warmly at me, almost apologetic that she still had to prosecute me for old charges.

She sat on the edge of her chair, pen in hand, legal pad propped on the three-inch ledge in the room reserved for confidential visits. Stress ravaged the soft skin beneath her pale blue eyes. She lifted her gaze slightly and asked me how I was doing. I stared at her, astonished. *How am I doing?* The question hit me hard. I wanted to laugh at its absurdity. *I'm hungry. I sleep on concrete. My bones are bruised. I've lost track of time. The light burns my eyes. I will go mad if I stay.*

But instead I politely answered her questions about Bernard. She owned me. She had the power to release me if she wanted. I was expendable, only as valuable to her as my testimony. My nerves shot, sleep deprived, so broken my legs actually shook, I wanted the interview to last hours. Starved for human contact, the prosecutor represented my only lifeline, my only assurance that my rescue was imminent. I think I surprised her with my recall. I knew the drug business, the language, the equipment used to manufacture large quantities of methamphetamine. In my former life I could have been Bernard's equal. When the questioning ended, she stood, smoothed her crisp navy suit, and clicked her pen shut. Interview over.

Wait, I wanted to shout, feeling like a zoo animal housed in the wrong cage.

<hr />

"Why am I here again?" I cradled the phone to my ear and struggled to keep my voice calm. White walls stretched the length of Solitary. My eyes played tricks on me. Shadows darted at the far end. Footsteps padded around me, belonging to no one. Voices faded in and out of earshot as if someone messed with the volume on a radio. Fear zipped up my spine. My breath came in short bursts.

"We couldn't get you back in the general population." Koz cleared his throat. His words crackled over the line. He sounded far away, gone already.

"How long this time?" I managed.

"Your preliminary hearing is only three days away. If you can make it until then . . ."

"Three days?" I felt sick. I couldn't last another hour in Solitary. I didn't have to continue. I could tell Koz this was the end of the road, and no one would fault me. The informant always had the final word. But it was risky for Koz to inform the DA's office of my identity. Leaks could get me killed. At least in jail I had a chance. *I could do this.*

"I'm pretty sure they'll drop the charges," I said.

><

My heart beat faster in the hole, louder, irregular. Sometimes the sound thundered in my ears, and I scrambled to the corners of darkness to shut out the noise. I shivered from sweat. Shadow people crowded the one glass portal, scratching to enter. I could hear inmates in cells next to me. Bubba asked me about the rats. He had sores along his legs and arms. He said the rats feasted on his cuts. I had never seen any rats. Pain throbbed in my temple. I stopped pacing yesterday. My legs ached. My toes were numb. A draft blew from an unknown source, felt like fingers on my neck. I ate rice clumps with my hands. Some of the white pieces dropped to the floor. I worried the food might attract critters. I envisioned tiny legs scratching through my skin.

"They're coming for my face," Bubba hollered. "They're chewing at my lips."

I rocked in my corner, hands locked around my knees. A prickly sensation tingled up my legs, like hypothermia, the last feeling before the body shuts down. Fever coursed through me; I sweated and shivered intermittently, and in the few moments I slept I dreamed of cold water. I smelled rain. I ran, my heart beating so fast it nearly burst. Layers stripped away from me, costumes, one after the other, leaving lumps, like bodies, in the desert.

Day 4, my clothes fit looser. I hadn't eaten for hours and the last food I swallowed came back up. We were lucky to have a communal shower. But I was sick, and sometimes Atkins took his time getting me out of my cell.

Sometimes he didn't come at all. And I wondered vaguely about the prison infirmary and whether inmates ever recovered from infection or illness. Whether it even mattered. Atkins mumbled something about my preliminary hearing and told me to "hurry the fuck up."

"But I don't have court today," I protested mildly as he ushered me down a narrow hallway and hustled me into a dark holding cell.

"What time is it?" I managed.

"Time to shut the fuck up," Atkins barked, and his face contorted like a banshee's.

He slammed the cell door shut and left me huddled in the dark for what seemed an eternity. After a while, another deputy appeared, opened my cell, searched me, and shoved breakfast at me. "Hurry the fuck up," he screamed as I shoveled runny oatmeal into my mouth. "You have the wrong day," I insisted, and I recognized the deputy. Mexican Hitler stared blankly at me, his mustache twitching above his lip. He squared his shoulders, shook his head, barked "Orders are orders," whisked my bowl away, and slammed the door shut. I waited in darkness again, shivering with fever. Lumps of oatmeal settled in my stomach and threatened to roll back up. *I wished they would hurry the fuck up.* Several minutes later, Atkins returned, ushered me quickly to my feet, down another skinny hallway to yet another cell where, this time chained to other inmates, I waited for the bus that would transport me from the San Bernardino jail to the Victorville courthouse. We shuffled outside, stood in our designated lines to board. Sun slanted through the dark sky and I realized it must be dawn.

Doors opened and three of us climbed inside the cramped space with bench seats designed for midgets.

"Sit the fuck down," the deputy ordered as I hesitated.

"I can't fit," I protested, pointing to the wedge of cushions and my large knees. The scene replayed like a cartoon.

The deputy stared at me, preprogrammed with his response. "Sit the fuck down."

"You don't understand . . . I can't fit." I raised my voice as if sound were the problem.

He glared at me and looked like he might explode. He couldn't care less that my body didn't fold that small, that all of us would have to sit in each other's laps to travel. He looked flustered. His face flushed. He barked the orders louder. "*Sit the fuck down! Sit the fuck down!*"

I was too ill to process his tantrum. I sat sideways, my knees bumping into the next inmate's chest, my chained hands resting in his lap. We rode in silence for forty-five minutes, bumping through the dark, my nose running, my body shaking. Like being in a coffin two sizes too small. When we finally arrived, the deputy ordered us out. He adjusted our chains, pinning my right arm close to my hip just in case I planned to escape. We huddled into a holding cell in the Victorville jail looking like a group of amputees. Bunks lined the walls, and I rolled onto one and fell into a restless sleep. As the hours ticked by, inmates complained, the chains cut into their wrists, their one pinned arm tingled with numbness. Mine felt like bread strapped to my back.

"I can't even take a crap," one inmate whined. "How am I supposed to wipe my ass with my left hand?" He had a point.

Finally, after what seemed several hours, I shuffled into the courtroom, feeling weak and nauseous.

"Can I have some water?" I noticed a paper cup and pitcher nearby. The deputy shrugged, and with shaking hands I poured water into a cup, spilling some on the ledge. I raised the paper to my lips but discovered that my chains didn't extend that far. I contorted my body, folded myself in half, bent my head low all in an effort to take a sip. Meanwhile, my fever raged. Sweat slicked my face. I barely registered the courtroom, my whole focus now on the cup. The inmate next to me chuckled, then yanked on the chain so that I spilled the contents.

Before I could react, the judge barked, "What is Falco doing here?"

The deputy, flustered, rifled through his paperwork, looking for my name.

"Take him back. Take him to a *doctor*. His preliminary isn't until tomorrow."

Now I *really* felt sick. It would take at least all night to return me to Solitary, only to start the process all over the next morning. And I knew better than to think anyone would summon a doctor.

⚞⚟

The next day in court, deputies, looking like rotten bananas in their brown uniforms, guarded the "chain" where most of us waited shackled together to hear our fate. Amid the buzz of attorneys, the occasional cough or sneeze, the musty smell of body odor and jail, the judge called my case. My preliminary hearing lasted five hours; the prosecutor displayed photos for the judge of members with shaved heads and graphic tattoos. One had inked GREEN NATION across his skull.

"They *want* you to fear them," she spat. "They *enjoy* inflicting terror." Her icy stare made me squirm. I wanted to shout out, "Not me, not me, I'm not one of them. I'm one of the good guys." But of course I understood that the lines were blurred. The courtroom stirred as SWAT teams, poised for action, blocked the exits. Reporters clustered near the back and furiously scribbled notes. Witnesses—civilians, police officers—testified but none implicated me. I felt invisible. Everyone spoke about the fake me in third person, which only added another layer of invisibility. One bar patron visibly paled. A column of dark hair fell across his left cheek. His fingers mere stubs, the nails bitten off. He frowned when asked to identify me and said, "*He* didn't do anything."

"Are you sure?" The prosecutor looked troubled. Her face relaxed from its perpetual mean glare and settled into surprise.

"He just stood there." Others who testified confirmed I had not participated.

Hope surged through me and then extinguished quickly as the judge read the formal charges against me: assault with a deadly weapon to cause great bodily harm and participating in a street gang. The State had enough probable cause to proceed to trial. The process could take months, maybe even a year, and with my bail still set at $500,000, I would remain in Solitary indefinitely. Worse, the investigation would stall.

"It's your call," Koz said. My obligation to the feds ended long ago with Twist's confession to murder. I didn't have to return to Solitary. But if I relented, if I gave up now, nothing would come of the Vagos infiltration, no indictments, no conclusion, no chill to their criminal activities. The ATF had no one else who could get inside. I swallowed, felt my world slip away as I stared down the long hallway in Solitary.

"Let me go to the prosecutor," Koz insisted. "He can dismiss the charges . . ."

"He'll have to dismiss them against others, too," I said.

"He'll have to know who you are."

It was a risk to leak information about my identity to the DA. But what choice did I have? I couldn't rot indefinitely in Solitary. Koz hung up, and I listened to the dial tone for several seconds, my only connection to the outside world. Atkins ushered me inside the hole; the automatic doors buzzed shut behind me. He became a disembodied voice, perhaps making it easier for him, for all of the guards, to dehumanize their subjects. If they couldn't see me, huddled in the dark, they could justify their cruelty, their apathy. By necessity they became one of us, immersed in a windowless cave, no companionship, no sense of time passing, forced to listen to night terrors and relentless pounding on the walls.

I shut my eyes to the noise: I tried to control the nightmares, but like muscle memory, images returned distortions of reality. My lit cave suddenly so white my eyes burned, the corners of my mouth melted. My space transformed into a vault filled with money; the gun in my hand a plastic toy. Then dust blew around me, fine and odorless. It formed large piles in the center of my cave. I lay on my back and spread my arms wide. I flapped like an angel. But then the whiteness fogged my vision. I had trouble breathing. The whiteness choked me.

Was this what it felt like to lose one's mind?

I lost the ability to distinguish between reality and illusion. I paced, screamed at the portal, at Atkins on the other side. This place housed the mentally ill or those on their way toward madness. I craved dialogue and sometimes I talked to myself, sometimes I answered Bubba. I smacked the damp walls, hoping he could hear me.

Then Atkins slid back the dead bolt. The sound made my heart flutter. I squinted at the sliver of weak light from the hallway.

"Move," he said.

I crawled to my feet. My wrists were sore from handcuffs. Leg irons chafed my shins. I was considered violent and dangerous. Doors buzzed open. I stepped from one cell to the next, put my hands through cutouts in the wall and felt handcuffs slap my wrists. The courtroom unfolded like a vision, and part of me worried that the people I saw shuffling papers, mouthing words, visiting with inmates were unreal, that I saw what I wanted to see. A gorgeous prosecutor with hooded eyes and thin lips nodded in my direction and I knew she knew my secret. Later, Kiles disclosed that the DA was "pissed" she hadn't been informed of my status, but it wasn't Kiles's job to reveal my work for the ATF; my current charges stemmed from State violations. The two jurisdictions had nothing to do with each other.

The judge took the bench, and he looked like a winged creature. He pounded his gavel. Attorneys flocked to him. They spoke in earnest; one cupped the microphone. This was my second bail reduction hearing. The prosecutor dismissed my charges. An audible gasp shuddered through the audience.

I was *free*. The thought paralyzed me; suddenly I was unsure what to do first, whom to contact, how to behave. I needn't have worried. I returned to my cave.

"It's going to take a few hours to do the paperwork," Koz explained.

"Sure." I could handle a few more hours.

I had no sense of time inside the hole, only a sense of slipping away. I had no obvious markers—breakfast, lunch, dinner, daylight, twilight, moon—to signal a beginning or end to my day. I had the stress of preparation, of waiting for an event to occur and wondering if it ever would. It was the same kind of anxiety I imagined old people faced day in and day out; to compensate for their anxiety they accomplished things earlier—ate, slept, awoke—just to get the activity behind them. There was satisfaction in completion, no matter how mundane the goal. Their lives focused on anticipation, waiting for the end when they no longer had to worry about time.

Midnight, twenty hours later, I stood outside the prison's walls.

><

I barely remember being led out of my cave, escorted by Atkins to four different cells where eventually I recovered my clothes along with thirty other guys in a communal holding cell. My girlfriend met me on the curb. I caught my reflection in the car mirror and shuddered: gaunt face, sunken eyes, grizzled beard, unkempt hair, layers of dirt. Night air through the open window filled my lungs. No one spoke. And despite my nausea, I was hungry. Veterans returning from war probably felt similar: shell-shocked, disoriented, relieved. Fear tugged at my conscience. Bernard still loomed large. By now he surely knew I had been in jail. Maybe he had even tipped off the Vagos.

As I slid my key into the lock, my hand trembled. In the dark, noise amplified. My heart beat faster. A trash lid clattered to the street. Startled, I fixated on a rat's tail inside a pizza box. Wind blew an empty cigarette carton across my boots. I glanced over my shoulder. The street was mostly empty. A homeless man pedaled a bicycle several sizes too small for his frame. No cars out of place. No rustling bushes. I opened the door and slid inside. I bent a blind and watched the dark street for sudden movement. *Bernard was out there. And it was only a matter of time before he found me.*

Eventually I fell into a restless sleep. Hercules curled at my feet.

I didn't leave my girlfriend's apartment for three days.

><

"You were right," Koz confirmed. Propped on pillows, the television set tuned to old *Road Runner* cartoons, I cradled the phone to my ear and shoveled in spoonfuls of Lucky Charms.

"Bernard knows about you."

I swallowed and slowly set the cereal bowl on the nightstand. Milk sloshed over my hand. My heart beat faster. Colored marshmallows dissolved in my throat.

"The DEA has an informant in the federal jail who knows about Bernard. The CI reports that Bernard knows your real name, cell, and unit. He commissioned the Mexican Mafia to do a hit."

"Did he give them money?" My chest constricted. That would have solidified the contract.

"The informant says they discussed payment."

"Discussed?"

"We don't know if he ever gave them any money." The unknown was worse. *What if he did? What if he didn't?*

I tossed off my sheets. Sweat drenched my shirt. Nausea settled in my stomach.

"How did Bernard—"

But I realized it didn't matter whether Bernard ever paid the Mexican Mafia to take me out; he simply had to leak my identity to the Vagos. I was screwed either way. (In the end, the government cut Bernard a good deal. As a three-time felon trafficking nearly four hundred pounds of methamphetamine, he received a fifteen-year sentence in federal prison.) When I finally ventured outside, I alternated my routes home, zigzagged between buildings, slowly pulled into my driveway and let the engine idle. But I knew that no amount of charade would save my life. The Vagos knew where I lived. And the Mexican Mafia could take me out in my driveway, one clean shot to the temple before I even opened my car door.

My paranoia was similar to a panic attack. Shadows morphed into silhouettes of familiar people. I jumped at sounds: cars backfiring, thunder, sirens. I had nightmares. Throngs of Vagos stormed my apartment, their fists like rocks against my head. Always I called Koz, the dial tone so loud it hurt my ears. My fingers fumbled on the keypad, thick and clumsy. I could never reach him.

11

The Son of Anarchy

I worried that my two months in the Murder Unit had stalled the Vagos investigation, but my performance in jail actually enhanced my reputation with the club, and at least so far, Bernard hadn't leaked my identity to the gang. Vinny, the former vice president, disgusted by Psycho's renouncement of his own gang, defected from Victorville and formed his own chapter called the High Desert. He recruited some of Psycho's minions. As a result, Psycho needed new blood, new loyal leaders. *Me.* I saw opportunity, a way to access the internal workings of the club and prove it operated as a criminal enterprise. But Psycho didn't like me much, not after I had emasculated him in the Murder Unit.

I needed another conduit, someone Psycho respected, someone Psycho liked and who liked me: Lizard. The gangster lived in his memories. He wove dark, intricate webs few could unravel. Most in the club barely remembered Lizard's accomplishments—whether he had any or members simply believed he had once been powerful hardly mattered. Members respected him. I used that. If Lizard liked me, others might like me, too.

My bond with him developed slowly, born out of practicality and mutual interest in motorcycles. His wiry frame held him together like rebar. He needed help with repairs; I needed an insider. He preferred to work naked. I pretended his choices were normal. And for several weeks, we had super-ficial conversations about mechanical parts and drugs. I fake-laughed at his jokes, presented myself as amiable, flexible, and a kindred sociopath.

And as long as we discussed his favorite subject—Lizard—he liked me.

Then one afternoon, Psycho held Church in Lizard's garage. Spoon and Wrench, both truck drivers, missed the meeting. Chains and Powder attended. Psycho looked particularly agitated. He paced between motor-cycles like a small general acutely aware that he had lost most of his soldiers. Rain lingered in the air. Psycho skimmed a finger across a dusty motorcycle seat: His eyes, gold flecks in the dim light, glinted triumphantly as he announced his plan: "No one wears a High Desert rocker without my permission." He ordered us to seize any violator's colors. (Vinny, of course, promptly changed his chapter's name to Death Valley). As loyal subjects, we supported Psycho's "great strategy" to regain his leadership. We flattered him, said he was clever, powerful, blah blah blah.

Rain fell, at first a drizzle, then large drops stained the concrete. Lizard stared at the water. He slowly undressed and stood in the shower. No one protested. No one said anything at all. The meeting continued without interruption.

"Fucking Rust." Psycho slid onto a motorcycle seat. He ranted about his pending assault charges, blamed Rust for starting the whole debacle. "I should kill him right now." He paused for emphasis, then shrugged. "I'm already going away for ten years. Why not make it twenty?" *Why not?* He watched me carefully as if I had just spoken the words aloud. Nerves skit-tered across his face. Lizard nodded, clicked his teeth, rested his chin on his cane.

But revenge against Rust would have to wait. Psycho had more pressing news. Members of the Mexican Mafia had contacted him as a "professional courtesy" to let him know that they planned to kill a Vago associate suspected of "snitching" on La eMe. The gang didn't want "innocents" to get caught in the crossfire.

"The rat lives in this area," Psycho disclosed.

My heart pounded. Bernard flashed in my mind's eye.

Powder suddenly puffed to life. "Do they know who it is?" His words floated over us like vapor. As vice president, he should have elevated his president, supplied his voice, dictated his decisions, but Powder was a title only.

"My lawyer knows. He said it was one of the dudes whose charges got dismissed. We'll find out when he testifies." Psycho also had information from "a law enforcement source" that the Vagos had been infiltrated by an informant in the "high desert" area. He had a source on the inside, an "old lady," who advised him that the DA's office planned to refile the murder charges against Twist.

"*Your* charges were dismissed." Psycho looked directly at me, his tone sharp.

"They dropped charges against *three* of us," I reminded him. (The other two were Walter and Joe, hang-arounds.)

I half expected him to order me to strip. Members fixed me with icy stares and I felt raw and exposed, like meat hanging from a butcher's hook. But Psycho couldn't risk more defectors. As captain of a mutinous crew, Psycho needed me. He dropped the challenge. His gaze traveled to Chains, the chapter's secretary-treasurer. The biker resembled a rock star, long hair, goatee, well chiseled.

"You're a fucking mess," Psycho scolded him. Thanks to his bookkeeping efforts, the club bled money. Bills went unpaid. Some members still owed chapter dues. Fiscal irresponsibility invited the scrutiny of the national secretary-treasurer.

"I need a volunteer," Psycho announced. "Someone who has actual accounting skills."

"I'm studying to be a paralegal." I perpetuated my lie.

Psycho chuckled. "Yeah, sure," he said. "Maybe you could help Chains."

Technically, I wasn't qualified. The rules required membership in the club for at least one year.

"Fuck the rules," Lizard slurred. He moved out of the rain, pounded his cane on the floor. His boxers drenched, he still commanded an audience. Psycho bristled at the outburst but considered Lizard's deviation. He was desperate. He studied me warily, then smirked. "Just don't go writing a book about us. You know, like fucking Billy Queen."*

I smothered a smile. Chains's face muscles relaxed. He stood quietly next to me as Psycho briefed me on my new "secretary-treasurer" position. I was to attend all Church meetings, take notes, handle the club's money issues, record dues, and, when the chapter acquired property—like guns or drugs—dispose of the evidence (after first notifying the ATF). The meeting notes had to be coded, Psycho advised, so as not to reveal the actual attendees.

Financial records had to be doctored to "make it difficult" for law enforcement. The Vagos' books provided proof that the club operated as a criminal enterprise. Each member paid club dues, belonged to a chapter, implemented a rank-and-file structure—president, vice president, secretary-treasurer, sergeant at arms. I reported to Tata, the international secretary-treasurer of the Vagos. (Though predominantly a Southwestern gang, the Vagos had chapters in Mexico, Canada, Nicaragua, and the Philippines.) Most of the Vagos' funds derived from illegitimate sources—gun trafficking, weapons, extortion—though some came from bona fide businesses: tattoo shops, strip clubs, runs, and the club's "legal defense fund."

Vagos chapters attended the monthly secretaries' meeting, held at Bobby Bajas in Rancho Cucamonga, California. Over salsa and tacos, Tata warned us about the Solos Angeles. The newly formed chapter had been "green-lit."

---

* William Queen, a retired ATF agent, wrote a book called *Under and Alone* about his infiltration of the Mongols.

Lights dimmed in the restaurant. I stopped taking notes. My recorder vibrated in my wallet. Tata dipped his taco into a blob of salsa and ordered everyone to purchase throwaway cell phones; the "Man" was watching the Vagos closely.

"We have to be careful," he said.

If any sergeant at arms caught any member "moving dope," he had permission to "run them down the road." Tata warned us about getting "too drunk" in bars. Alcohol was contributing to too many assaults. We needed to watch our step.

The Vagos nodded, absorbing Tata's cautions. Each chapter should "keep a tool chest"—weapons—so "they have them when they need them" and get rid of old ladies who were becoming "pains." No liabilities. No witnesses. He needed "clean chapters." He ranted about the Patriot Act and reminded members that "biker gangs" were not excluded; "police could enter anyone's residence without a search warrant and plant what they wanted to plant as well as tap phone lines."

"We should wear recorders," one member shouted. "The police do."

"That could pose problems for some brothers," Tata warned. He paused, swished his food around on his plate, and reconsidered. "Anyone who wants to wear one must report it to National."

⚞

While I absorbed my new position as secretary-treasurer under Psycho, I continued to work his rival chapter, Death Valley. I started by negotiating the purchase of an ounce of marijuana from a thick-necked member named Elmo. Wind bit into my face. The dark street glittered with broken glass. Elmo's house dead-ended like a drain. He quickly ushered me inside and my eyes adjusted to harsh white glare. I squinted, blocked the light with my hand. A couch, two end tables, and patches of shaved mauve carpet looked like debris left over from storm damage.

Elmo motioned toward the worn leather couch, where we both sat. My recorder pinched the inside of my thigh. Elmo's face flushed as he overstuffed a joint and offered me the first hit. He tested me, unwilling to initiate a drug deal unless he knew I was a stoner. But as an informant, I didn't have to pretend. I pinched the joint between my fingers and, without hesitation, inhaled deeply. The drug slammed into my lungs and left me instantly light-headed. I couldn't stand, couldn't form words. Elmo chuckled and balanced the joint between his lips. "That's good shit, isn't it?"

"Good shit." I coughed, hoping my head would feel less like a balloon soon.

Elmo blew smoke circles in my face. "Check this out. Yesterday, I shot at someone."

It took a few minutes for his confession to process. Elmo's voice, low and cold, replayed the scene: "Some dude" had beaten up his old lady in a bar, "gave her a black shiner." But the assault was no ordinary brawl. Elmo's old lady happened to be the international vice president's daughter. He ordered Elmo to exact revenge, to "take care of business."

"What happened?" I managed, hoping my recorder picked up his hushed tones.

Elmo stared at me and his eyes had a glassy sheen. Calmly, he explained how he had enlisted the help of a hang-around and together they had cruised in his ominous black Lexus through different neighborhoods until he spotted the attacker's car and opened fire. Bullets ripped through the victim's rear tires, but "unfortunately no one was killed."

Elmo shrugged, offered me another hit, and said, "Hey, at least no one saw me."

⚓

Thanks to my recorded conversation with him, Elmo was eventually charged with assault with a deadly weapon and sentenced to four years in prison for his drive-by shooting. His hang-around testified against him. Years later, Elmo appeared on *Gangland* and proudly displayed a new tattoo he'd inked in prison. The image covered his whole left side like a flesh mural. He appeared bare chested for the cameras and flashed his hanging rat. He had tattooed on the animal's belly FUCK THE ATF, and on the rat's forehead, he inked my confidential informant number.

I saw Elmo one more time on national television: He played an extra on the popular biker show *Sons of Anarchy*. I learned that many of the extras in that series were Vagos.

12

Hawaii

Vagos who could afford the trip attended the annual Labor Day run held in Kona, Hawaii, a beach resort famous for sportfishing, sunsets, and coffee. Although the club had yet to establish a chapter on Kona, their goal was always expansion into burgeoning drug markets. Hawaii provided opportunity for members, many of whom were either former or active military, to reconnect with their roots.

The Kona event attracted Vagos from California (South Bay and Hollywood chapters), Nevada, and Mexico as well as the many already established Hawaii chapters. Other local one-percenter groups like the Kinsmen, Devils Breed, and Satan's Brigade mixed with Hells Angels from the Oakland chapter who hoped to recruit them. My faithful surveillance team, composed of Koz, Carr, and Kiles, boarded the plane with me, passing through the metal detectors one pace behind Rhino and Head Butt. They reserved me a rental car and a hotel room at the Hilton that overlooked the Pacific Ocean.

Shortly after my arrival, Koz and Carr interrupted my view of the out-rigger canoes navigating frothy waves with a knock at my door.

"How do you like the accommodations?" Koz grinned, but I knew he hadn't come for pleasantries.

"Very nice," I said, glancing beyond them into the vacant hallway. The last thing I needed was to be seen socializing with ATF agents. But both assured me there were no other Vagos staying at my hotel.

Koz delivered his bomb: "But there *is* another informant." We spoke on the balcony.

"*Here?*"

"He's working for me," Carr supplied. "Started about eight months before you did."

"How do you feel about meeting him?" Koz cut to the chase.

"Give up my cover?"

"Work as a team."

It was risky to disclose my identity to another confidential informant. I didn't know him and I had no reason to trust him. What if he flipped on me and gave me up to the Vagos? Still, Koz had asked. I trusted Koz. He must have had his reasons, though he didn't tell me the informant's name or what area he worked.

"Okay." I blew out a sigh. Salt air whipped around us.

"Just so you know, he's against the idea," Carr said.

While I waited for the agents to make the arrangements, Rhino burst into my room. "Mind if I crash here?" A gold glow lit up his face as he tossed his things on the bed. Head Butt and Rhino's mother had become an "item" and commandeered the time-share his mother owned. He was "in the way." I suspected he was used to that.

As night fell, we headed to LuLu's bar.

The place had a strange familiarity: Garish wide mirrors lined the back wall, dim lighting framed ripped pool tables, music beat a heavy percussion.

The bar could easily have been transplanted from Victorville. The Vagos preferred the illusion of travel without the experience, predictable violence against a backdrop of calm. Nothing but the scenery ever changed.

And as the evening wore on, Rhino agitated over a cluster of Satan's Brigade playing pool. One racked the balls so forcefully he pocketed the eight ball and sent another clunking over the rail. It rolled close to Rhino's boot. In a flash, Rhino cocked back his fist and played the next shot. The member, knocked out, slumped to the floor. LuLu's transformed into a blur of stop-action clips as fists landed against jaws, chins, and chests, and sounds muted to scrapes of stools across concrete, low moans, and reflexive grunts.

To the Vagos, conditioned to attack, like windup soldiers in a makeshift war, destruction was an addiction: It was much more satisfying to damage human beings than to smash beer bottles or steal motorcycles. "Never let a patch holder hit the ground." The phrase originated after Vagos crashed a Halloween party in a sleepy suburban town, ordered the homeowner to leave, and then stabbed him brutally when he refused. While the first act may have been gratuitous violence, it flexed muscle and triggered a brawl, a second act that suddenly had meaning. Now members fought to defend their fellow Vagos; guests fought to avenge the death of the homeowner. The natural order of things had been restored.

By the time they stumbled out of LuLu's, leaving the place gutted, the purpose of the Kona run surfaced. Act Two began. In hushed tones, Rocco, a massive Vago from the South Bay chapter, announced that the Kinsmen had been "green-lit," though no one knew why. And no one asked. The Vagos had orders from the head of all five Hawaii chapters to take the Kinsmen's colors the next day on a blustery main street crowded with tourists. The call to action promised bloodshed, anticipated arrests, incarceration, and a likely logistical nightmare for the ATF.

Surrounded by water, escape would be difficult, if not impossible.

Back at the hotel, I slipped into the hallway to report the threat to Koz.

"That's it, go call your handler," Rhino slurred after me, and his tone, though joking, had an edge. But before I could rebut, he sprawled across my twin bed, fully clothed and with his head drooped over the side. In the morning he would have a raging headache.

"A few of us have been ordered to enforce the green light on the Kinsmen," I relayed to Koz in the parking lot later. We sat in my dark car, wary of eyes watching us. "We're supposed to operate like a tactical team or special enforcement unit of the Vagos." Rhino and I were the highest-ranking Vagos in the mix. We *had* to participate.

"Be a witness," Koz said.

⇒⇐

I rode the elevator up to my room. It was late. I hoped Rhino had left me a bed. The doors buzzed open two flights below mine and in walked Green Nation, the man whose tattooed head had flashed so prominently on the court's blank wall during my preliminary hearing. I had interacted with Green Nation at a Hemet Vago event. I had played him as a dope source. He looked at me, and his foot-long goatee thumped against his chest as he chuckled.

"*You.*" He shook his head.

Relief shuddered through me, so liberating to finally be myself, to finally remove my Halloween mask, to *let go.*

We spoke in hushed tones in the elevator: Green Nation (aka George) enlightened me about the "Kinsmen problem," reported that Woodstock, a member of the Puma Hi chapter, had engaged in a heated debate with a member of the Kinsmen just days before; afterward, that member surrendered his patch. Rumor swirled that Joker, president of the Vagos in Hawaii, had given the Hells Angels a "gift," an "81" support patch cut from the cloth of the Kinsmen's colors.

"The Puma Hi chapter is all active military," George elaborated. "They have connections to weapons." Woodstock stashed a Mossberg .12 gauge shotgun, a .22 revolver, and a .380 pistol in his bedroom and dismissed rumors that police thought he had taken the patch at gunpoint.

≫≪

The next morning, over pancakes and pineapples in the hotel café, we planned to take the Kinsman's colors. No one knew why or how, only that Tata had ordered the action. Never mind that only hours before Tata had held an emergency meeting in the parking lot of a nearby Home Depot to reprimand Rocco, Cowboy, Turtle, and Rhino for their random assault of a Satan's Brigade member in LuLu's. The Harley-Davidson rodeo event, he reminded everyone, was "public" and the club "didn't need heat."

But as I drizzled syrup over my bacon, Rocco, secretary of the South Bay chapter, scraped back his chair and left to make another phone call. He spoke to Joker, who said the Kinsmen was Woodstock's issue and the Vagos should not attack. I shoveled in a few bites of pancake. Rocco frowned, still conflicted. He left the table again, made a "follow-up" call to Tata.

"He says we should confront the Kinsmen and take their patches by force."

≫≪

While we vacillated between orders, eight Kinsmen gathered at the Midnight Riders event across the street. George and I finished our breakfast, sucking on a few pineapple wedges. Meanwhile, Koz and Carr watched from their cars across the street. Koz, who had once infiltrated the Vagos, and Carr, who had testified against the club, could not risk exposure. Kiles, dressed in impressive black and looking like a tourist, openly snapped photos of the Vagos, including the international president, Terry the Tramp. Motorcycles roared. Awnings flapped in the breeze, old ladies participated in a game of hot dog on a string. Hands roped behind their backs, they leaned sideways in the saddle and puckered up to bite the end off a steaming hot dog.

Amid cheers and whoops, we watched the Kinsmen, huddled together like a football team discussing the next play. We confronted two members from the Hells Angels Oakland chapter and wanted to know their "intentions" regarding the Kinsmen. The Hells Angels insisted they had no intentions regarding the Kinsmen; the Hawaii Vagos had the "problem" with the Kinsmen and their dispute should not become our issue. The Hells Angels were "on vacation" and had no plans to get involved. In truth, the Hells Angels would never defend a support club. If the Kinsmen wanted to patch over into the Hells Angels, they needed to prove their prowess.

Rhino reminded the two Hells Angels that it was impossible to "mess with just one Vago. You mess with one, you mess with *all* of us."

The decision whether to attack required a majority vote. Five of us, George and I, Rhino, and two patches, waffled for nearly thirty minutes. We stared at the Kinsmen as they mingled outside the Midnight Riders event. We thought about fighting, but action eluded us. And the more we huddled, stared and huddled, the more foolish we looked. George and I finally voted to attack; it made the most sense for our characters. But even as we gave our nods, panic shot through me. *How would we get off the island? With only one airport, we could hardly commandeer a submarine.*

Tourists strolled by us, ogled us like a curiosity, window dressing. Meanwhile, the Kinsmen clustered near the corner engrossed in the street theater, periodically glancing in our direction. The token Hells Angels waded through throngs of people; they reached the Kinsmen, whispered something urgent in their ear. The club bolted from the scene, and the Vagos, still debating what Woodstock or Tata would do, unwittingly avoided a war.

13

Street Vibrations

Shortly after returning from Hawaii, I attended the Street Vibrations Motorcycle Festival, one of the largest annual motorcycle events in the country and easily as famous as Sturgis or Daytona. Held on Center Street in downtown Reno, Nevada, the festival attracted thousands of Harley lovers from all over the country, mostly civilian wannabes but also a large conglomerate of outlaw bikers including Hells Angels, Boozefighters, Mongols, and Bandidos. The event, a celebration of music, metal, and motorcycles, also offered tours, live entertainment, ride-in, and stunt shows. Major event venues were planned at Harley-Davidson dealerships in Reno and historic Virginia City. Participants could view the latest creations at America's Finest Custom Bike Builder's Expo and check out the Tattoo Expo for body art extraordinaire.

I drove to the event with Death Valley members Vinny, who had a suspended driver's license, and Rust, who worried he might lose bike parts on the freeway. Mongols and Hells Angels roared past us, belching exhaust and smoke. They followed closely in packs, a blur of colors in tight formation, riding cannibalized Harleys, parts likely stolen or swapped for speed and style. Dust devils swirled around us on the freeway. I had just traveled four hours through mountainous terrain and small towns. As beer flowed, Vinny littered the road with empty cans. Knives winked from the floorboards. My recorder hummed inside my wallet. Then, in my rearview mirror, I saw lights flash, heard a siren chirp, and with dread, I pulled over.

A deputy's voice thundered through the bullhorn. My car, piled high with beer cans and a knife on the floor, was enough to get us in trouble. Worse, if the deputy ordered me to stand spread-eagled near the trunk with my hands on the hood, I was a dead man. In a pat-down, the cops would find my wallet tucked inside my pants, find the thin silver box that contained precious evidence, squint at the device, wag it in my face, and demand, "What's this?" before cold dawning hit them and they let me go. But it would be too late. The Vagos, like salivating wolves, would have already registered my recorder, and, with the deputy safely gone, tear me to shreds.

Nausea roared in my throat.

A portly deputy approached the car. "License and registration," he barked. My fingers fumbled for the information. Panic surged through me as the deputy returned to his car. Police always searched the wallet not only for identification but also for dope. Heaviness filled my lungs; it was over.

"Leave your wallet on the dash and exit the vehicle with your hands up."

I barely remembered to breathe. Working undercover demanded a strange mix of courage and improvisation. Luck, too, and at times I was inexplicably lucky, as if an invisible shield had dropped around me. I played high-stakes poker with a fixed deck. I wanted so badly to let the deputy know I *wasn't* my costume, I *wasn't* a badass. I was one of the good guys. My hands shook in the air. *Don't do anything stupid*, I telegraphed to my passengers.

I was sure we were all going to jail. The deputy ordered Vinny and Rust out of the car and they stumbled to the curb. *Be cool*, I mentally warned them. *He's got nothing on us. He'll let us go. Ride it out.* Tumbleweed blew across the freeway. Fear gripped me. The deputy steadied his gun and radioed for backup with his other hand. Wind scratched my

Members of the Vagos Victorville chapter. *Left to right:* Spoon, Lizard, Powder, Head Butt, Rhino, Wrench, Vinny, Chains. The child is a relative of a member.

Inside Psycho's motor home during Vago run. *Left to right:* Head Butt, Psycho, his wife, and Rhino.

My first Vago run as an official Vago hang-around, March 2004. *Left to right:* Head Butt and Terrible.

Sonny's memorial service held at the Motherlode in Hesperia, California.

The ceremonial burning of Sonny's cut at the Motherlode.

At a run in San Bernardino. *Left to right:* Rhino, Charles, Head Butt, Rancid, Terrible, and Powder.

Left to right: Rancid, Rhino, Head Butt, Rust, Vinny, and Terrible.

Charles's hotel in Hawaii.
Left to right: Charles, Rhino, and Hollywood.

In Hawaii. *Left to right:* Charles, Joker, (Vagos leader of all Hawaii chapters), and an unknown Vago.

At a run in Kona, Hawaii. *Left to right:* Hollywood, Rhino, Quicky John, Charles, Tata (international president), Head Butt, and Turtle in front.

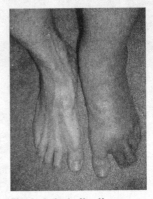

Charles's foot after the probate battles on July 3, 2009.

July 5, 2009, the day after being patched in. The Nazi flags given to us by our region the day we opened this clubhouse in the background. *Left to right:* ATF Special Agent JD, Milwakee Jack, ATF Special Agent Gringo, Charles, ATF Special Agent Bobby.

Cemetery in North Carolina, memorial run for fallen brothers of the Copper Region. *Bottom row, second Outlaw from the right:* ATF Special Agent Gringo. *Bottom row, fifth Outlaw from the right:* ATF Special Agent JD. *Top row, fourth Outlaw from the left:* ATF Special Agent Bobby. *Bottom row, second from the left:* Charles.

Cemetery in North Carolina, memorial run for fallen Copper Region Outlaws. *Left to right:* Brian, ATF Special Agent Bobby, Charles, Hollywood, Harry, and Alibi.

A party at clubhouse in Petersburg, Virginia.

Easy Rider Bike Expo Charlotte, North Carolina. *Left to right:* ATF Special Agent JD, Brett, Snuff, ATF Special Agent Gringo, and Charles.

Inside the Lexington, North Carolina, Outlaws clubhouse. *Left to right:* ATF Special Agent Bobby, unidentified outlaw, Vern, ATF Special Agent JD, Norm, and Charles.

ATF Special Agent Gringo displaying shotgun kept behind the bar at Rockhill, South Carolina, clubhouse.

New Year's party for the Copper Region. Although women were welcome, none attended.

Outlaws probate Hollywood fighting for his colors to become a full-patch member. The Outlaws member on the ground has a handgun protruding from his pants.

Outlaws probate Shia fighting for his colors to become a full-patch member.

Outlaws drinking at Petersburg, Virginia, clubhouse. *Left to right:* Rocket, Chris, Hollywood, and M & M.

cheeks. Several bikes whizzed past. *He's going to search the car. He's going to rifle through my wallet, he's going to find* . . . But he didn't. Instead, he made me blow into a portable Breathalyzer right there on the side of the road, and when I registered zero alcohol, he ordered me to dump out the beer and "slow it down."

"You could kill someone."

✄

After that I did slow it down. While we were stopped on the side of the road getting harangued by the deputy, Vagos and Hells Angels nearly started a bloodbath inside the convention center in Reno. Hours before our arrival, one Vago lingered too close to a Hells Angels booth; the Hells Angel swatted him away. The pair acted like children flexing muscle on a playground fighting over the one twisting slide. They both needed a referee, some instruction on how to break away gracefully without injury, without incident. The Vago whipped out his cell phone and dialed Vinny. "What should I do?" the disembodied voice panicked. "I can't just walk away."

A drunk Vinny put the Vago on hold and placed his own call to the international sergeant at arms: "Send as many Vagos to the convention center as possible." Like a general rallying his soldiers, the sergeant at arms prepared for battle from a safe distance. No one asked for details or justification. They were briefed on one fact: a Hells Angel had insulted a Vago. We learned later that within minutes of placing the calls, Vagos from other chapters streamed into the convention center, blocked the exits, crowded the packed booths in the hall, and hovered near the Hells Angels. Armed with Buck knives and pistols, they displayed an awesome show of force. For several tense moments, the Vagos and the Hells Angels squared off and leveled fierce looks at one another over the T-shirt displays until finally the Hells Angels relented.

No blood would be spilled that afternoon.

✄

The convention center boasted large banners in the entrance: WELCOME TO THE BIGGEST LITTLE CITY IN THE WORLD. The atmosphere inside was a mixture of electric noise, a cacophony of bands competing for space on nearby stages, and vendors selling grilled chicken parts, strips of steak, and booze. Motorcycle stunts and martial arts demonstrations drew crowds. Booths sold bike parts, T-shirts, leathercrafts. In a nearby ballroom, a tattoo expo buzzed in full force. Models volunteered their flesh canvas. Women with bare midrifts, leather-adorned bras, ill-fitting jeans, and head scarves paraded past me in a strange perversion of a masquerade ball. Amid the grinning skulls, vibrant colors, live entertainment, and loud pulse, violence suspended like a vapor, odorless, colorless, and deadly.

Sometimes it took unexpected forms. We left to go barhopping. We took a shortcut.

※

In an alley behind busy Main Street, a small shadow approached with a cigarette dangling between her lips. "Got a light?" She nodded at the prospect behind me. He spit his response, "Fuck off," and pushed her aside. The waif, unmoved, hissed, "Fuck you." The exchange rippled through the darkness like an electric current. Without warning, she lunged, scratching thin lines in the prospect's old lady. In a flash, their bodies tangled on the asphalt. Fists struck bone, skin dragged across bits of glass and decaying rats.

Soon other old ladies pummeled and clawed at the waif, knocking her to her knees. The woman shook a band of hair from her eyes. Blood drooled from her mouth and random flecks hit the side of my boot. With her front tooth missing, another old lady kicked her hard in the chin and whipped her head backward. A crowd gathered and formed a perimeter around the women. They cheered and mocked with the enthusiasm of spectators at a cockfight. It was hard to watch and not intervene; it went against everything I believed in. The wounded woman crawled, dazed and disoriented, and propped herself against a broken fender in the alley. And just when I thought she might surrender, a flash of metal glinted in the darkness and she plunged her blade deep into the woman's thigh. As blood gushed, the crowd scattered. Sirens wailed in the distance. The alarms were my exit cue, and as much as I wanted to help her, I knew I couldn't. The *real* war happened in dark, narrow spaces, to innocents. The gangs just pretended.

14

Close Call

After Street Vibrations, the transmission in my car exploded and I had no choice but to ride my bike, which meant I also had to wear my colors. It was like wearing a target on my back. Random motorists honked at me, flipped me off, and defiantly roared past me. The San Bernardino gang unit had a field day with me and pulled me over, harassing me (as they should have) regarding my gang affiliation, issuing me tickets for failing to activate my turn signal. They snapped photos of my various tattoos and hoped I'd sign a gang card confirming my Vagos membership.

I called up Kiles. "I got another one."

"Meet me at the Taco Bell on the corner." Kiles signed off that she had "fixed" the faulty turn signal.

The charade continued for several weeks until, shortly before Thanksgiving on a blustery afternoon, Bubba solicited me for a drug buy. He arranged to sell me cocaine in the back of his shop, Outlaw Tattoo. Koz met me first in a nearby café, handed me a recorder, patted me down for drugs, and gave me $350 cash to execute the deal.

"You okay with this?" he asked, knowing the inherent dangers. The choice to wear a wire or do a deal was exclusively mine. If Bubba decided to search me and found the device, he would not hesitate to put a bullet in my head. No questions asked, investigation over. But it was a risk worth taking because without the ability to preserve evidence, the government had no case.

"Sure." I shrugged, hoping I sounded more confident than I felt.

"We'll be right outside," Koz said. Wind smacked my cheeks as I pulled my leather jacket closed but made sure my cuts stayed exposed. With my hands shoved in my pockets and the recorder on, I approached Bubba's white Ford Bronco. He left the engine on. He was dressed casually in a Vagos T-shirt, jeans, and dark sunglasses. I wasn't worried about the actual deal; I had done hundreds in my lifetime, waiting near trash dumps, empty graves, and street corners just to exchange cash for drugs, to see the flicker of relief skitter across the dealer's skinny, haunted eyes.

But something stirred inside me on this afternoon. Cops often spoke of a sixth sense, an inexplicable "vibe" that danger lurked. The hair on the back of my neck pricked. My heart beat faster. Traffic flowed noisily on the streets behind me: The parking lot where Bubba idled contained rows of cars and bikes. A gun poked from Bubba's waistband. He had come alone. Without a word, he led me inside his fairly empty shop. Stragglers lingered in the middle of the day. Bubba motioned me toward a small back office. Guns were stacked along the walls and littered the desk. I flashed my cash and he slipped me the cocaine. I tucked the half ounce inside a slim pocket in my leather jacket; it didn't fit in my boot.

Within minutes, I steered my bike into rush hour: Anxiety fueled my impatience and I split traffic, my tires riding the white line. The shopping center where Koz and I had agreed to meet loomed just a few short blocks away. Behind me, Koz darted in and out of traffic like a dark fish. I changed lanes abruptly and forgot to signal. Marked San Bernardino sheriff's units descended on me with their flashing lights and sirens. Koz slowed and the deputies pulled us both over; they had seen Koz follow me. Panic gripped me; I had a large quantity of cocaine in my pocket.

Koz said nothing as the officers patted me down. Their hands skimmed my cuts and jacket, traveling over my bulging wallet but strangely missing the chunk of cocaine in the other pocket. Sweat moistened the back of my neck. My heart raced. Harsh wind slapped my face. Koz, who had been pulled over a few hundred yards away, flashed his ATF credentials and convinced the deputy he had followed me because I was a Vago. He smartly allowed the traffic charade to continue. If he hadn't, he would have risked my exposure and the integrity of the investigation. After thirty minutes, the deputies, satisfied that I had committed nothing more than a traffic violation, scribbled me a citation. But my relief quickly turned to dread as I caught Bubba's truck across the road, idling on the shoulder: He watched with interest as the deputies released me.

Another Vago from the Victorville chapter pulled up in his Chevrolet pickup and approached the deputies; Kiles told me later she recognized his passenger: a San Bernardino sheriff's deputy. The cop insisted he was off duty, a mere patron at the Vago's barbershop. But that didn't explain why the Chevrolet was registered to him. I figured the Vago knew about the cocaine buy and saw the cops pull me over. He didn't show up out of concern for my predicament; he came because he thought my bike would be towed and he wanted to offer to take it instead. There was no danger that the registration would ever come back as government issued. The bike belonged to me.

Kiles, who had watched the scene unfold from her surveillance car, appeared a few minutes later wanting an update.

"Are you going to arrest him?" she asked a fellow deputy.

"I just *know* he has stuff on him, but I can't find it."

※

And they never would. Although others continued to be suspicious of me, Psycho never worried about my credentials. He formed his own loose rules. Numbers mattered; the more members he recruited into his club, the more powerful his presence. He collected my club dues but often forgot about my application and patch fees and checked me off his list as "compliant." But the fact that I was never busted for the cocaine puzzled everyone. And I had no plausible explanation for my uncanny "luck."

At least once a week someone challenged my identity, until one rainy afternoon at Garcia's Mexican Restaurant, Psycho chewed a mouthful of pulled pork and remarked thoughtfully to Rhino and Head Butt that I couldn't be a cop. I didn't initiate drug and arms deals. I didn't ask for anything or do anything. But in truth, I had been buying drugs and guns from the Vagos every chance I could. I had just kept quiet. Head Butt glared at me and inhaled his refried beans. Rhino shoveled sizzling chicken into a fajita. My heart hammered in my chest. I had worked so hard to deflect attention, to be a flawed gangster, one who, unlike a federal undercover agent, didn't attend every planned motorcycle run or participate in every organized criminal transaction precisely because I didn't want to *play* a criminal, I wanted to *be* one. I had an advantage: I had already been one.

Psycho dipped his taco into a blob of salsa and said, "If I didn't know you, I'd have made you road kill."

He never made idle threats. I took a sip of water, crunched ice between my teeth, and smiled weakly, unprepared for his next bomb.

"Joanna told us about the letter." He chewed calmly and explained how my girlfriend had worked as a Vagos spy for the first three weeks of our relationship. My stomach lurched. *Now it made sense why so many of the Vagos thought I was a cop.* The room spun. Ice slicked my throat. I couldn't believe it. I thought I had smoothed things over with Joanna, thought I had convinced her I was studying to be a paralegal. My one foolish attempt to reconcile with my ex-wife threatened to topple the entire investigation. This was it. I couldn't believe I had been derailed by a woman, a woman I trusted. Sounds amplified in the dim restaurant, the scrape of a fork across a plate, the clink of glasses, a match flare. Sauces blended together. My hair stuck to the back of my neck, wet with sweat. I had imagined so many scenarios—bullet spray, a cold gun against my temple, a beating.

Psycho swallowed his taco. He bunched a napkin in his hands and said, "It's cool. She told us about your schooling."

My body deflated. I wanted to slide under the table, into the floorboards, down an invisible dark hole. Relief shuddered through me, then doubt, then panic. Did they really believe the paralegal thing? Was Psycho just messing with me? No way to tell. Then again, maybe Joanna had bought my story. Maybe she had successfully convinced Psycho's ex-wife that I was a student and not a cop. Maybe her disinformation campaign had worked after all. But while I stressed over my loose end, conversation turned to more pressing issues: rumors that the newly formed Arizona chapter of the Solo Angeles Motorcycle Club possibly contained an informant or, worse, an undercover agent. (In fact, the rumors were correct. The mock Solo Angeles included an undercover ATF operative, a Phoenix police detective, and two confidential informants.)

Psycho planned an officers' meeting at Lake Havasu to review possible solutions.

"We have to be smarter than the others," he cautioned and recounted the ATF's two other infiltrations involving the Mongols and the Hells Angels. He waved a fork at me and smirked. "For *two* years those fuckers never saw it coming."

15

Disappearing Acts

By early August 2005 I had established enough of a rapport with Vinny and members of his Death Valley chapter to propose buys of large quantities of cocaine. We flopped on his filthy couch in Hesperia. Bubba, a recent defector and the chapter's new sergeant at arms, hovered in the doorway and inhaled a joint. Cold emanated from him, like an open refrigerator door. He exhaled in my face and passed the joint to Vinny. My eyes smarted.

"Come back tomorrow." Vinny coughed. "I'll have the cocaine for you." He waved the joint at me. "If you give me a twenty now, I'll get some of this for you too."

I nodded and reached into my wallet for the cash and handed him a bill.

"Remember Hammer?" Vinny's words shot through me like a bullet. "Who knew that motherfucker would turn out to be a government snitch." He shook his head, and the room suddenly grew darker. A chill coursed through me. I remembered Hammer, a "hard-core" Vago imposter whom, according to Vinny, "everyone trusted." Vinny described the Vagos' pay-back plan, their failed attempt to hurl grenades inside a hotel room they thought Hammer occupied. A group of them had staked out the place af-ter dark, ready to unplug the pins that would "blow the motherfucker up." But minutes before the explosion, a "completely random" citizen opened the hotel door and scooped up his newspaper from the hallway, not Ham-mer at all.

They were about to murder the wrong man.

I put the joint to my lips, feeling sick inside.

"Sometimes people get lucky," Vinny said, "and sometimes they don't. Know what I mean?"

And as I drove away from Vinny's, the near miss replayed in my mind. Hammer was like me, like George, like any one of us who risked every-thing for intelligence, for the chance to stop a terrorist organization. Vinny was not my friend. He would exact revenge on a traitor.

"We should probably think about protection," George advised me later in private.

"What kind of protection?"

"*Witness* protection." His words floated between us, and for the first time I considered the notion that I might be in danger *for the rest of my life.*

※

But I still had to do the drug deal with Vinny. If I backed out, I would in-vite suspicion. If I continued, I risked getting caught. The next morning, I contacted Vinny as planned, hoping to collect the cocaine and marijuana he'd promised and be done. But Vinny blew me off, mumbled something about being sick from partying the night before. He postponed our meet-ing. I wasn't expecting that curve. When I contacted him again a few hours later and got the same brushoff, I panicked.

"Back off," Koz warned, uneasy about Vinny's sudden change of plans. "If you pursue it, you'll appear too eager. He'll just get suspicious."

I listened. I backed off. Maybe Koz was right. Maybe Vinny had set me up. But several days later Vinny pursued *me*, offering to sell me several pounds of marijuana, and I stalled *him*, "Wait until payday."

"Good idea." Vinny nodded. "I wouldn't want to get stiffed." He flashed a knowing look at his girlfriend, Lara, who hugged the edge of the sofa. She averted her gaze, picked at a thumbnail, and stared at the floor. When she looked up, fear watered slightly behind her pale blue eyes. I couldn't believe she was still with him, still taking his bullshit.

"Her girlfriend owes me money, six hundred dollars from a deposit on a rental property." Vinny filled in the gaps. He shrugged, slapped the pistol tucked into his waistband, and said, "I think I'll just kill her." His tone, all business, stoic and cold, was no idle threat.

"She's pregnant," Lara pleaded, her lower lip trembling. Vinny laughed, looked at me, and said, "Two for one."

><

I dialed Koz at my first opportunity. "What do we have to do?"

A trim, pretty female agent from the U.S. Marshals Service (USMS) agreed to answer preliminary questions about the federal Witness Security Program (WSP). George and I met her one rainy afternoon in a dimly lit warehouse that could have easily passed for a storage unit in a commercial construction zone. She shook our hands, smiled warmly at us, and briefly reviewed how her agency helped people disappear.

"We've successfully relocated more than eighteen thousand witnesses since the program's inception in 1970. No one who has followed our system has ever been harmed," she assured us. The space swallowed her. Concrete walls boxed us in.

She folded her arms across her chest and warned, "It *does* require some sacrifices."

"What kind of sacrifices?" George hedged.

"New identities, Social Security numbers, driver's licenses, names. We'll help with vocational training and employment opportunities." She flashed her smile again. "Think of it as a chance to reinvent yourselves." *No past.*

It sounded attractive, a reset button for my life. Living in the Now like an amnesia patient, only worse. I would know what I'd lost and be forced to forget. No trace deposits of my life. Complete isolation until it was "safe" to put on my new mask. Theoretically it sounded possible, but I knew that "three may keep a secret if two of them are dead."

What would that feel like to never trust again?

"I don't want to leave you with the wrong impression." The deputy marshal hesitated. "It can be . . . challenging to create a new identity." But she convinced us the sacrifice would be worth the risk. Through our testimony we would likely join the ranks of other "brave and noble" men who paid the price to crush Al-Qaeda terrorists or chill further mob violence.

We still had to be admitted into the program. The government worried about liability. No deputy marshal wanted to be responsible for relocating a homicidal sociopath addicted to violence into sleepy suburbia and risk a murderous encounter with a neighbor. Mostly, my sessions with the government psychiatrist confirmed that I could handle isolation and invisibility.

"How do you feel about that?" The psychiatrist removed her readers. She searched my face for cracks in the foundation.

"I know I'll never be a criminal again," I said with conviction.

She smirked, twirled her glasses. "Now I know you're lying."

I didn't like psychiatrists much, and I didn't like this one. But she could determine my fate. It didn't matter how I answered her questions; if she didn't like me, she would find a reason to reject me. She stood, smoothed her wrinkled navy slacks, and poured herself a mug of black coffee.

"Are you telling me what you think I want to hear?"

"No, ma'am." *I'm telling you what I want to hear.*

16

Endgame

In the last three months of the investigation, I occupied Rust's one-bedroom house behind his home in Lucerne Valley, an isolated plot of land situated on a hill surrounded by desert tumbleweed. By now I had left Joanna and needed a temporary place to crash. Rust, a member of Death Valley, welcomed the company, though most evenings he alternated between firing random buckshot from his back porch into purple sage and twirling his pistol in the air while he watched his favorite television show, *The Sopranos*. We sat in the dark, drank cheap beer from sweaty cans, and watched James Gandolfini's face flicker against blue tint. His character preached about respect and rats, and Rust leaned forward, elbows on his knees, face flushed from alcohol, and said, "If I ever found out *we* had a snitch, he'd be gone." Rust cocked his pistol for emphasis, pointed the barrel at the wall, and dry fired.

Note taken. Rust had an arsenal of weapons that included an AR-15, an SKS, a Sig Sauer, a .40 caliber pistol, a shotgun, and two Golden Bear bolt action rifles. He stashed a long rifle he camouflaged with duct tape in an attic crawl space because he feared it might be stolen.

One morning I noticed it missing.

"I took it to have a scope fitted," Rust explained and offered to give me his .12 gauge shotgun. He had duped a relative who worked for the Los Angeles County Sheriff's Department into checking the serial number on the weapon and confirmed it was "hot."

"I don't want it in my house," Rust said.

Meanwhile, Koz worried that I had become too soft, "too nice, too much of a gentleman" gangster. He didn't want me to be like "fucking James Bond," but he urged me to "stand up to the Vagos, be more aggressive." So far, I had never initiated fights. I had reacted to beatings. I had defended Psycho as any good minion would. But for all of my caution, I had telegraphed my difference. I needed to blend, deflect the "cop talk," be a "badass."

I could do that. At the next Church meeting, in Lizard's garage, Psycho complained that I was "spending too much time with Death Valley members." Maybe I needed a loyalty check. Head Butt agreed, said I was being "disrespectful." He smacked his fist into a cracked leather motorcycle seat. "We should pull your colors."

I glared at him. "Pull my colors?" I was living in Rust's house. "I'll pull them off right now, put them on the ground. If you can take them, you can have them. But I'll kill you first. I'll kill you, motherfucker."

Head Butt irritated me so much I almost convinced myself that I *would* kill him. Rhino put a warning hand on my shoulder as Head Butt snorted and shook like an injured bull. His breathing was labored. He balled his hands into fists. Spoon, the chapter's designated sergeant at arms, suddenly lunged at me and tackled me to the dirt. I pinned him down and shoved my knee into his face. Psycho joined in the scuffle, attempting to break us apart. Spoon clumsily deflected and accidentally tore Psycho's stitches from his recent surgery.

"You're a pussy," I accused, mindful that I needed to act more like an asshole. Psycho fined Spoon $100.

Days later, Vinny, having heard the story, yanked Spoon's goatee for fun. Spoon winced but otherwise didn't react.

"You're embarrassing." I shook my head. *Maybe I was overdoing it?*

"He's the president," Spoon defended. "I can't punch a president."

"I need someone I can trust." Psycho offered to make me cosergeant at arms.

✄

Occasionally Rust had houseguests. Vinny slept on his couch until his "domestic problems" resolved. And while I pretended to care about Vinny's sordid relationships, Koz sought indictments of key Vagos players before a federal grand jury. I supplied him intelligence for his search warrants, snapped photographs of weapons and drugs stashed inside members' homes, and confirmed addresses and identities of gangsters who moved frequently, drifted between trailer parks, used monikers, initials, and fake first names. The location of Rust's house posed a logistical issue; it was difficult, if not impossible, to conduct surveillance on a hill. We had to wait for Rust to leave before helicopters fanned above the rocky terrain noting the possible exits. Search warrants had to contain specifics, but when facts changed in the span of several minutes, details, too, had to be revised. I performed as one of several conductors in a giant orchestra; each instrument had to be tuned to the others, each note brilliant and solid. With the musicians set and the audience prepared to listen to perfect harmony, Koz stopped the show. "Can you find me Twist?"

I hated the idea; it would be like looking for an electric eel in a deep ocean cave. After a few false leads, I finally tracked Twist down at a seedy meth house. When he answered the door, his eyes resembled cracked glass. Tiny red veins streamed from his pupils like spokes. A Nazi swastika flag fluttered above him. Terrible waved me inside. He was smoking speed and offered me a taste.

"You know I don't do that, bro." I reminded him again that I was a stoner. My eyes smarted in the haze. I sat on the edge of the couch as Twist paced, cupped a phone to his ear, and crackled to life like a spitfire. Meanwhile, Terrible refilled his bowl with speed. The scene played like a stop-action clip building to the big climax.

Twist clicked his phone shut. Determination blazed in his eyes. He retrieved black leather gloves from a box in his room and meticulously pulled on the fingers. Then he reached beneath his bed and retrieved a steel pipe.

"Some dude is talking shit about me." Twist planned to take care of business.

"You coming?" He looked at me. Terrible took his last puff and sprang to attention.

I felt sick inside, my whole body tense. "Right behind you." I had no easy exit. I might have been a Vagos imposter, but I was not about to be an accomplice to murder.

"We should drive separately," I managed. "In case you need to leave quickly."

Inside my car, my hands shook on the steering wheel. I dialed Koz and told him, "If Twist beats this guy with a pipe, I'm going to smash his head in." It would mean the abrupt end to the investigation. But Koz agreed. "You can't be a witness to murder." I considered that it might take forty blows to collapse a man's skull with a steel pipe. I had little time to find a suitable weapon. Car doors slammed. Twist and Terrible marched across gravel to the victim's front entrance. I lagged a few paces behind, assessing my options. Twist banged on the door. A wiry man with a smashed nose and greasy ponytail answered. Maybe it would only take twenty blows. His eyes widened to saucers. Twist stood sideways, one hand skimmed his pipe.

"Why you talking shit about me?" Twist was the bully on the playground accusing his classmate of stealing his ball, only he was armed and not at all interested in fair play.

The man cowered, his knees visibly buckled. He dissolved into tears, deep rasping sobs. "Please," he begged, "please. I didn't say nothing."

I spotted a brick on the ground. Their voices sounded like snapping dogs. Terrible turned his back to the victim, folded his arms, and balanced against the house.

"Please." The victim pissed himself.

I grabbed the brick, my heart racing. This was it.

"Let's get the fuck out of here," Twist said suddenly, apparently satisfied that the victim had not disrespected him. The brick slipped out of my hand. It hit the pavement with a soft thud. The next day authorities picked Twist up. He never knew I had betrayed him. He blamed the arrest on his girlfriend, whose car he had "borrowed" and never returned.

≈≈

Vinny proposed that I officially switch chapters, renounce Victorville and transfer to Death Valley. While the proposition was flattering, I already had the main players of Death Valley on criminal violations. I didn't need to work them. In fact, I would rather have infiltrated the Hollywood or San Fernando Valley Vagos, since those members had yet to be targeted. But I had run out of time; government raids were scheduled to occur in a matter of days.

Still, I needed Psycho's permission to formally leave the Victorville chapter. Predictably, he was less than eager to help me out; in fact, he threatened Terry the Tramp that if he ever "saw that motherfucker [meaning me] on the streets, he would take [my] colors." Tramp accepted Psycho's warning as sufficient permission to allow me to switch chapters.

"Bring four hundred dollars cash tomorrow and meet me at Terry the Tramp's house," Vinny advised.

I didn't have that kind of money, so I borrowed it from Rust. "I'll pay you back tomorrow," I lied, knowing that the next day more than eight hundred law enforcement personnel planned to execute search warrants in five counties, including his.

Until then, I stayed in character. As promised, the next day I arrived at Terry the Tramp's house in the middle of the afternoon. Vinny hugged me warmly, vouched to Tramp that he had "known me for years" and wanted me in Death Valley. Tramp approved me instantly and allowed me to switch over as soon as possible. I handed Vinny my four-hundred-dollar transfer fee and left Tramp's house, bright sun burning my cheeks, my heart pounding.

That was the last exchange I ever did with the Vagos.

⇒⇒

At dawn the next day, March 9, 2006, twenty-five Vagos members and associates (including Psycho and Twist, seven chapter presidents, one vice president, one secretary, one treasurer, and seven sergeants at arms) were arrested on firearms, drug, assault, and murder charges following one of the largest and most ambitious coordinated law enforcement probes ever conducted in Southern California. The three-year investigation, Operation 22 Green, involved over eight hundred personnel from the ATF and local police and sheriff's departments, and spanned five counties, Los Angeles, San Bernardino, Riverside, Orange, and Ventura. Law enforcement seized 134 firearms (including Beretta and Mossberg 12 gauge shotguns, SKS assault rifles, and TEC-9 assault weapons), 305 grams of methamphetamine, 46 grams of cocaine, $15,000 in currency, explosives, four stolen motorcycles, and thousands of rounds of ammunition.

Of the twenty-five, all served time pursuant to plea bargains: Terrible received fifteen years concurrent in federal and state prison. Psycho, who had no prior criminal convictions, received one year for the assault in Mickey McGees bar and one strike.* Vinny accepted a strike and one year for selling me marijuana. Rust served concurrent one-year prison terms and one strike for the assault and the stolen weapon he sold to me. Powder, who had sold me the stolen shotgun, accepted five years' probation and two strikes. Bandit took one year and one strike for the Mickey McGees assault. Bubba accepted two years and a strike for selling me cocaine. Rhino, too, struck a deal.

---

* Three strikes laws, also called habitual offender laws, require state courts to impose a life sentence on anyone convicted of three or more violent crimes or felonies. Twenty-four states have three strikes laws.

Following his arrest, he agitated in custody, paced the confined interview room.

"We know about the murder," the lead homicide investigator prompted him.

"Fuck you," Rhino spat back.

"We know you were with Daniel Foreman [Twist]."

"I don't know what you're talking about."

"No?" The detective played him Rhino's recorded confession. He told me later that the blood drained from Rhino's face.

"What do I have to do?" He relented and accepted fifteen years in prison in exchange for his testimony. The prosecution reduced his charges to voluntary manslaughter and attempted burglary with a gang affiliation.

❧

The raids marked the end of my undercover role and the beginning of my new invisible life. I felt conflicted, not because I had any regret about my impending betrayal of the Vagos, but because I was about to leave the familiar. For three years I knew my role, and the culmination of my life's work was about to unfold. Hard-core, violent gangsters would be subdued, led away in chains and handcuffs, their rank and stature in the criminal world suddenly emasculated, reduced to rubber sandals, pastel jumpsuits, and faded memories.

They were nothing behind bars.

They would never be anything again.

17

Vanilla

After the raids, an ATF SWAT team gave me twenty-four hours to fold my life into one suitcase. At least in the interim I could choose my temporary relocation, a nondescript Residence Inn in Oxnard, the strawberry and lima bean capital of California. Situated a hundred miles from Victorville, the area was still considered Ventura County, and as far as I knew only one other Vago lived in Oxnard. I needed to stay fairly close to Koz in order to collect money from him, since I could no longer work. Koz assured me my limbo status was temporary, "three months max," but Koz had never before placed an informant into the WSP.

George arrived that same day and settled into a suite next to mine. The transition was no doubt more difficult for him since he had a family and a baby due. I couldn't imagine burdening a loved one with such secrecy. Not only did he have to become temporarily invisible, she did too. At first it was strange living out of a suitcase, buying groceries, cooking meals in my room that transformed into a miniature apartment, saluting the hotel concierge each morning as I headed for the gym or walked Hercules. Several military personnel also occupied the suites at government expense; some had lived there for years.

We were warehoused people, in limbo, waiting for our lives to restart.

By summer, the football field behind the Residence Inn converted into the Dallas Cowboys' training camp and I was fortunate enough to receive VIP passes to the practices. George's routine differed considerably as he tempered his wife's growing restlessness and concerns about the impending birth of their first child. With nothing to occupy my time, I enrolled in online classes through Liberty University and decided in my new life I would be well educated and well employed. I worked toward my bachelor's in biblical studies.

But I was restless. I didn't know how to still my mind. Working the Vagos had been an addiction. Living in the hotel, cut off from myself, was like withdrawal. I needed something to revive my inner core, to fuel my sense of purpose. I knew why I had infiltrated the Vagos, not to work off charges (although that had been my initial reason) but to contribute, to do good in the world, to be part of a solution, not a problem. The hotel was safe, but it was killing me. I didn't know how to be done. I imagined that cops forced to retire felt similar angst. I panicked. What would life after the Vagos look like? I had nightmares of stocking shelves in Walmart, working the graveyard shift, adjusting, adapting, accepting my new vanilla life.

And I couldn't stand it.

≫≪

The specter of prison also loomed large. Now that the Vagos case had ended, I fully expected to be sentenced pursuant to my 2002 plea agreement for drug conspiracy charges. And while I hoped I would receive probation, I had no expectations. So when Koz called me one morning with the good news that he and John Carr had convinced the U.S. Attorney's Office to drop all charges against me, I thought I had won the lottery. I was free, my life a complete do-over.

I wanted so badly to get it right. No mistakes, no lapses, no apologies. Like the lone survivor of a deadly plane crash, I had been given a gift, a second lease. I couldn't live vanilla. I needed to be involved in something big. I had read about the bloody history of the Quebec Biker War between the Hells Angels and the Rock Machine. The Canadian Hells Angels operated like drug cartels and ran a billion-dollar business. The turf war between the two claimed hundreds of lives, including an eleven-year-old boy's who died when a car bomb exploded outside a biker hangout. It also bred one of Canada's most prolific contract killers.

I contacted a biker expert in Canada and offered my skills. He connected me to the Royal Canadian Mounted Police (similar to our FBI). A suit met me in a diner near the beach in California. We spoke in hushed tones over steak and eggs. He said I impressed him. He might be able to use me. But as the weeks wore on, he grew discouraged. His agency suffered from budget cuts due to the recession and the Olympics. "There are other provinces looking for similar help," he said and suggested Ontario. "You should resubmit next year."

After nine months of hotel life, I proposed, as Koz handed me my $3,000 cash for expenses, that I find something cheaper nearby. I didn't see the point in wasting government funds for a hotel room I might occupy indefinitely. I quickly found a condo in Oceanside in San Diego, two blocks from the beach. Fresh paint coated the walls. A wooden deck overlooked the swells. George moved into a house next door. We fished on the docks each night at sunset. Even if we caught nothing, the lapping of the waves, the salt air wet on our faces, and the sand on our clothes enveloped us with calm. Those quiet moments, Hercules' head on my lap, were some of the happiest of my life.

Three more months passed, and one early evening George's face glowed bright in the golden dusk. He plunked his poles and bait on the dock and grinned. "I got a kid now," a baby born to legally invisible parents.

Life was good. Life was really good. But I knew it wouldn't last.

※

A few days later, George left. It was hard saying good-bye to him, my only friend, the only witness to my life. I would never see him again, never know where he lived, how his child developed, how his life evolved. I would never know the ending. Mine was a cutoff life. Koz gave me a week's notice I was leaving, and I planned my exit. I found a prime kennel for my dog, one that boasted a swimming pool, gourmet meals, and a large play area for "proper socialization." Hercules rested his large head in my lap, his dark eyes over-bright, expectant, our connection to one another almost spiritual. He *trusted* me, knew without a doubt I would return for him.

After midnight, with wind howling through the vents, there was a knock at my front door. I tossed off my sheets and pulled on jeans and a T-shirt, my heart pounding. *This was it.*

Koz smiled as I padded into the hallway. I still didn't feel ready. I had no idea if my destination was cold, warm, or rainy.

"Pack layers," Koz had suggested.

※

What followed was a blur: We drove in silence to LAX, a mixture of fear and excitement coursing through me as I watched headlights smear the darkness. The deputy marshal who met us at security smiled warmly at us, extended her hand to Koz, and nodded to the duffel bags. "You have your things?" An awkward moment passed as she mistook Koz for me. I understood her confusion; Koz looked every bit the informant, with his chiseled features, blond goatee and mustache, bedraggled clothes. I cleared my throat. "I'm the one you're here to take." She absorbed my clean-cut style and fresh-washed tan with some hesitation, unsure whether we had played a trick on her.

"This is the end of the line." Koz shook my hand and I felt my lifeline sever. The deputy escorted me quickly through the metal detectors. I had no identification, no credit cards, no photo. Guards looked through me like I was a ghost already. I boarded a plane as a fake person and settled next to a woman who bloomed like a flower in a red blouse with yellow spots. The black runway dazzled with pin lights. Turbulence rocked the plane as we flew through thick clouds and lightning. Flight attendants scurried down the aisles and placed miniature cans of Sprite and club soda on my fold-out tray. I stared into the black night alert and more focused than I'd ever been in my life.

And as dawn bruised the sky, we landed in Minneapolis. My heart raced. Cold blew into the plane. Was this to be my new home? Although it was early March, snow dusted the runway. Another deputy marshal met me in the waiting area. He smiled, shook my hand, and hurried me through another security gate. Weather postponed my next flight, this time to Albany, New York.

"We're going to have to put you up in a hotel until the blizzard passes," the marshal said.

I felt like displaced luggage.

The next day I flew to Albany, where winter lasted another month and I waited in the Hilton for my next flight. Snow covered the streets. Day blended into night. I stood at my window, steaming coffee in hand, absorbed in a white, quiet world, my life suspended again. The television flickered behind me, my only window to the world, my only human contact. Albany was not my final destination.

"Any preferences?" Koz had asked me early on where I thought I might want to end up. I liked Virginia. My online university had a campus in Lynchburg and I thought it would be nice to attend live classes. But of course I had no control over where I would finally live. I might have enjoyed the wait more had I not been so stressed about my dog. Hercules had been with me since he was six weeks old. He was my only family. An indoor dog, he was accustomed to sleeping in my bed, curling in piles of blankets at my feet. If I lost him, I really didn't think I could survive this new loneliness.

"I promise I'll take care of him for you," Koz assured me, even offering to split the kennel cost. He must have heard the panic in my voice. Koz had always been kind to me, decent, a real human being, but when he offered to look after Hercules for me, he saved my life. No one had ever showed me such kindness. He called to report Hercules' antics, his sleeping and eating patterns, and his general mood. He was like a concerned parent with a new infant. And as I cradled the phone to my ear, I relaxed.

I chose a new name in Albany. But it would take another month to get identification with that name and a new Social Security number. In early May, with wind whipping around my coat collar, I boarded a plane for my final destination. Deputy marshals escorted me once more through the metal detectors, up the ramp, through the final gate. As passengers found their seats, I tried to guess by their attire where I was headed. Some wore floppy straw hats, striped shorts, suits. Then the flight attendant announced over the speaker: Norfolk, Virginia.

When I landed, I had no formal identity, no driver's license, birth certificate, or passport, nothing to prove my existence. My challenge: to find a place that would accept an invisible man. Illegals accomplished as much every day. After much searching and rejection, I settled on a quiet crime-ridden black neighborhood in Portsmouth, near the beach. The one-bedroom house had a den and a fenced yard and plenty of room for Hercules.

"He has to fly out before June," I told Koz. "Once the temperatures climb over eighty degrees, it'll be too hot for him." There were no flights in the middle of the night to Norfolk. Hercules had to be crated and placed in cargo long enough to make it across the country and not melt. As the days ticked by, I grew more and more concerned. If Hercules didn't board a plane in the next couple of days, I would have to wait until the fall, and by then . . .

My heart raced as Hercules emerged from cargo. He had lost fifteen pounds, but his eyes lit up when he saw me. He practically slid across the tiles into my arms. It was the first time I thought I might make it.

18

Once Upon a Time

Deputy marshals warned me early on that most who entered the Witness Security Program could not survive the isolation, could not perpetuate the lies. Typically, participants lasted two years before they voluntarily reentered the world and lived exposed. As an informant *and* a Vago, I had an identity: I was either a good guy or a badass. My costumes generated respect and fear, sometimes a mixture of both. I slipped effortlessly between my two personas, and in "off" hours I dissolved into myself. But in the WSP I was no one.

Strangely, the lying bothered me the most even though I had been deceptive about my life since I was nineteen years old: first as a drug dealer, then as an informant, and now as a completely revised person. I never imagined that lying could be so stressful. In the WSP I survived; I didn't live exactly. In the end, I really lied only about why I relocated from Southern California to Virginia. The rest was the truth. I *had* legally changed my name to Charles. I *was* a college graduate. I *did* leave Southern California to start anew in Virginia. I stayed as close to the truth as possible. But disclosing only limited information made it difficult to form friendships, and I realized that I had unwittingly entered another kind of prison with new rules and codes of conduct. I was not free and I never would be.

Nightmares invaded my sleep; Bernard's shadow loomed above my bed. I felt his presence like eyes watching me, far ahead of me, controlling me. I still had no idea whether he had paid someone to end my life. The unknown was more unsettling than the known. At least if I knew, I had a chance. I could prepare. In limbo I had real fear, even in the program. And it wasn't just Bernard's darkness I felt; the Vagos, too, filled my room with a heaviness.

Church became my peace. I found energy in its walls. And though I told no one at first that I participated in the WSP or had infiltrated the Vagos, I did confide in my pastor. He felt safe, like a conduit to God. The pastor absorbed my secrets, absolved my darkness, and slowly gave me permission to exhale. It took a year for the nightmares to dissipate. Simple tasks like purchasing groceries sometimes made my hands shake and my heart race. If the cashier frowned or cleared his throat or looked at me sideways, familiar rage bubbled to the surface. I wanted to punch him for no reason, to react on raw impulse. I felt like a soldier returning from war, and I imagined I experienced similar post-traumatic stress.

I had trouble dating. I wore a costume and a mask and mostly listened to the pretty fixtures across the table, watched their delicate hands lift wineglasses to their lips, push food around their plates with shiny forks. But then one night I had dinner with Monet* and I knew I was in trouble. The last woman I had let into my circle nearly had me killed. But Monet presented a lesson in trust. Strikingly pretty, reserved, and intelligent, she tested my commitment to the program. I had to let my guard down, to believe she would protect me. Slowly, I let her into my world.

➤✖

---

* Pseudonym.

In early December 2007, I received word that Twist's murder trial was scheduled to begin. I had been in the Witness Security Program for seven months. Deputy marshals made arrangements for me to fly from Virginia to Los Angeles. They booked multiple planes routed through various cities across the United States so that no one could track my movements. When I finally landed at LAX, several deputy marshals ushered me into a nondescript Suburban sandwiched between a convoy. For the briefest of moments I felt what a celebrity must, only my paparazzi were dark snipers hidden in courthouse towers or abandoned buildings, waiting to put a bullet in my brain. I thought of the Vagos, who had military and Special Ops training, and my heart pounded. Murdering an informant would put a notch in their belt. But I was well protected; the Suburban had bulletproof glass and I was surrounded by U.S. marshals and ATF agents.

At the federal courthouse, I followed several deputies through the judge's secure entrance to the underground rooms beneath the jail. Mine, similar to a hotel suite, had no windows, no phone, just a speaker button I could push when I needed to communicate. Koz supplied me with a bottle of cold water and wished me luck. After giving me preliminary instructions, the doors closed and I sank, exhausted, into plush blue sofa cushions.

Time passed slowly while I waited for my turn to testify. I had no reservations about betraying Twist. In fact, I felt relief; because of me, a violent sociopath would finally be removed from the community. Twist killed like a machine, indiscriminately, impulsively, and left a trail of human debris. It would feel good to nail his coffin. People warned me that I might feel conflicted when I testified, might hesitate to turn against a "friend," someone who respected me and vouched for me. But I had no regret, no remorse. I had conviction.

Neither Twist nor the Vagos loved me or each other; they loved the idea of me and their brotherhood.

➤✦

Rhino testified in his jail clothes. He looked scared and pale, a far cry from his Vagos persona. The courtroom overflowed with Vagos and curious spectators. Kiles sat next to Twist's family. She blended in easily, unassuming, coy, amazing. They had no idea she was a detective, no idea she had been so instrumental in orchestrating the success of Operation 22 Green, no idea that she had so much to do with Twist being on trial for murder. Rhino's mother came to watch, too, perhaps to support her son, perhaps to support the club. She entwined her arms through her young husband's, Head Butt. Thirty years her junior, she connected with him mentally even though by day she worked as a bank president and power player in the city council. She wore her costumes well. Perhaps she needed both identities, yearned to live life on the edge, with risk. Maybe she needed to wake from her numb existence and feel something again, however misguided and confused.

As Rhino exited, I shuffled to the witness stand. He had testified under duress, pursuant to a plea bargain for lesser charges and a reduced sentence. He had no loyalty or sense of "brotherhood" for his fellow Vagos. He had a sense of self-preservation. They all did. The whole idea that Vagos would defend each other, even die for each other, was bullshit. Code, club, colors was all illusion and delusion. The seduction of being someone else was an addiction.

Strangely, Rhino's twin brother, who had never been a Vago during Rhino's involvement, decided to prospect for the club after Rhino went to prison. But that wasn't the strange part. The truly bizarre footnote was that they allowed Rhino's brother to join at all, considering that Rhino became a snitch and at one time the Vagos had put a hit out on him. The revolving door swung again, and in the end no one really cared about a person's past. They were all opportunists. They fulfilled the Now. Loyalty was fleeting.

For them. But I had no question what my purpose served. Twist stared at me from the defense table, his gaze cold and penetrating and inhuman.

A chill coursed through me as I recalled the night I had planned to kill him.

As I raised my right hand to be sworn, the prosecutor moved in for the jugular: "You used to be a drug dealer, didn't you?"

Yes. A million years ago, I used to be a criminal.

PART II

Operation Black Diamond: Black to Black

Which is better—to have laws and agree, or to hunt and kill?
—WILLIAM GOLDING, *LORD OF THE FLIES*

19

First It Rains . . .

Life in the Witness Security Program progressed at a moderate pace, safe but dull. I settled into routines, found work as a mechanic and earned a decent wage, but I couldn't imagine the rest of my life. With no past, no apparent future, and only a mundane present, I simply existed like a broken appliance left to mend someday on a warehouse shelf. But more than that, I couldn't bear to live my life perpetually hidden. I needed purpose. Monet married me in the program. She contracted to disappear with me, to protect me. But I didn't want her sacrifice. She deserved to be safe and free. And the only way I knew to accomplish both was to return to my life undercover, but this time, as a well-paid informant.

Canada offered its informants—they called them "police agents"—$1 million to infiltrate the Hells Angels. But the Royal Canadian Mounted Police had no paid positions available, so they referred me to their law enforcement agency, the Ontario Provincial Police (OPP). The Hells Angels operated largely as a cartel in Canada; the club had subsumed seven other biker gangs and represented the "highest concentration of

Hells Angels in the world." The OPP needed my help to infiltrate the club in Ontario, so they flew me to Buffalo, New York, to discuss the particulars. In a dimly lit café with wind howling around me, I proposed a four-month contract for their consideration: $10,000 a month until I got inside the Hells Angels.

But the recession took its toll on the OPP as well, and the department had no funds to finance an infiltration. Unwilling to let the opportunity drop, I proposed getting inside a Hells Angels support club in the United States, preferably one with a chapter in Virginia Beach. The Hells Angels barely had a presence in Virginia, but they wanted one and they were actively recruiting the Merciless Souls. I figured if I prospected for the Merciless Souls and subsequently patched into the Hells Angels, I could transfer to Canada.

Meanwhile, I commuted forty miles each way to work and began to notice a Mongol presence in my area. The one-percenter bikers roared past me wearing bottom rockers that boasted BALTIMORE. Predominantly a West Coast gang headquartered in Southern California, the Mongols only sporadically dotted some East Coast cities. And they had formed a fledgling chapter in Virginia Beach. I decided that while I waited for the OPP opportunity to materialize, I could work the gang part time.

⫘

Koz put me in touch with Gringo, an agent out of the ATF's Richmond field office located ninety miles from my home. He said he was "working something big" but disclosed no details.

The following week I arranged to meet Gringo ten miles from Richmond at a pizza restaurant. He arrived on his motorcycle, dressed in full Mongol cuts, wearing a Baltimore side rocker. His "prospect," special agent JD, also wore a Mongol prospect patch.

"*You're* the Mongols?" I laughed.

Over several slices of pizza, Gringo explained the agents' odyssey: He and JD had started a Mongol "community impact investigation" in Baltimore six months prior with a goal of curbing drugs, but after encountering administrative roadblocks, they transferred their case to the ATF field office in Richmond and joined the Virginia Beach chapter of the Mongols. But they had yet to switch their rockers.

"You commute from Richmond?" I asked.

"Technically our chapter has three official Mongols, but the president is an enlisted soldier. He's currently out to sea. So is the other one. I'm the acting president." Gringo grinned.

"How did you . . ."

"We *applied*." Gringo explained the extensive process involved in becoming an accepted full-patch Mongol. The club demanded a birth certificate, relatives' names and addresses, employment and criminal history for the last ten years, even tax returns. Preparing an undercover identity involved an elaborate operation. Gringo and JD had to create fake records—including school, credit, and work history—that corroborated their fictitious lives. I quickly realized the difference between our respective roles: Gringo and JD had the administrative support of the ATF to doctor records. I had no one. Gringo had already been "approved" by the Mongols to become a full-patched member thanks to the help of a confidential informant. JD, however, still waited for his paperwork to clear.

My heart sank as I listened to the requirements. Like hell would I complete an application for Mongol admission or expose my past or my family to that kind of scrutiny. And I couldn't exactly borrow another agent's identity without attracting suspicion from the ATF. Never mind that I was technically still in the program.

But I was in luck. Apparently on the East Coast, the Mongols required official credentials only if a prospect wanted to become a full-patched member. I could be a part-time Mongol prospect and avoid a background investigation altogether. Distance helped. Gringo convinced the two official Mongols in the Virginia Beach chapter that the reason they hadn't seen me yet was that I lived damn near eighty miles away.

✕

At first my dip back into undercover life was unremarkable. I was too part time to really participate much in the bar scene. And I hadn't committed to the Mongols since I still hoped the OPP opportunity would materialize. But one chilly September afternoon in 2008, Gringo asked me to attend an "event" at the Virginia Motorsports Park in Dinwiddie—a possible "war" brewed between the Pagans and the Hells Angels' support club, the Merciless Souls. The Pagans, who had long claimed Richmond as their territory, planned to intimidate the fledgling gang. They requested members of the Outlaws Motorcycle Club and us Mongols to assist in their cause. The three clubs tolerated each other's presence mostly out of guarded caution. They shared a common enemy—the Hells Angels—and a joint goal—to impede the club's territorial growth. None of them could survive a Hells Angels sweep. The Pagans respected the Outlaws because they feared them. By designating certain regions of the East Coast Outlaws territory, the Pagans maintained their own stronghold on larger parts of Virginia. The few Mongols who occupied the East Coast had no support from their West Coast chapters, and politically the club functioned much like an independent party trying desperately to capture the majority vote by advancing a minority platform.

Gringo, JD, and two Mongol hang-arounds obliged. I followed Gringo in my clunky Honda Civic as he sped through traffic toward the racetrack. Doubt swirled in my head. *What was I doing? I was part time for a reason.* Inside the park, an army of Outlaws and Pagans squared off a few yards from the Merciless Souls. They formed a blur of colors, like misfit cowboys, prepared to reenact their own version of the gunfight at the O.K. Corral. Police scattered in the bleachers, some blending with civilians, others guarding the entrances and exits.

Snuff, president of the Manassas chapter of the Outlaws, shifted next to me, the skull and crossed pistons on his cuts flapping in the breeze. His trademark black leather beret kept his ponytail in place. His mostly gray beard extended to his belly. A former competitive power lifter in prison, he now used a cane. His patches telegraphed his commitment to the Out-laws, his willingness to exact revenge, even murder: SNITCHES ARE A DYING BREED, AHAMD (All Hells Angels Must Die), ADIOS (Angels Die in Outlaw States), GFOD (God Forgives, Outlaws Don't). He sneered menacingly at members of the Merciless Souls, his eyes narrowing to slits.

The Merciless Souls grew increasingly agitated at the Pagans' and Out-laws' presence. They stood in defensive posture, arms crossed, mad dogging us, inviting a confrontation. Each side waited for a signal to fire, and I had no doubt Snuff would charge headlong into the crowd randomly shooting. And the agents and I, woefully outnumbered, would be caught in his bul-let spray. Tension rippled over us. Deputies milled around us, and I won-dered if any would interfere.

After an hour of staring at one another, the Merciless Souls finally dis-persed.

⋙⋘

The big standoff almost compelled me to grow out my short-cropped hair and prospect for the Merciless Souls. The Hells Angels had no chapters yet in Virginia, and I was fairly confident the club would absorb the Merciless Souls and anoint them as the first Virginia Hells Angels chapter. After three months of working undercover as a part-time Mongol, I decided to defect.

"Nothing's happening," I complained. "There aren't enough Mongols here to make an impact."

Koz suggested I watch the evening news. That night on TV, an anchor-woman with serious eyes and a wide smile reported on Operation Black Rain, a "massive undercover investigation" that "resulted in the arrest of thirty-eight members of the Mongols Motorcycle Club, including the club's president, Ruben "Doc" Cavazos. Federal authorities also served over 160 search warrants in California, Ohio, Colorado, Nevada, Washington, and Oregon. A total of 110 arrest warrants . . ." As her voice filled my living room, Koz debriefed me.

"While you worked the Vagos, *I* worked undercover in the Mongols."

"*You* were part of Black Rain?" His revelation stunned me. Of course I had no idea, and his ability to move effortlessly in and out of the investigation was a testament to his skill. I wanted to be that good, that incognito.

The fallout from that investigation had huge implications for our Mongol infiltration. Not only did Black Rain devastate the Mongol leadership on the West Coast, but a federal court also banned use of the Mongols' logo (a ruling that was later overturned); gang members could no longer wear their colors. Unable to flaunt their identity, Mongols had to revise their club code. Full-patched members now blended with prospects. Their whole rank-and-file hierarchy disintegrated. Lars, the Mongols' national president, rotted in federal custody. During the raids, government agents seized the Mongols' paperwork, including pending applications from prospective members, partially completed background investigations, "research" on possible informants, and the club's bylaws and constitution. We no longer had to prove or explain our status to the Mongols. Members had no means of checking our credentials. And Lars was no help. If we said we were Mongols, we *were*.

Even our chapter president, who briefly returned from his sea post, accepted our status without further inquiry. The new laws emasculated him; we suddenly all looked alike, dressed now in T-shirts, soft colors with the Mongols logo embroidered on the pocket. Real tough guys. Black Rain's crippling effect on the Mongols organization made us reevaluate our purpose. We had less need to conduct another full-scale federal investigation into the same biker club. Few Mongols inhabited Virginia Beach, and most of the other clubs in the area either liked or tolerated the Mongols' presence.

We debated whether to infiltrate the Pagans, but Gringo worried about exposure. He and Koz had previously investigated the Warlocks, the Pagans' chief rival. There was always a chance some Pagans might recognize them. But the Pagans shared an alliance with the Outlaws; if we infiltrated the Outlaws, at least the Pagans would treat us well.

I was conflicted. I wanted to work the Hells Angels and relocate to Canada. But that option still hadn't materialized and I was open to other possibilities.

Meanwhile, as Mongols we continued to frequent bars in Richmond, mixing with Pagans and Outlaws, until one night changed everything. The catalyst came shortly before Thanksgiving in 2008, when the agents witnessed what Snuff would later describe as an "unfortunate" incident involving a black male patron and members of his Manassas chapter. In the Hard Times Cafe, a Depression-era parlor tucked into a street corner in Fredericksburg, two Outlaws, Alibi and Jason (Snuff's brother), decided to "have some fun" with a customer.

"Got a light?" Jason dangled a cigarette between his lips: A black man obliged. But when his match flared in the murky darkness, Jason, without provocation, put his fist through the man's face. Since he "wasn't going to get laid" that night, he figured he "might as well hit a nigger." The force of Jason's punch propelled the man to his knees. Alibi, a stubby Outlaw who resembled a tree trunk, struck the dazed and bloody man again, this time fracturing his eye socket.

"He has to have surgery." Snuff took a pull on his beer, and his words chilled me more than the cool winter air funneling through his garage. He had canvassed the restaurant, worried about witnesses, assured that they knew the script: Alibi punched in self-defense. Snuff tossed his empty bottle against the wall and shot Gringo a hard stare. "I suggest you lie, too."

Jason snickered. "Hit any niggers lately?"

Alibi, too, begged JD to "lie to his lawyer," "testify falsely" at his pending trial. "That's what a brother would do."

✖

In early January 2009, we decided to become brothers. At first I refused, still hopeful Canada would materialize. But then JD reminded me that Outlaws had chapters in Canada; I could infiltrate the club in the United States, transfer, and still work for the OPP.

JD looked relieved. "Good. Because we already told them you were in."

20

Outside In

We are not marauding sociopaths . . . we have rules.
—Outlaw to a reporter

The American Outlaws Association (AOA) was officially established in 1965. A precursor group originated in Chicago in the 1930s and eventually spread throughout the East Coast, Canada, and Europe, with chapters formed in France, Norway, Belgium, Great Britain, Germany, Thailand, and Sweden. Recently, the AOA established chapters in Russia and Japan and boasts one of the largest motorcycle clubs in the world. The various chapters are grouped into color-coded regions. The Copper Region, which included North and South Carolina and Virginia, consisted of seven active chapters. Milwaukee Jack served as the Outlaws' national boss. And like the Vagos, the AOA implemented a rank-and-file structure replete with a boss, vice president, enforcer, and secretary-treasurer. Prospective members first had to "hang around" the club for at least one year, demonstrate their commitment to the organization, and eventually obtain a club sponsor to prospect. That process could last at least six months or more.

As Mongol full-patches, we planned to become a prospective chapter of the Outlaws composed of agents and informants. But the Mongols, angry that the Outlaws had seduced us, insisted that the leaders of both clubs meet to discuss the politics of defection. Not that recruitment required permission, but tolerance was appreciated. The Mongols and Outlaws, after all, still had to coexist in a small territory, and with a common enemy it made sense for them to play nice. According to the club's strict rules, we needed five members and we had only thirty days to find a clubhouse. If we failed, we would be relegated to probationary status through the Northern Virginia chapter under Snuff's leadership. That wasn't going to happen.

At first we attempted to recruit the Mongols' Virginia Beach president (as well as the other member and the hang-arounds) to be our fourth member; with him mostly at sea he could fulfill a number without actually being a participant. But he refused. He was a devoted Mongol with no interest in defecting. He needed the identity, especially after losing his position with the Naval Special Warfare Development Group.

Nevertheless, he had a prized "war trophy" he wanted to sell, a Russian-made automatic AK-47 that he "found" buried in warehouse debris on an abandoned Iraqi military base.

"I could use the money," he confided in Gringo and offered to toss in his bike for good measure.

"I plan to report it stolen anyway," he added, "and file a fraudulent insurance claim."

He sold Gringo his motorcycle for $1,200 and reported a theft with the Fairfax County police. But when the Mongols president learned that his insurance company had denied the claim, he offered Gringo two ballistic vests and another AK-47 in lieu of his immediate repayment. He should have known Gringo would never accept a bike with a lien.

"I was low-hanging fruit" for the agent, the president confessed as he later pled guilty to selling illegal weapons to a federal agent.

✄

The Norfolk field office, nearly eighty miles from Richmond, attempted to find us recruits. Naturally they wanted to avoid using another federal agent.

The expense and the safety measures that had to be implemented each time the ATF dispatched one of their own into the field posed a bureaucratic nightmare. But they had a possible candidate, an informant and former drug dealer who had recently completed a prison sentence. He sounded promising. I arranged to meet him after work in a local bar.

"Tell him you're a federal agent," Gringo suggested. "Explain that you're infiltrating a biker club but don't tell him which one." The lie was a necessary precaution. If we decided not to use the informant, the less he knew about us and our operation the better.

The informant arrived fifteen minutes late for our date at Cheers. Tall and skinny, he had a deformed arm that flapped at his side like a wing, an alcoholic bloom, and sweaty cheeks. A gold skull necklace swung from his neck. Baggy pants hugged his hips, exposing red boxers. We were already in trouble. He extended his deformed arm in greeting, and the appendage reminded me of half-kneaded dough. *This was Norfolk's finest?*

"Electrical wire accident," he volunteered and slid onto the stool beside me. Reeking of alcohol, he ordered more shots and recounted in slurry detail several versions of his life story. I didn't believe a single word, but we had limited time to pull together a chapter of misfits.

"How did he seem?" Gringo asked me later.

"Confused."

"But will he work?"

"We're desperate," I said.

"Can he ride?"

"Only a street bike."

We decided to test the informant—we named him Claw—to make sure his backstory contained no holes, no missing details that might incite suspicion and compromise the entire investigation. The Outlaws always tested newcomers, wary of police informants and undercover operatives. They had protections in place—brutal initiation rites, interminably long prospecting periods, and verbal jousts. We were actors, method actors; we couldn't pretend on the surface we were other people. We had to *be* our identities through and through, and if we didn't rehearse, didn't challenge the fake histories we created for ourselves, the Outlaws would sense our deception and reject us like a foul odor. The details had to be perfect, flawless. Claw had to give the performance of his life and remember his lines. He made me nervous; I had always relied on my intuition when I infiltrated the Vagos. Now, for the first time, my fate rested with my team's deliverance.

"Tell him *you're* the ATF agent and *we're* the Outlaws," JD suggested. "Make up a backstory about how the two of you met. We'll grill him."

Claw climbed into my car: His hands shook and he wore the same disheveled baggy clothes as the day before. Not a good sign.

"You ready for this?" I asked.

He nodded, stared into the street. "Pumped. Let's do it." His enthusiasm telegraphed his inexperience. No one I knew had ever been "pumped" to infiltrate a violent biker gang.

"How do we know each other?" I quizzed him.

"We met in a bar?"

"What bar? Where? We have to be specific."

"Bailey's?"

"No good. That's in Richmond. How long have we known each other?"

"A few months?"

"At least a year. We met in Portsmouth, at the Foggy Point."

I took him there the next day so he could memorize the smells, the menu, the neighborhood—just in case the Outlaws demanded more detail. After several days I asked him, "Think you got it?"

"Let's do it."

⋙

I took him to our undercover house to meet the "bad guys." Gringo and JD, dressed in prospect cuts, lounged on pink couches. Claw walked beside me, half my weight, looking like a cutout from a cardboard poster. The agents suppressed a smirk, careful to stay in character. They spent the next few hours interrogating him, role-playing, asking him how he and I knew each other, until Claw looked like he might expire from the pressure.

"How did he do?" I asked Gringo later.

"He passed."

Claw became #4.

But we still needed a fifth member, and time was running out. Days before our deadline, the ATF relented and supplied us with Bobby, a qualified federal agent, medic, and experienced Green Beret with two completed tours in Afghanistan. Well-groomed and soft-spoken, he disarmed us with his calm demeanor and relaxed style. Hardly the profile of a trained gentleman killer, Bobby oddly blended well into the biker culture. With our fifth member firmly recruited, it was time for the club of misfits to find our clubhouse.

The Outlaws had several in black neighborhoods, convinced that police were less likely to "harass" them if they remained hidden in plain view. I searched dilapidated rental properties but settled on an abandoned tire warehouse in an industrial area of Petersburg. The building, tucked between boarded-up businesses and gutted streets, provided perfect seclusion for drug deals, clandestine conversations, and unexpected night visitors. Situated one mile from the only Hells Angel living in the area, the ATF promptly wired our warehouse for sound and video. With one flip of a switch we could record every conversation and transaction. Video streamed twenty-four/seven as a safety precaution. Attorneys could never accuse us later of selective editing.

～✕～

Members gave us a housewarming gift: a pair of Nazi and Southern Confederate flags. We draped them above our bar and over the picture of Adolf Hitler. Inside a wall, the agents hid their government credentials. With our cast selected, we rehearsed. As vice president of our chapter, I developed plausible histories, reviewing the details of when, where, and how I met each of the agents. Our chapter boss, Gringo, and I pretended we were longtime dope traffickers who, for ten years, smuggled shipments of marijuana from the West to East Coast; in those pre-9/11 days, airport security rarely checked luggage. Eventually, I met Gringo's "partner," JD. My adopted name, Chef, solidified my role as a former methamphetamine cook. The best lie was closest to the truth. I knew a lot about drugs, too much, and sometimes that knowledge backfired.

Later, a hefty Italian Outlaw from Florida would call my bluff after an impromptu visit to our clubhouse. He spilled over our barstool, snorted lines of coke in front of us, and announced matter-of-factly that he had "close connections" to the Gambino crime family and we'd be wise not to "fuck with him."

"I know what you're playing at." He wagged his pudgy finger in my face. His icy tone chipped at my resolve. Still, I shrugged, wiped down the counter with a wet rag, and quietly imploded. "You're the informant." His finger traveled over the rest of us as one by one he picked us off. "You fuckers are the federal agents."

He meant to jar us, to gauge our reaction. If we bristled, registered alarm, even blanched, we would give away our identities. I didn't look at the other agents, didn't flinch, didn't want to give them any opportunity to struggle. The Outlaw laughed and tapped his fingers on the bar to an invisible drumbeat.

I played along. "How come I'm the informant?"

He shrugged, his cheeks peppered red. "You know too much." He qualified after reflection, "definitely too much about drugs."

✕

Bobby joined our mix as a mock Mongol hang-around. We pretended he'd supervised me for three years when I worked in his tree-trimming business. Claw played himself, a deformed, drug-addicted criminal. He blended well as our prospect.

※※

In addition to our government-issued motorcycles, I purchased a van. My experience in the Vagos prepared me well for grit, sleep deprivation, hard concrete flooring, and open fields with rocks for pillows. The van at least provided shelter and thin carpet that wasn't stained with cat piss. I took comfort in the knowledge that if I closed my eyes, no one would step on my head or dribble beer in my ear.

21

War Games

The Outlaws' main objective was to hunt and kill Hells Angels. As predators, the club strategized regularly about impending turf wars with their rival. They baited Hells Angels' support clubs (the Richmond area had only two) like the Desperados, hoping to lure them onto foreign turf and entice them to battle. They feared that the Hells Angels might absorb the support clubs and become an amorphous powerful mass on the East Coast. To thwart that effort, the Outlaws staged assaults. One, at the Cockade City Grill in downtown Petersburg, erupted into a full riot. The Outlaws' plan: Dispatch three small-boned Outlaws, dressed in full regalia and colors, to enter the bar and initiate a confrontation with members of the Desperados. The expectation: The Hells Angels would join their comrades inside and unwittingly submit to be ambushed. The strategy: Outlaws, those not wearing colors, armed with assault rifles, brass knuckles, and revolvers, would man the perimeter, trapping the rivals inside. The players: the agents, Les, the Outlaws' Copper Region North Carolina vice president, and Alibi served outside as human barricades. The orders: Shoot to kill.

The night of the big "showdown," I contracted food poisoning and spent hours vomiting up spoiled mayonnaise in a nearby hospital. But Gringo recounted the details. As Desperados filtered through the large double doors of the bar, a blizzard of violence hit them. Fists dented faces and tabletops, brass knuckles slashed flesh, beer bottles shattered glassware and countertops and slammed into walls. The Cockade City Grill dissolved into a blur of bodies. Desperados fled. One took a bottle to Gringo's head; a jagged glass edge left an angry red gash above his left eye. Gringo struck his assailant with his baton. Fighting spilled into the street. One Desperado, cornered by Outlaws, brandished a Bowie knife, the blade glittering in the darkness. Les drew his revolver; his finger flirted on the trigger as he prepared to drop the gangster like a rag doll. Bobby and JD firmly gripped their guns. It was kill or be killed. Then a siren wailed in the distance. Bikers instantly dispersed; violence rippled like stones over the scene.

"You think you'll make it to the next one?" Gringo teased me.

I smiled weakly. "The poison's almost out of my system."

Gringo laughed. "It'll never be out of your system."

Nurses gave Gringo fourteen stitches.

＞＜

Apart from impromptu fights, bartending proved to be our biggest challenge as prospects. I didn't know the first thing about mixing drinks, and I didn't want to learn at three o'clock in the morning surrounded by bored Outlaws amped up with coke. Probates gave us "on-the-job training" for two weeks in our regional clubhouses until we became proficient at combining Crown and Coke, Jack and Coke, screwdrivers, and Bacardis. The rehearsals helped, but I wasn't ready for long shifts behind the bar: After just two weeks of training, we received word that a Florida Outlaw had crashed his motorcycle into a guardrail. We were summoned to his funeral and expected to bartend.

The Outlaws commandeered the state of Florida, home to more than half the chapters in the country. I dreaded the twenty-hour trek to Ft. Lauderdale. The agents and I rode for two days in tremendous heat, humidity, and patches of rain, passing through the Carolinas and Georgia, grabbing cheap motel rooms when we could, until we arrived at an impressive property spread over acres of immaculate lawn. The Outlaws' clubhouse in Ft. Lauderdale flaunted an inside *and* outside bar covered with a gorgeous canopy. A lake shimmered in the background and reflected rows of chrome. A boat docked near the shore looked like a promising place to sleep. But the pristine scenery hid a sinister undercurrent: alligators. Some creatures lounged on logs in banks of sand. Others slept with their mouths open. Tents pitched along the grass blew dangerously close to the waters. They, too, made inviting bait. I made it a goal to stay awake for the next two days.

"Keep busy and keep your head down," one probate warned us. Then he told us about "batting practice." Calmly, he recounted how a handful of Outlaws, bored and drugged one night, messed with two probates behind the bar. They ordered one to stand in front while they balanced an ashtray on his head.

"They took turns with the bat," the probate said, and all I heard was *whoosh whoosh whoosh* as I imagined them swatting close to the victim's head.

"The other guy just watched as his partner bled, and when it was his turn, he ran."

The story horrified me. The agents and I just looked at the probate, dumbfounded. No one was going to whack anything off my head.

That night we hustled behind the bar, mixing drinks, stocking ice, filling glasses, until our legs burned with exhaustion and our hands shook from the repetition. We slept only two hours, curled in our tents by the lake, wind howling around us. The next morning we mounted our bikes and rode to the funeral home in large packs, in pairs, twenty-five across, three feet deep, muscling over lanes of traffic, blowing through red lights, cutting off other motorists. I never felt more stressed, more exhausted in my life. I hugged the rear; the noise was deafening. In front of me, a sea of black-and-white vests; to the side of me, bodies; to the rear, more bodies.

We rode in tight formation, so close my knees practically bumped the next bike.

And still a large civilian roared close by, pissed that my tires straddled a piece of his lane. He didn't get it—the seriousness of a motorcycle gang. He didn't get that the Outlaws didn't play fair, didn't care, would have bumped him off his bike and run him over like roadkill. I waved the motorist away, hoping he would take his exit cue, but he persisted, coasted next to me, shouted into the wind, "Move the fuck over." He managed to squeeze between me and another Outlaw. Spit flew from the corners of his mouth. The fool was going to get himself killed. Desperation took over and I kicked his bike's gas tank, the force propelling him into the next lane. The motorist struggled to control his bike, glanced at me stunned, and then slowly pulled back.

He didn't know it, maybe never would, but I had just saved his life.

In the biker world, no one expected to survive. The funeral ended two days later like punctuation, ellipsis at the end of a sentence, continuation after pause. Attendees forgot the reason they traveled all those miles to pay their respects to the body in the box who looked oddly unreal, a waxy replica of themselves. With just two hours of sleep the whole weekend, the highway home stretched before us like a dark mouth ready to swallow us whole. The agents and I, exhausted and worn, nodded off, barely able to steady our bikes. We pulled into a motel to nap. I didn't think I would make it. None of us did. Sleep enveloped me like a heavy fog and at first I thought I dreamed the call.

"There's been another death," Gringo mumbled over the phone.

It took me a minute to process his words.

"An Outlaw crashed his bike leaving the funeral."

Our attendance at any memorial service was mandatory. But the thought of repeating another biker funeral on the heels of the one we had just left nearly finished me. I was done. My body couldn't do it. Mentally, I protested, "I'm not going." Investigation over. I didn't care.

I hung up, fell asleep. The phone shrilled again.

"We don't have to go," Gringo breathed. Relief shuddered over the line.

❧

Three weeks later, we attended the national Daytona Run, an annual three-day event held in Florida. Hundreds of Outlaws from surrounding areas attended. My wife, pregnant with our first child, was expected to deliver in less than three weeks, and the last thing I needed was to ride to the hospital dressed in colors and on a motorcycle. Instead, I drove my van and towed our bikes to Atlanta. Rain pelted the streets. But weather was no deterrence. In Atlanta, the others mounted their bikes and fishtailed the rest of the way to Daytona in heat and wet. By the time they arrived at the clubhouse, they looked like the others, bedraggled, weary, and coated in sweat.

Sun poked through the clouds just in time for our first task: guarding the Outlaws' bikes. As Snuff had so delicately explained, "Why the fuck would we entrust amateurs with our lives?" The real posts—protecting the clubhouse and scouting for Hells Angels—were reserved for members only, since they could carry a gun and "shoot on sight." Hot tar seared through my boots. Clothes clung to my body like a second skin. We had "volunteered" for twenty-hour shifts, alternating between guard duty and bartending. Periodically we slept, sometimes for a whole three hours.

Heat beat my face. Occasionally, members threw us bottled water. But after the first few hours, fever raged inside me. Fire burned in JD's cheeks; a red band circled his throat. Neither of us had sunscreen. My throat was parched, but I dreaded the long path through the clubhouse to replenish water. The gauntlet made me easy prey for members. And instinctively I knew that if I ventured past their roving gaze, I would never quench my thirst. They would find other, far worse tasks for me to perform. I stayed thirsty.

Snuff added to our tension. He hobbled toward us, his cane clicking on the concrete. Despite the tremendous heat, he wore a leather trench coat. His beret shielded the sun from his eyes. He circled us, whacked us in the shins with his cane, then, for "fun," whispered in the shell of JD's ear, "I'm hunting Hells Angels." Then, without provocation, he whipped out his Buck knife, pressed the blade to JD's throat, and chuckled. "Seen any yet?" JD flinched.

We were both unarmed and surrounded by gangsters with weapons clipped to their hips like accessories. Snuff slid the blade into JD's throat, pressed his thumb into the wound, and licked off the blood. But before JD could react, Snuff turned his attention to me. He slapped the knife against his trench coat, moved closer to me, and pressed the long blade to my throat. It nicked my skin and a hot trickle of blood stained my vest.

"How about you?" he sneered, and I thought he might be crazy enough to drop me right there, "just for fun." Snuff had no filters, no limits, no *feeling*. If he could beat a stranger senseless in a bar in front of a crowd, he could certainly cut me.

I swallowed, my nerves shot. Buzzing sounded in my ears. My world suddenly shrank: every detail amplified, Snuff's foul breath, the prick of cold metal on my skin, burning in my eyes. This was not how I imagined my end, slit for slaughter. Rage mixed with fear as my mind raced with exit strategies. Snuff enjoyed watching my light extinguish. As a skilled sociopath, he controlled when and how and whom he would blame for my end. I was certain JD was scared, too. Somehow we had to extricate ourselves from this scene, scream "Cut," fire the crazy actor from the set. Snuff had deviated from the script. *Where was the fucking director?* Then, as if reason suddenly returned to Snuff, he removed the blade from my throat and disappeared through the crowd, his black trench flapping like crows' wings.

We stood there, chrome from the bikes glinting in the sunlight. Members strolled past us; prospects ran errands. General commotion stirred the air. If Snuff had slashed our throats and dropped us like burlap sacks on the pavement, would anyone have noticed?

❧

At last, we moved inside to bartend. As my eyes adjusted to the dim bulbs, a blast of heat and sweat hit me full force in the face. The bar stretched twenty feet long, framed by a wall scribbled with the names of fallen Outlaws. Dizzy and dehydrated, I pushed through the standing-room-only crowd to relieve Bobby. He pulled JD and me aside and reported his narrow escape. His shift had just started when Spot, a Florida Outlaw, spit into his mixed drink and ordered the four prospects behind the bar to "line up" in front of him. He had excused Bobby, whose shift had just begun. The other prospects apparently had spent the last three hours "fucking up." They bristled at Spot's command and stood shoulder to shoulder and flinched, already anticipating their punishment. Spot punched, and with each blow, blackened their eyes. *Pop. Pop. Pop.* Fist struck bone.

"Now make me a *real* drink."

Shakily, I wiped beer steins with a damp towel as the beaten prospects resumed their posts. Alcohol sloshed over their hands; beer foam blew into their swollen eyes. They behaved like beaten dogs, cowered in the back of their cage, head bowed, paws forward, waiting for the kick, the scold, the burst of anger that racked their body with pain. They stayed for the reward, the promise of rank advancement. A flurry of women hustled past; most resembled hags, smashed-in faces, missing teeth, purple stains beneath their eyes. I couldn't imagine why they stayed. Reduced to slaves, "property of Outlaws," they lived to serve the men who beat them. I watched one drop a french fry. An Outlaw kicked the tray of food from her hand, smashed his boot into the mess, yanked her hair, and dragged her face to the floor. On her hands and knees, she lapped up the leftovers.

All around me casualties worked. Though the women "volunteered" for the job, I couldn't imagine they bargained for such cruelty. Few of them stayed, and those who did survived as hollow, addicted shells. As long as they had utility, the Outlaws tolerated their presence. As a result, none of us worried much about dreaded "female tests"—Outlaws used women the way they used drugs, as a quick fix. And they didn't much care whether we got high or not.

But they did care whether we fucked up. And I didn't want a black eye. Gringo and I approached bartending like a military drill. We served every beer chilled, stocked the refrigerator with ice, emptied trash in the fields, and kept a frenzied pace. My rescue came an hour after my shift began. Outlaws rumbled about Hells Angels sightings. And the regional Outlaw boss, Les, asked, "Does anyone have a car?"

My hand shot up. Soon, Les, a bull named Johnny, a cunning gangster others called the Devil, and Gringo climbed into my van. In the cramped darkness, armed with revolvers, automatic handguns, and my collapsible baton, we scanned the busy streets for the Enemy. Heavy percussion beat the night air as bands competed for audiences. Les ordered me to double-park. Surrounded by attractive people and dizzy lights, we entered bar after bar, hunting for Hells Angels. To patrons we must have looked like beasts: oversized, dirty, grizzly. We moved with single-minded purpose. It felt like rehearsal for a strange road play. Dressed in costumes, grim masks, and battle armor, we prepared for confrontation. But in the end, we only faced ourselves.

The Devil complained we were "chasing ghosts." He flashed me a wide grin and winked as he unveiled his plan to "kidnap me later" to party. But the only thing I wanted to do was sleep. At noon the next day, we finally had the chance. Though the van had no air-conditioning, temperatures soared over 100 degrees, and the humidity was cloying, Gringo and I crawled inside, sweaty, smelly, and exhausted. It was good to escape. It was good to have a van.

⚞⚟

By day four, I needed a hospital. Feverish, blistered from sunburn, dizzy from sleep deprivation, I barely remembered the ride home. By day five, I had contracted pneumonia. Confined to a cot in a white room and plugged with IVs, I drifted off to my safe place, my subconscious. Soon I would welcome a son and once again explain to my wife why I had to leave.

Although I returned home more often than the undercover agents who saw their families only once a month, the transition proved stressful. Typically it took me two days to adjust to "normal." As a rule, I never spoke about my experiences with my wife. The less she knew, the better for her psyche. And she didn't want to know. Like a soldier returning from war, I learned to compartmentalize. When I was home, I shut down and shut out friends; it was too difficult to form and maintain relationships that necessarily revolved around lies. I could never tell people who I was, what I did for a living, why I couldn't come to the church picnic.

Some experiences are too profound to translate: war, military service, and life undercover. My only friends all lived like me, all understood the trauma, the restless sleep, the need to watch mindless cartoons at night sprawled on the living room couch. I escaped through movies—mostly comedies, the dumber the better. At home, my day job crowded my thoughts. I was Chef 24/7 not because he was a fictional identity I created but because he was me. He had to be. I couldn't turn off my role, couldn't pretend that I became an Outlaw sometimes and then a husband others. Undercover was my identity. I not only acted like an Outlaw, I learned to think like one.

I had lived my whole life undercover; I didn't know anything else. I thrived on high risk the way a snowboarder loves helicopter drops over fresh white cliffs. My wife thankfully accepted my addiction, my need for adrenaline and complete rejection of all things mundane. It didn't matter whether she ever said a word to me when I was home, as long as she was there: Just looking at her quiet silhouette brought me comfort.

22

David and Goliath

Our Petersburg clubhouse, situated nearly two hundred miles from other Outlaws chapters, typically discouraged night visitors. But occasionally strays surprised us. It was Memorial Day weekend 2009, and we had spent the night celebrating at local bars in Richmond with Outlaws—Les; M & M, boss of the Rock Hill South Carolina chapter and Copper Region enforcer; Harry; and two stragglers, a probate named Bovine and a full-patch, Brett, a former wrestler who lived perpetually high on coke.

Well after midnight, we moved the partying to our clubhouse and simply rewound our night. Hospitality generated good business relations. Bobby and I rotated tending bar until Les finally drifted off to sleep on our couch. He looked mangled, damaged, like a doll without stuffing. In sleep, masks slipped off. Harry and Brett alternated between shots and spoons of coke. They snorted thick lines on our bar in plain view of the video cameras. Bovine served them like a mangy butler, answering to quick finger snaps, to his new name, Probate, and to indiscriminate expletives. He reminded me of Claw, anxious, twitchy, a distinct liability.

We used Claw sparingly. He satisfied our body count and tagged along mostly on mandatory runs. Otherwise, we kept him well hidden. He didn't complain. In fact, I think he was relieved. Bovine lowered his gaze to the floor. He looked discolored, ashen, as if the strain of being a slave had already thinned his resolve. His left eye was ringed yellow with the end of a shiner.

Bobby bantered easily with Harry, regularly refilling his beer stein, feigning interest in his drug exploits, and behaving like a friend. An older gangster in his midfifties, Harry resembled a retired Nazi officer, sleek head, swastika tattoos on his biceps. His raucous laughter echoed in the clubhouse as he drank and picked cocaine residue from his nostrils. But as the night faded, newfound rage simmered beneath Harry's demeanor and he sneered suddenly at Bobby, "I don't *like* you."

Bobby's jaw slacked. His smile instantly vanished. A pall of apprehension hung in the air. Bovine jerked his head up, his neck corded with tension. He stiffened his legs apart, ready for his orders. Harry's outburst rippled over the room like a vibration.

"I don't like you," he repeated.

Worry creased Bobby's face. None of us knew what had happened. One minute Harry and Bobby were engaged in collegial conversation, the next, Harry pounced.

"Who the fuck *are* you?" Harry spit and I knew it was the cocaine talking. He slid off the barstool, his hands balled to fists. We stashed AK-47s in our clubhouse with the pins deactivated. Harry's gun protruded from his waistband. My knife blade chafed my shin. We poised for reaction. But Harry surprised us.

"Stand in that corner and don't move until I say so." He snapped his fingers at Bobby, motioned to the wall, and scolded him like an insolent child. "You can't fucking talk to a full-patch like that. Who the fuck do you think you are?" Startled, Bobby stood, back to us, facing the wall. It was late. I was tired. I had been partying for hours and now I just wanted them all to leave. But Harry and Brett, wired from coke, stayed. And as long as they did, Bobby faced the wall.

His punishment bothered me the most. It seemed so basic, so unin-
spired, so . . . strangely ordinary. Here we had endured sudden punches, cuts
to the throat, veiled threats, action/reaction, what seemed to be the natural
order of things in the Outlaws' world. And now, for the briefest of moments,
their masks slipped and we saw them, who they *really* were, not actors at
all, not tough, not one percenters who maimed and killed for fun, not anything at all. It was hard to fear the known.

❧

Soon boredom inspired cruelty. Brett charged spontaneously like an ele-
phant, wrapping his thick arms around Gringo's throat and pinning him to
the scratchy green carpet, his elbows and knees pressing into Gringo's chest
and groin. Forced to wrestle for several minutes, sweat dripped from Gringo's eyes as he grappled with Brett and pinned him down for the count.
Brett sprang from the ground and immediately choked me from behind.
"Get out of this one, fucker." He laughed, a ball of muscle, half my size, but
strong. He played dirty and loose. And though at one time I had trained in
Brazilian jujitsu, I succumbed, white spots punching my eyelids.

M & M whistled, clapped loudly, and Brett released.

"How about a rematch?" He squatted, breathed in my face.

I scrambled to my feet, still dressed in my cuts, and tackled Brett to the
ground. I pressed my forearm into his throat. He wriggled beneath me, strug-
gling like a wild boar. My weight crushed him. No one cheered or grunted.
No one dared. His sour breath in my face came in quick bursts. I tugged at
his vest, pinned his elbows to the carpet. Shadows circled me. *Feud-frenzy,
feud-frenzy*: Chants repeated like percussion. But the rounds lasted too
long, three to four minutes. Our limbs tangled together, we grunted like
animals. Finally M & M called time.

We broke apart. Brett rolled to his feet. His sweat stained the carpet.
Dizzy and spent, I struggled to stand. Then I saw M & M's right hand shoot
up. Round two, his voice boomed through the clubhouse. We were the
entertainment, expected to perform like gladiators in an arena: prospect

against full-patch. I had no choice. I lunged at Brett, grappled him to the ground, body-slammed him into the thin carpet. His face flushed, shiny wet. We sparred for several minutes, ground fighting until wind rushed from Brett's lungs. My body burned with strain. Dawn seeped through the windows. Fleetingly, I worried about repercussions. If I beat Brett, would I then be forced to fight the others—Gringo, JD, Bobby? Would the matches continue without relief?

M & M, perpetually high on coke, called time. Brett stumbled to the bar and vomited into the sink. He grabbed an ice pack from the freezer and shoved it against his head. Shock slid behind his eyes. I dropped into the couch, dizzy and exhausted, my body numb with fatigue. M & M worked the room. He next paired Gringo with the probate and Bobby with JD. The latter pair went easy on each other. On M & M's orders, they stripped their cuts. Chains and rings glittered on the counter. The match began. Mock wrestling, the agents circled the carpet, lunged, pinned each other in joint locks. They wrestled for several minutes: grunts, moans, pants. The fighting continued. I didn't move, didn't think the matches would ever end. Every muscle in my body tensed. Two hours later, spent and needing rest, I stumbled outside into bright sun and left the others to fight well into morning.

Guilt shuddered through me. Their day had just begun. Not only would they continue to wrestle each other, but they would also contend with the ATF as they were debriefed and justified Operation Black Diamond. The investigation demanded massive outlays of money, electronic surveillance, mountains of paperwork, and dependent cover teams. Not only did the agents balance a split life between being mock gangsters and family men, but they also placated the brass, including top officials in Washington, D.C., who wanted nothing better than to shut down the investigation. Pressure to produce results added to the agents' strain.

Though I participated in none of the internal negotiations, I imagined the conversations. Tensions erupted between cover crew and agents as each accused the other of being unsympathetic. We weren't "partying," we were building trust. Rapport necessarily produced drugs, confessions, conspiracies to kill. Even so, surveillance teams quit regularly, tired of the hours and what they considered reckless disregard for their time. But the nature of undercover work sometimes made it impossible to warn them of sudden plans, impromptu visits . . . wrestling matches that extended far beyond their shifts.

⚒

Exhausted, I needed to get home to my family. I passed the cover team parked across the street. Steaming coffee rested on the dash. I called them as a courtesy, otherwise they might sit indefinitely in the street waiting for their exit cuc.

"What's going on in there?" one piped over the line, sounding a little too eager.

It took me a minute to answer, vaguely wondering what it would take for them to charge inside and rescue us.

"You looked like you were having fun."

I hung up.

⚒

Apart from the physical exertion prospecting demanded, I worried about ambush and lone snipers from the Hells Angels. Even the act of pumping gas stirred anxiety: We traveled in pairs, making sure one of us always kept a lookout for strays, for shadows, for things out of place. Each time I left the clubhouse, I scanned the cameras angled toward the street and driveway looking for dark cars parked askew, for silhouettes on the corner, for abandoned bikes. I altered my routes home and checked for tails, worried gangsters might discover my real home. If I parked my van overnight at the undercover house, in the morning I checked underneath for bombs.

The Hells Angel who owned a tattoo shop a mile from our clubhouse posed a perpetual threat. He served as the puppet master for the Hells Angels' supporters like the Desperados and the Merciless Souls. And he let it slip where the agents lived in their undercover house. The Merciless Souls taunted us, left us flyers and cards in our mailbox: "Come play with us, faggots." They challenged the agents to a brawl a week later in the Southern Star, a bar situated a few miles from our clubhouse. They arrived on their bikes, a pack of twenty armed with bats and mouthpieces.

They dismounted, paced the curb, already agitated. One, who looked like the club's leader, swaggered up to the glass where the agents were drinking inside, tapped his bat on the window, and said, "Come outside, fuckers." When JD didn't budge, the leader marched inside and hovered menacingly at the agents' table. Dressed in black cuts and orange piping, he wore embroidered hammers and a skull with red-devil eyes. MERCILESS SOULS blazed across the top rocker; RICHMOND adorned the bottom. Gringo swallowed a sip of beer, shook his head. "*You* come inside." He slid his gun on the table. The leader's face contorted. He looked constipated as he clicked his tongue over his mouthpiece. As he left, he swung his bat hard, shattering a beer bottle into the street.

Neither side moved. Each played the other's bluff, knowing the slightest provocation would ignite a firestorm. Like a chess game, the players lined up their pawns, positioned their bishops, and debated whether to storm the castle. The agents worried that the Merciless Souls might summon reinforcements, might enter the Southern Star smashing posts and patrons searching for deliverance. Tension punctuated the air. But after an hour of posturing, the gang relented, secured their bats to their bikes, and sped into the darkness like demons.

➤✕

The Merciless Souls spread rumors that our chapter was composed of government agents; *real* outlaws, after all, would have shot them by now. *Probably right.* Over the next few weeks they tested us, appearing suddenly at eateries and bars in our neighborhood like dark ghouls, until one day the threat increased.

Summer heat drifted through the open windows in our clubhouse. Red lanterns flickered inside the Italian restaurant across the street. Quiet swelled with strange foreboding. We heard them first, the roar of bikes rumbling in like a storm. The token Hells Angel in our area led the pack. He parked in front of Louie's, trailed by three prospects and a dozen Merciless Souls. They dismounted, bedraggled, unkempt, long hair blowing away from their faces.

"What are they up to?" Bobby racked his shotgun and ran onto the sidewalk. Wind swirled around us. Gringo moved inside, grabbed his revolver, and said, "They want to play." JD produced his Glock, and I stroked my machete, my breathing heavy. This was it. I waved the lone Hells Angel over with my blade and no doubt made the cover team squirm. But I knew what I was doing. If we were going to survive an ambush, we had to deflect fear, beat them at their own game, put them in check first.

The Hells Angel smirked at the gesture and ordered his minions to remain outside while he devoured a pizza. He took his time. The Merciless Souls paced on the curb, wielding bats and guns. They moved in bursts, like charged bolts, and I had no doubt that if commanded, they would rush at us. The three Hells Angels prospects stood apart, perfectly still, loyal as dogs. After an hour, a patrol car swished through the street.

The uniform zipped down his window. "Everything all right?" I guessed the cover team had called him. His presence was hardly a comfort. He came alone. No helicopters whirred overhead. There would be no takedown, no tumbles, all very civilized and orderly. He was no doubt as scared of us as we were *for* him, each of us helpless to stop the other from ambush.

"Everything's fine," JD lied, and his hand shook as he waved the cop away. *Keep moving*, I mentally shouted, *floor it, get the hell out of this neighborhood. Whatever you do, stay in the fucking car.* Thankfully, the deputy listened and slowly disappeared around the corner.

We didn't need cops. We needed reinforcements. We called members from the Devil's Grip, a Pagans support club. We needed backup and fast. The Hells Angel would soon finish his pizza and our situation had not improved. Within a half hour, members from the Devil's Grip rolled up, apparently without the Pagans' blessing.

Across the street, the troops huddled: Hells Angels, Merciless Souls, and now a smattering of Desperados. Tensions mounted. Meanwhile, we paced our clubhouse, weapons loaded, thoughts racing. *What would we do if someone actually fired the first shot?* The Devil's Grip strutted on our porch, pumped at the specter of war. They were soldiers waiting for their general's command. But after two hours of posturing, the crowd dispersed. We "celebrated" our victory by inviting the Devil's Grip inside and opening up our bar. The oppressive heat gave way to sheets of rain *tap-tap-tapping* on our roof. The night had just begun.

As the drinks flowed, tension electrified the atmosphere. Forced laughter punctuated conversation. Strain worried our brows as outside the street glistened with fresh rain. A neon sign, with one missing letter, cast dull red shadows over our walls. Then I heard it, a low rumble that at first mimicked thunder and evolved into a distinct roar. All of us instantly sobered as gold headlights swished through the dark. They had returned, Hells Angels and Merciless Souls. They parked in front of a neighborhood bar and dismounted. We called the Pagans. And waited, separated by glass, until someone dared to move his bishop.

But as the hours ticked by, nobody moved.

⇝⇜

The standoff only fueled tensions between the Outlaws and Hells Angels support clubs. They hunted us, we hunted them, and it was only a matter of time before one side produced casualties. We rode for hours, sometimes several hundred miles a day through congested neighborhoods, lonely freeways, commercial zones, searching for the elusive enemy. I never stopped to think what I would do if I found one. But smartly, the Merciless Souls hid, and in those rare moments when they did emerge crazy bold, we ducked. And so the war games continued.

⊃⊂

The threat of violence increased. Outlaws arranged to ambush the Merciless Souls one afternoon at a local Harley-Davidson shop in Richmond. The owners hosted a public event—raffles, a barbecue—and they invited the Merciless Souls. But as Outlaws descended the night before to stake out the local bars for stragglers, their presence served as deterrence. A light drizzle fell over plainclothes police officers who surrounded the shop the next morning. Undercover detectives set up surveillance at the gang's clubhouse, hoping to follow members foolish enough to head toward the dealership. They enlisted the help of local police to pull gang members over for real or imagined traffic violations.

Rain fell harder, and I waited hours in the parking lot of the Harley-Davidson shop, knowing that no Merciless Souls would ever appear.

When the afternoon proved a bust, the Outlaws regrouped, determined to continue their hunt. They convened the following afternoon at a local Hooters, propelled by rumors that Merciless Souls dined inside. But when we crowded the entrance of the restaurant, prepared for a confrontation, ordinary people stared back at us, their plates full of burgers and french fries, their mouths gaping with curiosity at our costumes.

"They must have changed their plans," an Outlaw grumbled. Plans always changed. The Outlaws, unfamiliar with the Richmond and Virginia Beach area, often revised their murder plots based on errors in direction. We stayed one step ahead of their bungled efforts, and because we knew the area well, no matter how many times the Outlaws rode through unintended neighborhoods or targeted the wrong restaurants, the surveillance team followed not far behind.

The support clubs propagated quickly, nearly tripling in size in a matter of months. Membership attracted the young street fighters, paramilitary types who lusted for blood. Soldiers already, the Hells Angels dispensed with further "training" and simply recruited them.

"What's the plan?" Claw whimpered, clearly uncomfortable with all the hunting.

"We play," Gringo replied.

"We scare them," I tempered, knowing we first had to target their puppeteer. "Let's put an Outlaw sticker on the asshole's front door."

We drove to the Hells Angel's home and I left him the Outlaws' signature, a skull-and-crossbones emblem. It had the effect we wanted, like a stalker who leaves dead roses on his victim's windshield. We let the Hells Angel know we saw him, watched him, and waited for him. After that, the Hells Angel never messed with us. He didn't want trouble. He had a family, a job, and now he knew we knew where he lived. He played the game well. Both sides did. We continued to move around our pieces on the board, mindful of the king and checkmate.

⫸⫷

But the Hells Angels and Merciless Souls weren't our only threats. The following week, Alibi paid us an impromptu visit. He rumbled into our neighborhood blasting racist country lyrics, which was strange since he looked half Puerto Rican himself. I marveled that no one attacked him or deflated his tires or spray-painted something profane on the curb. He dismounted his motorcycle, bulking his shoulders like the school bully, mean and hard in his costume, but alone on the playground I suspected he would wilt. All of us could take him in a fair fight. But nothing about this game was fair. We played on his turf, by his rules, his interpretation.

He lumbered inside our clubhouse and ranted about the Hells Angels threat. At the bar, he rolled a joint stinking like sour cabbage. A squatty version of Snuff, Alibi inhaled and passed the joint to Gringo. It wasn't the first time in the investigation the agents and I had faced the specter of drugs. But even so, spontaneous deflection was difficult. Excuses, without corroboration, could get an agent in trouble. The Outlaws had spies who would investigate and unravel any unrehearsed story. Never mind that ATF policy strictly prohibited ingestion unless the agent deemed his life in danger.

But even that option offered little consolation; if the agent did consume the drug, he would have to emerge from his personality as soon as possible and utter *on tape* his reasons for ingesting and why he had perceived his situation "life threatening." Gringo's face reddened and I could tell he hesitated, debated his options—paper or bullet, neither was attractive. Alibi studied Gringo through a billow of smoke. His eyes watered slightly. Seconds counted in his nonverbal play, and I grabbed the joint.

"He doesn't do *weed*." I laughed, hoping I sounded convincing. I balanced the joint between my lips and inhaled deeply. A veil of smoke hung between us. Alibi looked guarded. I was a stoner, a recovering meth addict. That was my story.

Gringo lowered his gaze. I had no doubt he would have played along, would have fake inhaled the weed just to dodge Alibi's bullet. But it was easier for me to take the fall. I had no ATF repercussions.

Claw didn't get it. "If he can do weed, how come I can't do coke?"

⊱⊰

There was a lot that Claw didn't get. In fact, we worried early on that his recklessness might compromise the investigation. Stumbling home from an Italian restaurant in our neighborhood one night, he spontaneously whipped out his extendable baton and nearly whacked the shins of a civilian.

"What the hell's the matter with you?" Gringo snarled at Claw, pulling him aside like an insolent child.

"I'm an *Outlaw*." He slurred his words.

It was time for an intervention.

"You're not getting this role thing, are you?" Gringo snapped.

"Sure I am," Claw said. He dropped into our clubhouse couch. Bloodshot eyes blinked at us. His cuts swallowed him.

"No, you're not. You're *not* really an Outlaw. You're a *fake* real prospect."

"Sure." Claw picked his nose with his pinkie and I worried that he had done a line of coke.

"And *I'm* not an ATF agent," I said.

Claw's eyes widened. "No shit?"

"*We* are."

He blanched, leaned forward on the couch. Fear etched into his face.

"You fuck up and we're going to know about it," Gringo warned.

Claw sobered. "I haven't fucked up."

⬧⬧

Our Petersburg chapter fell into the Copper Region of Outlaws, but few members actually lived in our area. We had to travel over 250 miles to North Carolina in order to participate in Outlaw functions. The distance proved challenging as we rode in torrential rain, sleet, hail, and sometimes snow. Rain knocked our helmets like rocks. Most times I sped through slick streets behind the smear of red taillights into mist and fog and cold. By now I had become an expert at riding, but I never got used to the speed or the ape hanger handlebars.

"We should split up," I once suggested to Gringo. With Outlaws spread thin in so many states, it made sense to stretch our resources, widen our net. But the brass balked at the idea—too expensive, too dangerous, and logistically too difficult to provide government protection for us in multiple states.

"But *I* don't need a cover team," I offered. And though the agents supported my proposal, the bosses were emphatic. We compromised and participated only in mandatory national runs. War, after all, necessitated travel. It also required reconnaissance missions. And just as we gathered intelligence on Outlaws, they checked us out as well.

⬧⬧

One night, Norm, a ranking Outlaw from a North Carolina chapter, joined the agents and me at the Southern Star for drinks. The agents guarded Norm's bike in the parking lot and chatted up members from the Devil's Grip while I entertained him inside. Conversation mostly focused on hunt-

ing Hells Angels but sometimes bounced, like a bad radio frequency, between discussion of chopper parts and Norm's latest cocaine trip. Just as the
evening waned and I debated my escape, a large civilian blew into the bar,
matted hair like seaweed, bold tattoos bordering his arms. His face, red and
sweaty, looked crazed. Two women huddled nearby at a table; one, distracted by the human storm, flicked a panel of blond hair over her shoulder
and jutted her chin into the man's waiting fist. He moved like a machine,
snapping his hand back, punching the woman in the head, blackening her
eye, cracking the bridge of her nose. Blood smeared his knuckles. The woman's wails resounded in the bar like a wounded animal's yelps.

Norm barely flinched as the scene unfolded like sport, a flash of aggression between mismatched athletes. He swiveled on his stool to watch, gulped
his beer, and absorbed the fight as mindless entertainment. The woman's
girlfriend sprang from her stool like a windup toy and pummeled small
fists into the man's back. He shrugged her off like clothing, then wrapped
his hands around her throat. Instinct propelled me forward as I yanked the
beast off her and leveled a blow so hard the man stumbled backward into a
table and flattened the legs. Wood splintered. The man, now down on his
knees, shook his head as if he had dislodged reason and picked through
debris on the floor to find it again. My fist struck his temple.

The agents, distracted by the commotion, rushed inside but didn't interfere. Instead, they watched in stunned horror as I grabbed the civilian
by his coat and tossed him through the front door.

"Fucking bitch is my wife. She's *mine*," he snarled. I kicked him hard in
the ass, watched him grovel on all fours on the curb.

Norm didn't move. He studied me carefully, sipped his beer. Silence
settled over the bar like fine dust. Fans clicked overhead. I wondered if I
had not intervened, would Norm have simply allowed her to die, allowed
the man to squeeze her throat until she passed out, bluish and pale, on the
restaurant floor? The thought chilled me. And so did another: Had *my* actions perplexed Norm? I reacted with conscience, like any human being
unwilling to watch an innocent die. But compassion did not compute in

the Outlaws' world. The woman was property; another man's. I hoped I hadn't blown it.

Wood chips blew around me. No one moved. No one said a word. Like a tired cowboy in an old western, the Outlaw shifted, unfazed, quietly sipping his beer. The agents, winded, slowly backed outside. I waited for the fade-out, for the scene to change. My one impulsive act—being a decent human being—may have cost me my cover. But soon the tableau changed as patrons righted the splintered table and the bar sprang to life again. I hoped Norm had disappeared into an alcoholic stupor and the images he saw distorted and rippled across his memory like a mirage.

"He almost bumped us." Sweat trickled down my cheek. No Outlaw would ever rescue a woman, but an Outlaw would appreciate a prospect protecting a ranking member. Norm bought it, and after that incident, every chance he got he bragged about the "prospect who sacrificed" for him.

≫⋙

Later, I collapsed into the puffy pink chair in our clubhouse. Norm's presence lingered over me like a foul odor. Exhaustion enveloped me. The moment provided pause, space between the ugly and the light. I so rarely sat, so rarely said nothing. I needed to decompress, to process the night. I needed to go home. We all did. I said my good-byes, altered my route, zigzagging down broken streets with graffiti-sprayed stop signs. Restaurant signs with missing neon letters flashed through my car windows. Gold headlights blinded me. Panic sometimes rushed at me like a dark wave, drowning me in its force. I took a moment. At traffic lights, I idled until cars beeped, until I thought I could breathe again.

I arrived home to a dark house and the smell of grilled hamburger. My wife had wrapped a patty for me on a plate and left it on the counter. Hunger stabbed at me. I shut the front door, slid back the dead bolt. But instead of sleep, I settled onto the couch, flipped on the television, and lulled to white noise. In a few hours, I would return to that lonely place, to the underworld, inhabited by undercover operatives, where my life completely transformed. My clothes, the pictures in my wallet, even my favorite CDs in the family car would all be left behind. And as I turned the corner of my sleepy suburban neighborhood, I would become Chef—Outlaw, Renegade, Hunter—mentally tough enough to lie without losing my mind.

23

Dignity

The night we visited Big Mike's clubhouse in Hickory, North Carolina, Brian, a fat, short, newly patched member, proudly displayed his colors. He looked like an accountant. His reward: twenty-four hours of reprieve. No rules. No consequences. No random beatings. Normal was his privilege. And his celebration began in earnest. Beer flowed, music blared. Probates hustled behind the bar, some already with black eyes and others with fresh shine. Brian's success inspired them. As the night wore on, a dull ache pressed against my temple. I thought only of sleep. It was well after midnight. I had been on my feet for more than seven hours.

Brian, drunk and exhilarated, cradled a beer in his hand; gold liquid spilled onto his lap. A wet stain darkened his jeans. His cuts were still clean, still crisp. Addicts draped his arms, kissed his neck, dragged long nails through his cropped hair. Brian smiled, chuckled, enjoying the attention. Finally, he begged off and dozed asleep in a back bunk.

The crowd thinned. Harry; Johnny, the chapter's enforcer; and his sidekick, Rocket, disappeared periodically into a private room to do lines of coke. The agents and I continued to serve the three well into morning; Brian's snores punctuated Johnny's agitation. He sniffed, brushed fine powder from his nostrils, and looked ready to burst. His studded rings glittered in the dim lights. He nudged Rocket and Harry, and their whispers reached a crescendo. The trio disappeared into a back room and returned minutes later, laughing. But the sound reverberated like a threat. Brian had dozed off still wearing his colors. No self-respecting one percenter ever fell asleep with his cuts on. The Outlaws messed with Brian, tugged at his vest, punched him in the head as he slept. I heard the thuds, the grunts, the whispers. I knew what they were doing to Brian and I could do nothing.

Finally, Johnny emerged from the dark back room, sweaty and flushed, and snapped his fingers at JD and me. "You two, go to sleep." Bobby and Gringo stayed to work the bar. Dread followed me into the hallway as I headed toward the bunkers. An icy chill lingered in the room. Four bunks lined the far wall. No blankets, just bald mattresses. I sprawled fully dressed across the top cot, reversed my cuts, threaded my arms through the sleeves, and shut my eyes. On the upper level I figured I was safe from Johnny's abuse.

JD settled into the bunk below me. A pall of apprehension hung between us. Brian flashed in my mind's eye. He looked every bit the pasty-faced rotund accountant dressed in violent costume. But stripped, he still faced himself. Predators like Johnny pounced before they abandoned prey. I recalled Johnny's rings, the size of my wrist. One strike could easily slice open flesh. Darkness enveloped me and I fell into a restless sleep. I dreamed that Brian's face melted.

"Get the fuck up," a voice boomed.

Shortly before dawn, the beating began. Sound penetrated the thin drywall. JD shifted below me, his legs slid over the side of the cot. Hard thumps shook the room. Neither of us said anything. Brian's screams rattled the silence. I envisioned his blood streaking the wall, his face shredded by Johnny's rings, Johnny's hand a swollen mitt.

"I love my colors," I heard Brian sputter.

"I can't hear you," Johnny boomed.

"I love my colors," Brian shouted.

"You don't give a shit about your colors." I recognized Rocket's disdain.

JD's breathing labored. He dropped to the floor, his hand skimming his gun. The clubhouse, filled with sleeping Outlaws, was an arsenal of automatic weapons. Johnny, Rocket, and Harry, each armed with his own revolver, could simply pull the trigger and sound the alarm. We would be dead in an instant as we rushed to protect Brian. Gringo and Bobby would have no time to react. The cover team would never know what happened. Our room grew suddenly darker, smaller. Sounds amplified: moans, softer thuds, like listening to wolves devour a rabbit. A wave of nausea roared in my throat. Separated only by plywood, our room shook with each punch. Rocket panted from exertion. Harry egged on the beating. JD and I inched toward the door, our shadowed faces taut with tension. Mentally we reviewed our options—listen and do nothing; react and risk a firestorm; react and blow our cover; react, investigation over. We opened our door.

But before we could react, Johnny yelled, "Get the fuck out of here," and Brian bolted, his face shredded like fruit pulp.

➤≪

"He had a reprieve," I said. That night I dreamed of exits. Flashing red signs with missing letters. Each door I opened led into wind, white space, mirrors. Panic shot through me. I couldn't believe they'd lied. They had a code, rules of engagement. Betrayal did not compute.

Brian's beating shook me up, rattled all of us. The forty-eight-year-old full-patch had nearly lost his life over club colors. He had followed the rules and trusted there would be no deviation from club policy. Johnny was the rogue, dangerous and unpredictable. Brian didn't let it go. He insisted he deserved to be an Outlaw. He called the Copper Region boss, Les, to report his assailants. Furious that two members had violated his orders, Les stripped both of their patches and demoted them. Johnny and Rocket, now reduced to mere Outlaw probates, served at *Brian's* whim. Harry "retired" for six months. When he finally returned, he probated for sixty days. As further punishment, Les ordered each of them to pay a $100 fine for their "insubordination" and endure a black eye.

That Brian returned to the Outlaws at all stunned me. He had a chance to reconsider, to resume life on the outside, but he traded the title Accountant for Outlaw, seduced by the promise of power.

Later, at Brian's federal trial, the prosecutor would ask him why he didn't leave when he had the chance.

"I was scared. What was I going to do on the outside? Who was I going to be?"

➤➤

Maybe that was the problem—a person like Brian needed to be reprogrammed, retrained to live outside much the way I had learned to live inside. But more than my costume, my survival depended on camouflage and mimicry. In order to blend with the animals, I had to perform like one, absorb their vicious racial slurs, condone their denigration of women, pretend to be just like them.

It wasn't a role I could afford to screw up.

What really aroused the Outlaws was denigrating whole categories of people. And as much as I hated the idea, I developed a way in, a midget routine that appealed to their base sensibilities. The Outlaws already regarded little people as "pets." One recited the story of Puppet, who hobbled with a cane, drank his own urine as part of a stage act, and once, during a wrestling match, stapled his opponent's head "for fun."

"We should put them on an island," the Outlaw quipped, "and issue everyone hunting licenses." He roared with laughter, swiveled on his barstool, and sloshed his beer onto his pants.

Through my disdain I forced the comedy, broke terrible, tense moments with my twenty-minute "midget routine," always acutely aware we might *all* die laughing. My jokes did backfire, and to my horror, the Outlaws morphed my already tasteless rant into something even more perverse, sex with Bridgett the Midget, an infamous porn star who stood only three feet tall.

"We should get her for you." M & M, the chapter's enforcer, winked at me and I filled with dread.

I could handle drugs, sleep deprivation, even physical brutality, but I couldn't handle Bridgett.

"They bought her for an evening," one confided to me later. "We made a prospect hump her in the parking lot, over and over, like a fucking chain."

❀

I stressed about Bridgett, worried the Outlaws might surprise me and prop her in a doorframe, behind the bar, in a shadowy back bedroom. The specter of her little body terrified me. I knew they would do it. They would think it funny to watch a giant maneuver a tiny woman. They might turn the whole thing into sport, make others watch. The idea repulsed me.

"I can't do it," I warned the others.

"Tell her you're married." JD laughed. "Lie. Say you did it, then pay her off." But I wasn't amused; dignity mattered, even for Bridgett.

She so distracted me that my guard slipped. As Bobby wiped beer steins and restocked the ice behind me, Les's question flew at me like a random dart.

"How did you two meet again?" He wiped foam from his lips with the back of his hand. Bobby and I had reviewed our history a thousand times before, but now I stumbled over the lines.

"He was my boss at a tree-trimming business." The words dried in the back of my mouth.

"No shit, that's what *I* do," a young prospect piped up. Thin and pale, with a sprinkling of pimples across his cheeks, his revelation jarred me. What were the odds that someone actually worked as a tree trimmer? Sweat slicked my hands. Maybe he would disappear.

"What's your biggest bar?" He pressed. *What the fuck was a bar?* Gringo appeared like punctuation and shoved chunks of ice into the refrigerator. He heard the banter and sensed my growing tension as I fudged an answer, "My biggest bar . . ." I stared at the ceiling as if the chipped paint held the answer.

"Forty-eight inches, right?" Gringo interjected as he dropped a bag of ice on the floor. I swallowed, grateful for his rescue.

"Yeah, that's it." My heart slammed into my chest. The prospect frowned, shrugged, apparently satisfied with my answer.

Later, I called a tree service company and learned that "bar" was actually slang for "chain saw."

That night I crawled into the van, but sleep eluded me. Bridgett floated into my conscience.

24

A Patchwork Black

It is as inhuman to be totally good as it is to be totally evil.
—ANTHONY BURGESS, *A CLOCKWORK ORANGE*

The Fourth of July marked the club's largest mandatory annual run, attracting Outlaws from all over the world. Milwaukee Jack, the Outlaws' national boss, summoned leaders from other regions, and prepartying began days before. Gringo and I wound our way to North Carolina on July 1, speeding in formation, splitting the double-line highway divider and traveling so close to traffic we could have spit into car windows. Hot sun dehydrated us. We stashed provisions this time: sunscreen and bottled water. Claw and the other agents stayed behind to entertain Outlaws traveling from distant regions who needed temporary quarters.

Upon arrival, Gringo and I assumed our usual posts: guard duty and bartending. As the only two prospects serving fifty or so Outlaws, we were run ragged. Twenty-hour shifts morphed into thirty without rest. Sleep, when we were lucky enough to grab it, occurred in the van, in blazing heat and sticky humidity. Anxiety ripped through me as I hustled drinks and ice. I didn't want a black eye. After a while, I couldn't feel my legs; they tingled with fatigue. By day two I worked on automatic pilot, jerking toward commands and sounds, moving, always moving, until suddenly my momentum shattered.

"I need to talk to you." An Outlaw ushered Gringo aside. Tall as he was wide, sweat stained his armpits and slicked his forehead. His tangled braid swung like a whip behind his back. A smile died in the center of his eyes. A chill came over me as Gringo disappeared with him. He and I had always discussed escape plans, what to do if suddenly cornered. We rehearsed it like a fire drill. But my mind blanked. I forgot the distress signals, couldn't remember the requisite time to wait. I poured beer, wiped the counter, dropped blocks of ice on the floor, and felt the dizzy pull of panic.

Crazy thoughts filled my head: *Someone had recognized Gringo. He had successfully infiltrated the Warlocks in Northern Virginia. Snuff's chapter was in Northern Virginia. Maybe a Pagan had spotted him, ratted him out. We were being set up, ambushed. That's why Les and M & M had ordered us to arrive early.* For the first time in the investigation, I felt real fear.

Surrounded by assault rifles, machine guns, machetes, and wasted Outlaws, I had no defense, no way to alert the cover team. I made excuses, said I had to use the restroom, and spent precious minutes straining through the dark clubhouse in search of Gringo. *Where the fuck had he gone?* Our escape plan seemed ridiculous now. We had talked about bolting for the train tracks that bordered the forest outside the clubhouse; when we were clear, one of us would call the cover team.

I didn't know when to leave. We hadn't discussed time. I returned to the bar, hoping my face masked my panic. My hands shook as I poured more alcohol. Two hours ticked by. I heard no sounds of torture, no gurgling, no screams. I saw no Outlaws emerge with bloodstains. Another hour passed. The train tracks loomed in my thoughts.

We were all in this together. We all had to emerge triumphant as a *team.* This operation was no solo act. *Where the fuck had Gringo gone?* As Outlaws blurred around me, anger coursed through me. Even in war there were rules of engagement and there were crimes. We had a pact, an unspoken bond, the agents and me. We defended each other, we sacrificed. But not like this. I had imagined a shoot-out, a chance, not this quiet coward-ice, picking us off one by one. By the third hour, I really panicked, worried that if I acted too soon I might jeopardize the investigation, and if I didn't act at all Gringo might pay with his life.

"I need to pee," I mumbled and bunched the wet rag in my hand. I slipped into the hallway, listened to voices for high-pitched inflections or anything that signaled distress. The clubhouse, surrounded by fields and for-est, also bordered a nearby abandoned warehouse. I hadn't thought to check there. Fans blew in most of the rooms, but the hallways lengthened like hot tunnels. I decided if I didn't find Gringo this time, I would approach Les and make up a story: Gringo's old lady had a car accident and the hospital called. Just as I rehearsed the lines in my head, I caught a glimpse of Gringo through an open window in the warehouse. He was working the bar. My body relaxed. He looked tired and sweaty but very much alive.

In my nightmare, I heard bullets, deliberate shots to the back of Grin-go's head. His words floated above me: *They asked me to work the bar, man.* A train rushed by, its low whistle like a warning. I startled awake, drenched in sweat. Gringo stirred beside me. We had slept maybe two hours. Sud-denly I couldn't breathe. Pressure pushed against my chest. With the Vagos, I worried about my own safety. Now, as a team member, I felt re-sponsible for the cast. We all did. Today was too close.

"Do you think Snuff knows?" Gringo curled on his side. The glare of parking lot lights flooded our van.

"If he does, he would have already shot you." My back faced him.

"He asks a lot of questions."

"He messes with everyone." I sat up. Tired as I felt, sleep eluded me.

"What if he *knows?*"

We debated Snuff for another hour, and finally I said, "What can we do about it?" *Shut down the investigation?* All of this was dangerous, life-threatening gamesmanship. Paranoia was part of the play. All Outlaws sniffed out rats. At least once a week, wherever we went someone challenged our credentials.

⧓

Relief arrived the next day as Bobby, JD, and Claw joined us. Hundreds of Outlaws streamed through the clubhouse ready to party. I worried about Claw. With his weak arm he wouldn't last two minutes behind the bar. I envisioned him with bruised eyes and an injured shoulder. Gringo assigned him to food service.

"With the women?" His jaw dropped but relief skittered across his face. He knew better than to protest.

"With Coach," I qualified. "You'll be safe with him." The Outlaw was a chef and one of the few "happy" bikers.

Claw nodded and ducked out to mold sandwiches in the cafeteria.

⧓

I dragged to my post outside feeling dehydrated and sick. Gringo, too, looked ill. We had worked nearly forty-eight hours without reprieve, and the two hours we stretched in the van hardly qualified as rest. I wasn't sure I was going to make it. The others had rented a hotel for the weekend. I was ready to trade with them. Pain shot through my legs as I forced them to stand. Just when I thought I would collapse, Milwaukee Jack changed up our routine. With his hands on his hips, his gray beard fluttering in the breeze, he barked at several of us prospects to spray-paint a large white circle in the grassy field behind the clubhouse. The fumes made me nauseous. This couldn't be good. Crouched on all fours, sun on my neck, my cuts soaked with sweat, I knew painting would be the easy part. Les bobbed next to Milwaukee Jack, a sardonic smile on his face. When we finished, he announced we would be the entertainment. We had to submit to "gladiator matches."

Jack ordered all of us prospects and probates to put our names in a plastic container. He asked for volunteers. No one raised his hand. Jack reached into the bucket and paired us off with probates. Mine, ten years my junior, matched my size, but his veins bulged beneath his T-shirt. Humidity drenched us before we even began, and I dreaded the thought of his sweaty body tangled up in mine. There were no rules, not really. The objective was to win, toss the other person out of the white painted circle. Still, Les's voice droned on: two men per fight, one fight at a time, and fights last as long as they have to.

A hush fell over the large crowd. On Les's signal we dropped to the grass, each of us scrambling to pin the other first. Our legs and arms roped together. Adrenaline shot through me. The stench of sweat and body odor gagged me. I hadn't showered for days. I pushed the probate's shoulder blades into the ground. He winced in pain. But I didn't let up. Instinct took over. And suddenly it wasn't about winning or losing, it was about feeling. The crowd faded into the backdrop. It was just me and the probate, and as I threw him out of the circle and heard the crowd erupt, sharp pain shot through my left foot. It throbbed and swelled, suddenly heavy as a brick. I hobbled to the side, wriggled out of my boot. My foot had turned a sickly gray like spoiled meat.

><

By the next morning, my foot had lost all feeling. I improvised, popped Tylenol, soaked the foot in a hotel tub, and dragged it along for errands.

"Now you know what *I* deal with." Claw flapped his deformed arm at me.

><

Meanwhile, Gringo continued to worry. He thought he recognized faces among the guests; a woman who served him a ham sandwich looked familiar. He knew her from his Warlocks investigation. He was concerned she had seen his photo displayed on the Warlocks' Web site. But her dull gaze held no hint of recognition. Still, doubt lingered. At any moment the parts might click. She could snap her fingers, cry foul, and sick an army of angry Outlaws on him. And as cameras flashed, Gringo instinctively ducked behind another server, a move that aroused suspicion.

"What the fuck is *wrong* with you?" Snuff barked instantly at him.

"Nothing, I'm . . . I just don't like being photographed."

Snuff's face contorted. He pulled his invisible sword from his sheath and prepared to lunge. "Why? Are you a fucking cop?"

Gringo pretended to be insulted. He bristled. His face reddened. "What the fuck?"

Tension rippled between them. I forgot to breathe. Then the lines in Snuff's face smoothed. He relaxed, laughed. "Shit," he said. "Of course you're not a fucking cop. *That* would be suicide."

Snuff continued to test Gringo. He solicited him for drug buys, smacking him hard on the shins with his cane as if he were a goat, ordering him to purchase cocaine from his associates. Hand-to-hand buys could often be the riskiest. I envisioned Gringo exchanging cash with shadows, brokering deals in hushed tones, outnumbered in hollow corners, unsure of quality, quantity, or even safety. When I could, I initiated the buys with the agents, inserted myself as a foil just in case we got ripped or played. Under duress, when Gringo bought drugs for Snuff, there were no human barriers. Hours later, Gringo returned with the cocaine. He looked sweaty and pale. I never asked for details. Snuff nodded appreciatively, took the stash from Gringo, and consumed most of the coke on his own. Then he hobbled into the crowd and offered "hors d'oeuvres" to the guests, small samples of cocaine. Meanwhile, another Outlaw approached Gringo with party favors, shoveled him handfuls of oxycodone pills and several "muscle relaxers" for "the stress."

Later, Gringo would tell jurors he "lived in sort of a nightmare."

Despite my grossly oversized foot, I still hustled drinks for the Outlaws for damn near five hours before the national boss, Milwaukee Jack, swaggered into the humid space looking like a lumberjack and announced an impromptu meeting with patch-holders only. The air sizzled with tension as the crowd thinned. The remaining members exceeded three hundred. My foot throbbed. Jack ushered the agents and me in front of a small platform stage in the center of the clubhouse; I felt like a prized pig. Stress coursed through me. We were hopelessly outnumbered. *If this was some kind of target practice . . .* Fierce faces stared at us, drunk, high on cocaine, their throats scarred with tattoos. Some wore SS lightning bolts on their cuts, boldly telegraphing recent kills.

As my heart raced and my breathing labored, I thought about death and whether it would hurt. It wasn't true what people said about life being reduced to short fast clips. My past didn't replay for me, only my future. My wife. My son. My absence in their lives. Cold dawning hit me. I had risked everything. I glanced at Bobby, Gringo, JD—they, too, had sacrificed. If it ended now in a volley of bullets, no one would know they died heroes.

Jack broke the tension. "You fucked up," he boomed. "We're going to take your colors." The room inhaled. My heart thumped. When had we fucked up? Maybe Gringo had been right after all? Maybe Snuff did know about us. Then, as if an invisible flag waved, Outlaws suddenly stormed us. Random fists clawed at my vest. Sour breath brushed against my neck. I struggled, blocked Outlaws with my body, and grabbed my cuts. *Fight. Fight. Fight for the colors.* Instinct took over as members punched, pummeled my chest, stomped my bruised foot. Cheers, claps, congratulations resounded around me. Drenched in sweat, sore, and completely stressed out, we watched North Carolina's boss, Les, grinn and hand us our coveted diamond one-percenter patches. It took me a moment to focus, to adjust to the news that we had made it, we were Outlaws.

Jack raised his right hand. "Repeat after me. I, state your name . . ."

I struggled to stand. Sharp pain stabbed my stomach. "I, state your name." My two hours of sleep had taken their toll. Laughter erupted around me. The agents coughed and panted next to me, their faces flushed and sweaty. Then one by one, each member congratulated us by punching us hard in the center of our one-percenter patch. By the fiftieth hit, I felt nothing but numb. Then one Outlaw surprised me. He bolted from behind and thrust his fist into my solar plexus. The force knocked the wind from my lungs. My eyes watered. When the beatings tapered, celebration began. Congratulatory howls reached a crescendo. I was hugged, backslapped, and baptized in beer. I hobbled around the stage, giddy with pride. *Damn, I had patched into one of the most brutal biker gangs in the world.* We were the fireworks.

⋙⋘

As full-patches, we had access now to the internal workings of the club. Not only could we openly purchase guns and dope and record every detail for future prosecutions, but we also could listen, without scrutiny, to death plots. The confessions broke like dams as almost immediately we were briefed on the Outlaws' mission: hunting Hells Angels. They looked like us, smelled like us, were armed and drugged and dirty like us. But they were the "enemy combatant" and they had to be eradicated.

Les put his arm around my shoulder, completely drunk. It was three o'clock in the morning. Bodies fell around us, deep asleep. My foot now resembled a rubber appendage, something unreal and beastlike, a limb from a movie set. The pain kept me sharp. Les's breath in my face, sweetly rotten, warned if we saw a Hells Angel we *had* to attack; if we hesitated, he would "pull our one-percenter patch" and "everyone would know we were a coward." Like a scarlet letter, we would be branded, targets for ridicule. Les's face turned pepper red, as if the thought of murder aroused him. It was late. We gathered around our clubhouse bar. I poured Les another, hoping he would continue his rant for the cameras. Murder had suddenly become a focal point, and it was no longer a matter of *if* it would happen, but *when* and with what device.

⋙⋘

The next morning, we prepared to return to Petersburg. Still incapacitated from my gladiator match, I couldn't ride my bike back. Instead I traveled in the van with Claw. Milwaukee Jack surprised us and said he would be "honored" to ride home with us. And as he mounted his bike, my heart sank. I didn't want to ride five hours with Claw. I wanted to be in on the action. They sped in tandem, riding the 220 miles along the freeway, outlaw and agent side by side. Back at our clubhouse, we invited Jack inside our fully wired lair. We sent Claw away, concerned that his mouth would get us in trouble. As the sun set, we clicked on lamps. In the dim haze, Jack offered us "tips" to "get" the Hells Angels, especially the stray who roamed our neighborhood.

"We are at war," he reminded us and slammed back more beer.

He grew increasingly agitated as we shared with him our problems with the Merciless Souls. Jack had an easy solution: "Just put a cap in them." He formed his fingers into a gun and pulled the trigger. I hoped the cameras got a close-up.

As he stood to leave, he handed each of us a patch. "Sew it on your cuts when you get a chance," he said. I stared at mine, at the bold embroidered SNITCHES ARE A DYING BREED.

25

Black Dawn

A month later we returned to North Carolina and the Hickory clubhouse to attend the Copper Region Open Air Meeting, where we again prepared to discuss war plans against the Hells Angels and hear about the gang's home invasions on neighbors who strayed too close to the Outlaws' clubhouse. A light drizzle fell. Thunder rumbled across the gray morning, full of foreboding. I whispered good-bye to my sleeping wife and son and strapped on my full-face helmet. I had purchased it only a month before, wary of the novelty caps the others wore. Nothing particularly compelled me to do it; I guess safety was my line in the sand.

I played reckless, but I didn't want to be reckless. I had a family that needed me alive.

As I gripped my ape hanger handlebars, cold shivered through me. It was early autumn and the leaves changed from green to bloodred to gold. The scenery was my only clue that days ended and new ones began. My breath swirled around me in white vapor. There was nothing extraordinary about the morning. It was just a feeling I had of moving in fast-forward. I had heard that people who experienced trauma—a plane crash, a fire, a death—had strange stirrings moments before the crisis, heightened awareness, warnings. Most wished they had listened. Sounds and smells were more pronounced, colors more vivid. Some called it intuition, energy, inexplicable shifts in tempo. For me it was something deeper, something spiritual.

I should have listened.

The streets, slick with rain and diesel fuel, pulled my tires toward dramatic dips and curves and threatened to spill me over. Bobby kept pace with me. JD and Gringo sped in front in their baggers, so far ahead they formed a red smear against the approaching Blue Ridge Mountains. Claw rode behind in his car, and our cover team picked up the rear. Rain pelted my head. We fit an image, an illusion of freedom with rules. And though I was now a veteran rider, the appeal of biting wind in my face, fog in my headlights, and dark silhouettes in the distance was lost. So, focused on not crashing and keeping my front wheel steady, I had fleeting thoughts of turning around, of stopping. But adrenaline coursed through me. Gringo weaved dangerously ahead as he detoured to a famous falls at the summit.

Soaked and stressed, I protested. At the base of the mountain, a voice in my head warned me: *Turn around.* "This isn't a good idea," I yelled into the wind as rain washed gravel and dirt onto the road. Bobby blurred into the scenery a few paces ahead. Gringo and JD had disappeared around the bend. My bike wobbled. I was going too fast. I cared less about waterfalls and overlooks. I wanted to arrive at our destination intact. Cliffs rushed at me, steep and wet and green. Rain splashed into my eyes. The road curved sharply, vibrated beneath me. My arms ached with tension, and I drifted, my tires sliding into the grass shoulder. The impact was like hitting ice.

Then suddenly I was no longer riding; I separated from my bike, watched it slam into the guardrail at fifty miles an hour. I sailed through the air, weightless, over jagged rocks and edges, over my bike, the handlebars, the chrome. Then, as if the film fast-forwarded, I descended with a thudding impact. I felt no pain, just tightness in my chest as if I were underwater trying to breathe. Then a strange knocking in my head, a flutter of light like a shade being pulled up, then snapped down. The impact had knocked the wind from my lungs.

"Chef?" I heard Bobby's voice, distorted, hollow like a voice in a dream. "Chef?"

My eyes startled open. Bobby loomed above me, his face stricken, ashen.

"Tell Gringo to slow the fuck down!" I managed, but it didn't sound like me.

I couldn't breathe. I felt light-headed. I needed my inhaler. I reached into my front pants pocket.

"Don't move." Bobby put a hand on my shoulder and reached for his medic kit. Fear skittered across his eyes. His usually calm face covered with gray beard tensed. Subtle changes in his coloring, a reddish flush on his cheeks, telegraphed what he saw.

Can't breathe. He must have heard me because he retrieved my inhaler. *Remove my helmet.*

"Bad idea," Bobby protested.

My fucking helmet. I was screaming inside; it felt like my head was going to explode. Bobby relented. He removed my helmet, held the inhaler to my mouth, and a rush of air flooded into my lungs. I wanted to vomit. Sharp pain stabbed my knee. Bobby worked methodically and, with a pair of shears, cut away my pants. He inspected my bluish-stained skin. Gringo huddled nearby, tension stiffening his shoulders. He cradled his helmet. Wind flattened his beard and pulled at his cheeks. Worry flickered across his face. I wanted to shout, "I'm fine. I'm okay. I'm intact." Sirens wailed. An ambulance launched off the road and rumbled toward me. Dull ache hit my shoulder. State troopers arrived and their patrol cars navigated the steep terrain.

"You all right?" JD's voice came at me in slow motion.

My shoulder throbbed and I had a slight ache in my neck. Medics wrapped me in a collar. Disdain covered their faces. They looked at me and saw a criminal, a biker, an Outlaw. Fleetingly, I worried they might cut through my vest to treat me. Even disoriented, I thought about character and reaction. I was an Outlaw outside, an injured informant inside. I thought about my bike.

The ambulance doors closed. Almost instantly, pain shot through my shoulder and neck. At the hospital, staff injected me with medication through IV drips. The room spun. Smells of bleach assaulted my nostrils. Cold blew across my bare toes. I gripped my vest tightly to my chest. *Fight for your colors*—the mantra was ingrained in my head even in my medicated state. Only when Gringo appeared did I dare release my cuts. He folded them reverently and tucked them beneath his arm. They were safe. It didn't matter that I was broken, that I was in a hospital, that pain numbed me. There were no reprieves. Brian's ordeal still smarted in my thoughts.

I shivered in my thin paper robe. Bruises on my legs darkened and spread. A fresh-faced nurse drew back my curtains and wheeled me down a long hallway toward a drafty room. I needed an X-ray. I might have a broken neck, she said. At first I didn't register her words. She spoke a foreign language. *A broken neck? Not possible. I felt fine. I could still wiggle my fingers.* Then fear mixed with panic as visions of my mom resurfaced. She had suffered a broken neck after a fall down a flight of stairs. Screws bolted her together. Fine hair sprouted like tufts of dead grass between bare patches of skull. I worried she might rust and separate.

In the X-ray room, cold shuddered through me.

Pressure pushed against my bladder. I needed to pee.

"You can't," the technician cautioned. He was young, early twenties, hunched over a chart. He didn't look at me. I was Patient, not Outlaw, not Person.

"I *have* to pee," I insisted, but none of my muscles worked. I was too doped up. And as the minutes ticked by, I started to hyperventilate. Frustration formed a dull headache. Propped in the wheelchair, my neck in a collar, I panicked. *What if I never peed again? What if I never walked again? How was I supposed to live?* I hadn't called my wife. I didn't want to tell her yet that I was broken.

The technician, maybe sensing my distress, handed me a paper cup.

I wobbled to my feet, afraid I might fall over. I swayed, held the cup in front of me, parted my robe, and tried to pee. Minutes passed and still no progress. The technician stared dully at me, waiting patiently for me to finish. Nothing came. My muscles, too relaxed, could not release urine. I became acutely aware of sounds, the hum of the air conditioner, the click of the technician's pen. I watched shadows, my giant shape on the wall, suddenly reduced to human bodily functions. This is what I had become. *Pee, damn it.* The thought that I might pee from a plastic bag terrified me more than any Outlaw raid. After seven long minutes, warm liquid flowed into the cup.

⋙⋘

"Good news," the doctor said, pulling up a stool an hour later. "Your neck is fractured, but there's no damage to the spinal cord."

A fractured neck? How was I supposed to work with no neck?

But my right shoulder had suffered a rotator cuff tear that required immediate surgery. Instead, the doctor prescribed strong pain medication and the hospital released me after four hours. I guessed it was because Chef had no medical insurance. My other identity did, but there was no practical way to clear up the confusion.

⋙⋘

"If we hurry, we can still make the regional meeting." Gringo eased me into Claw's car. My mind, so fogged from drugs, barely processed his words. Blinding pain incapacitated my right arm; my neck was immovable and in a brace. I wanted to quit. But I couldn't. I was a private contractor and I needed the work. I needed the ATF to pay my medical bills. I had a stable fracture. I could do this.

The thought of lying on the floor or in the van repelled me. "I need a hotel," I mumbled. *Plenty of ice and a decent bed. Hotels at least had ice machines.* At the regional meeting, members blurred into the walls. Their voices buzzed in my ears like white noise. Bosses discussed war. It was no longer enough to assault and maim Hells Angels; we needed to kill them, earn our SS bolts if we committed "extreme acts" of violence against them. *Okay. Got it.* Mentally, I had checked out, drifted to a calm place full of bright color and soft sounds.

After two hours in blinding pain, a prospect finally drove me to my hotel. I "slept" awake, my arm packed in ice, propped up, throbbing. When I closed my eyes I saw shadow figures moving against the wall, each lighter than the other, the last practically floating toward the ceiling. They were me, and I was slowly fading out. In some nightmares I couldn't move at all, my body stretched across the bed like a morgue slab. I couldn't lift my head, couldn't feel my limbs, completely dead inside. Then Gringo appeared in the doorway, his eyes overbright, a large grin on his face as he steered in my custom-built bike perfectly designed for paraplegics.

⌇

Claw confided one night over drinks that he "couldn't take it anymore." He looked particularly agitated, his face sweaty and flushed. His shoulders shook. My accident had really "fucked him up" and he "just didn't know anymore" whether he was cut out for this assignment.

"You're quitting?" I took a pull on my beer. I felt sorry for Claw. I doubted whether he was cut out for any assignment.

Claw shook his head. Fat tears snaked down his cheek. He brushed them away with the back of his hand. In the dim lights he looked even thinner, as if he had been squeezed through a taffy machine.

"I don't know, man. I don't know."

"You *can't* quit." I was incredulous.

"I can't do this no more." He ordered another beer, told the bartender to put it on his tab.

"You're an Outlaw."

He looked at me, his eyes watery and bloodshot, his breath stinking of alcohol, and said, "You don't understand, man. I might *die* doing this."

After that conversation he disappeared, and it took the agents nearly two months to find him. But it didn't matter much. Once we were full-patches we no longer needed the requisite five members. We could manage with four.

✖

One month after the accident, I squeezed in a shoulder surgery. After a six-hour operation, doctors implanted screws into my bone and prescribed pain medication every four hours. Three times a week, in between being an Outlaw, an occupational therapist stretched out my arm, but the pain only increased. I wasn't getting better. I wasn't healing.

26

Masks

Halloween lasted three days. The Outlaws rented an old-style western town near Unadilla, Georgia, that resembled a Hollywood movie set: Wooden signs identified brothels, hotels, and saloons. But inside, the buildings were shells: hollow, drafty spaces. The Outlaws planned to party, not play war games, and though the town was situated on acres of property, five miles from the nearest civilians, they arrived armed, with pump-action shotguns, revolvers, chains, bullwhips, crowbars. And children. The bikers pitched tents and parked RVs on the property. Sleeping bags lashed to motorcycle handlebars, girls straddled the little seats looking like twigs snapped from highway debris. Support clubs like the Black Pistons clustered in some of the abandoned buildings. Different chapters rented whole sections for the run.

With my arm still wrapped in a sling, I chose a hotel. The closest one had a crooked floor, warped linoleum, and a toilet that never flushed. The Outlaws stocked the fake saloons with alcohol. Empty six-packs piled high in the dusty center of town. Some blew onto porches like tumbleweed. By day, sunlight and beer had lulled the bikers into a stupefied calm, but as night fell, the camp transformed into a kind of animal pen. Outlaws spooked each other, pretended to wander as ghouls into the mining shaft. They posed behind iron bars in the makeshift jail. One Outlaw swaggered through town as the mock sheriff, drew his weapon, randomly aimed, and pretended to fire. Children dressed in fairy costumes and as superheroes paraded through the fake stores looking like flashbacks of the Outlaws' former lives. I wanted to rescue them.

Their parents asked for drugs instead of candy. One member strolled through the crowd pretending he was the town medic. He wore readers and carried a leather satchel stuffed with oxycodone and handed out little "treats." Prostitutes offered "tricks."

Snuff hit me up for pain pills.

"Sorry, man, it's my last one and *I* need it." The lie was close to the truth. My shoulder throbbed. I still iced it regularly.

Snuff's lips bent in disapproving commas. "It's always your last one."

A few hours later he tried again, and again I put him off. "I don't have any on me."

"Why the fuck do you always run out?" Snuff shot me a hard look as he stumbled through the crowd.

Later that night he joined us around a bonfire. Sparks flew from the flame and sizzled by his boot. He stabbed his cane into the dust several times and I had the distinct impression he wanted to smack it across my shins. Snuff didn't need a Halloween costume; he was already a freak in long leathers and a scraggly beard. And after a handful of oxycodone, his eyes glazed white. He snarled and spit, transformed the way a full moon transformed a werewolf.

In the orange glow, Harleys gleamed at the edge of darkness. Faces obscured, bodies became silhouettes. The women who stayed disappeared into the empty building shells, props themselves. Giggles, groans, and grunts punctuated night sounds. An Outlaw named Bull lit a joint. Even seated, he spread massively wide like a beer barrel. He fit into Halloween with his stringy oriental beard and thick jowls. He personified the Out-laws' physique, subsisting on a diet of hamburgers, donuts, beer, and pills. Gringo sat cross-legged in a circle. Fire spit between us, flames towering over our heads. Bull inhaled and bragged about his skills as a marijuana dealer. He was a "professional" with over twenty years of experience. He nudged Gringo and confided that his career aspiration was to establish "a large marijuana distribution network from Montana to Maryland."

"Next time I come, I'll sell you a pound of high-grade shit." Bull passed his joint to Gringo. "In Montana we all carry medical marijuana cards." We had to bust him in another state.

I held my breath. Gringo huddled too close to Bull to reject his offer. Heat from the fire made me light-headed. *This was it. We were done.* Gringo took the joint. There was no way to rescue him. I watched him touch it to his lips and fake inhale. Panic shot through me as I scanned the faces around the fire, looking for subtle changes in expression, an eyelash flicker, a jaw twitch, a forehead wrinkle. But incredibly, no one noticed. And Gringo played it beautifully. He never flinched, never wavered. Cool. Smooth. Only his eyes watered slightly as he passed along the joint.

Bull, meanwhile, prattled on, and I hoped the drugs had anesthetized the crowd long enough for us to exit. Snuff lost interest in the bonfire and wandered off; the pills he had ingested on an empty stomach no doubt left him jittery and depressed. Random shouts split the dark like buckshot. Faces around the bonfire distorted into long howls. Chills coursed through me. Wind picked up. And before the joint made it around to me, I whined about my shoulder and stabbing pain. Bull stared dully in my direction. Gringo took my cue and scrambled to stand. As he did, his wire protruded from his neckline like a stationary horsefly. He had worn it all day so he could transmit sound in real time. The microphone, usually concealed inside his clothing, bobbed conspicuously. *How long had it been sticking out like that? Had anyone noticed?* Shock slid behind Gringo's eyes. Neither of us spoke as we drifted from the circle, turned slowly, and waited for the bullet.

✳

At the hotel, we stressed about the exposed wire, replayed what-if scenarios in our head. Did they see it? Did they not? Finally Gringo laughed it off: a spooky phenomenon, an inexplicable pardon. Next time he would be more careful. *Yeah. Yeah. Yeah.* I didn't sleep. My arm throbbed. I padded down the hallway for ice. The stained mustard carpet with its black spots looked like a thousand eyes watching me. Slowly, I returned to the room and sat on the bed. Sheets bunched at my feet. The ice numbed my arm. Spilled moonlight cast a cool blue glow over us. We were all awake. We said nothing. Soon, we would return to Halloween town. None of us would wear a wire.

✳

No one stirred until dusk the next day, when an Outlaw named Shia appeared like something recycled, used plastic spit into a new mold. His brown eyes bugged behind thick glasses. A mustache of sweat bordered his mouth. His cuts cropped above his protruding balloon belly. Rumors swirled that Shia's wife pushed him into prospecting for the Outlaws, hoping the role would "toughen him up" and transform him into an eligible Outlaw.

He boldly displayed his coke and a loaded revolver strapped to his hip. I baited him, asked him if he had any extra for JD and me. Shia smiled, waddled off to call his drug source, and within the hour motioned us both inside his sedan. He resembled a bloated child with a gun. In the shadowy dark parking lot of Halloween town, I slid into Shia's passenger seat and JD climbed into the back. My knees practically brushed my chest.

Shia held up his stash, his "nose candy," and with a wide stupid grin, plunged a rusty spoon into the fine white powder. My nerves already shot, I was in no mood to deflect him. Shia offered JD a taste. I caught JD's surprise in the rearview mirror. This was a test we couldn't flunk. A light drizzle splashed across the windshield. "Fucking rain," I barked. We had only seconds to improvise. If Shia picked up our foul scent, he would pounce. JD took the spoon. I shifted, joked about the cramped space, his car being too small and my body too wide.

Shia jerked at my tone and his attention drifted long enough for JD to toss the powder.

"That's good shit." JD broke the tension and pretended to pick his nose with his pinkie.

Shia grinned, swiveled to the front, and handed me the spoon. Metal glinted in the half-light and I felt my face flush. I knew addicts, knew their single-minded purpose, knew what blow did to a person's brain. We had been tested before with drugs, but never like this, never this close. Shia's revolver shined near my thigh; headlights from passing cars lit up his face like lightning flashing over a field. JD repeated my dance and distracted Shia long enough for me to dump the coke. Shia took our cash, gave us a quarter ounce, and opened the door. He wobbled off like a desperate rat in search of more trash.

27

Raw

Shia resurfaced throughout the investigation in different forms. A week later, Brian showed up unexpectedly at our clubhouse toting a prostitute and a bag of speed. Bobby and I entertained him. All night Brian baited me, desperate for me to taste his "shit." Meanwhile, his date spread on our couch looking like a doll missing its stuffing. Sickly and used, knotted blond hair, pale arms puffed blue with track marks, she was Brian's prop. Part of him spilled over her legs as he shared the couch with her, the hilt of his gun flashed on his hip.

"What kind do you have there?" Bobby engaged him.

Brian smiled, wiggled free from the woman, and proudly slid his .380 onto the bar in prime view of the cameras. The night stretched into dawn, and finally, when Brian's stash dwindled, he slapped his prostitute awake and headed for the door. "Can you leave me a line?" I called after him, knowing he had only a small portion left. Brian hesitated. I had deflected him all night. He trained his small nervous eyes on me and relented. He plunked his bag on the counter and said, "Take the rest." I nodded, watched him leave, watched him stuff his doll woman into the backseat of his sedan and squeeze his dumpy self behind the steering wheel. In a few hours his life would repeat: The woman in the backseat would stir, chilled and disoriented, and he would pay her again with drugs to be his date. He would tell her he was something, a real Outlaw, a real outcast.

⋊⋉

Next time *I* asked for weed.

But that backfired, too. "How come you never have any on you?" an Outlaw challenged me once. I made up excuses: I couldn't carry weed with me when I rode. What if I got stopped by the cops? The Outlaws continued to test us. They brought coke to our clubhouse, urged us to do lines with them on the floor. Gringo shook his head and said, "Not in the open," motioning to the partyers, some of whom we had invited inside from the local bars. In order to look the part of a legitimate chapter, we threw frequent parties at our clubhouse, always prepared for the unexpected visitor.

"We don't know who they are," Gringo explained. "They might be cops."

And one by one the Outlaws filed into the restroom, Gringo, too. He flushed his stash down the toilet, and when he emerged minutes later he looked like the rest of them, red nosed, wide-eyed, and fidgety. He should have received an Oscar for his brilliant performance.

JD deflected further suspicion by offering me up as entertainment: "Do your midget routine." Foam flew from his beer mug and settled in his goatee. Outlaws gathered around on our pink sofa chairs eager to hear my profane one-liners.

"How come I'm the show?" I laughed uneasily, put down my dirty rag, and assumed my best Vince Vaughn impression.

"I wouldn't mind having midgets for the clubhouse. We could make *them* hustle for drinks."

"They're not human, man," one Outlaw roared. He flashed yellow incisors at me.

"Can you imagine if my old lady was a midget?" I began, and I regretted the line as soon as I said it.

"We've never *seen* your ol' lady." I knew where this was going. Bridgett again.

"She probably flew off the back of your bike," another heckled.

"I'd strap her on with bungee cords." My routine was working. Not only did it distract the Outlaws from further drug pushing, but it endeared me to them, protected my cover. No way could I be a cop or an informant if I was as disgusting as them. Still, I kept a fake photo of an infant boy on my cell phone just in case anyone probed. And I told them my old lady couldn't come around because she watched my kid. They didn't care, not really, they just wanted to unnerve me.

"I should have a mini-me, a mini-Chef."

They roared. "I could prop him in the corner, drag him with me on a leash, or clip him to my chest in a baby sling."

"You could dress him up in minicuts," one Outlaw shrieked with laughter.

"You could make *him* fight for you."

"Midget wrestling." I pretended to endorse the idea. Their laughter echoed in the room, made the hair on the back of my neck bristle.

"Fuck that. We should just toss them from the rooftop and watch them splat on the cement." They cackled, cheered, toasted. I was a big hit. I detached from them, from their hollow faces, from their darkness.

And as they funneled out of the clubhouse, one texted me midget porn. He winked. "Until we can get Bridgett."

❊

As promised, Bull arrived several weeks later from Montana. He showed up at our Petersburg clubhouse in the late afternoon and brokered a marijuana deal with Gringo; he could deliver three pounds of marijuana worth over $13,000. Gringo made him a partial payment, earnest money in the amount of $2,500 in government funds. But Bull never made it back with the drugs. The agents made sure police stopped him in possession of five pounds of marijuana and two assault rifles.

➤≈≤

My dual life took its toll. One morning, early, in bitter cold, I sat in my car with the engine on. Heat blasted my face. Flurries blew around my wife and newborn son framed in the doorway of my house. Still dressed in pajamas and slippers, she waved good-bye to me. A smile stained her face. She had long ago mourned the loss of me. Guilt wedged in my throat. I couldn't stop being undercover, couldn't stop being husband and father, couldn't stop being broken or hunted. My family, my job seduced me. I wanted both, needed both. But at times the pressure to deliver nearly cracked me. There was no "time off" in war, no "safe zone." I compartmentalized my family, kept them contained in a field fenced with barbed wire.

The agents and I returned again to North Carolina and the Charlotte clubhouse. I followed behind them in the undercover car as the agents fishtailed through sleet. Still groggy from pain medication, and with my arm in a sling, we entered the clubhouse prepared to discuss hunting humans. Gringo tucked his wire inside his thick cable sweater. Winter blew around us. JD's trench coat swallowed him. Bobby wore a mask of calm. Only a bluish tint around his lips telegraphed his half-frozen state. His cuts, stiff from cold and wet, glazed with ice. Our boots left puddles on the concrete. Heaviness filled the air.

Les, now the Charlotte chapter vice president, ushered us into a back room. The space resembled a large closet and smelled of wood chips. Unease itched down my spine. This was different, against pattern. Prospects bolted the two doors behind us. The clicks resounded like bullets loading in a chamber. Plywood boarded the windows. Something was up. M & M was propped against a crate looking like a muscle. Had we just walked into an ambush? Shut in, closed off, it would be impossible for the cover team to reach us in time. Panic raced through my head. Had they seen Gringo's wire after all? Did they know he was a federal agent? Did they know I was an informant? Reason took over; they would have shot me by now, dropped me on the concrete and watched my blood drain; the agents they might beat silly, pull their patches, and kick them out, but they might not kill them. *Me, they would kill.*

Ten other Outlaws from our region joined us. They all looked nervous. Eyes dropped to the floor, hands folded across chests, winter in their cheeks.

"You've heard about Ivan?" M & M briefed us. The Tennessee Outlaw had recently kidnapped a sheriff's deputy at gunpoint and threatened to shoot him. Ivan had reliable intelligence that the deputy, who was posing as an Outlaw, was actually undercover. After threatening to torture the deputy, Ivan, in the end, simply confiscated the deputy's colors.

"We're taking precautions." M & M folded his arms and barked, "Everyone strip."

Nerves slicked my body. Gringo blanched. Rifles and shotguns lined the walls. If the Outlaws found Gringo's wire, we were as good as dead. The cover team would be too late. With an injured shoulder, I had no way to return fire. Thinking quickly, I yanked down my pants, wriggled out of my boxers, and flashed my ass in the Outlaws' faces.

"You want a piece of me?" I hoped my spectacle was enough of a distraction. Bent over, head between my legs, I gauged M & M's reaction; he smirked, shifted uncomfortably, flustered, but before he could protest, Bobby took my cue and stripped. Slowly, he unbuttoned his jeans, untangled his legs from stiff, ice-flecked denim. He tossed the jeans to the side and, in his underwear, modeled for the members, sashaying his hips as if he were in some kind of drag queen beauty contest. Les snickered; the prospects chuckled. M & M bristled. I whistled, tried to stall the audience. Gringo was next. Bobby prolonged his production, pretended his arms were twisted in the sleeves of his bulky sweater. He was the headless horseman. We had only seconds. JD unbuttoned his trench coat. *Gringo was next.* The room spun. Overwhelming sadness gripped me.

This would be my last image, a cold, white, boarded-up space. I thought of rabbits, when they died, how their eyes snapped final shots like camera flashes. Gringo visibly paled. This was it. I wanted to thank him, tell him he'd saved me, gave me such a life. I hoped he knew I forgave him for riding so fast. He looked up, stared at me with wet eyes, and winked. Fear shivered through me. I knew all of us felt the tremor. But we were outnumbered. The end would last only seconds.

But then something miraculous happened. M & M had had enough; we "were taking too long." "Leave your coats in your car and come back in so we can do this quickly."

Relief etched into Gringo's face as he bolted outside into the winter chill, exhaled by his bike, and slowly unraveled his wire.

~✕~

Later I reminded Gringo of the party in Brockton and Monster, the chapter's regional boss. He'd feasted on lobster, tore soft white meat between his teeth, sprinkled paprika on a claw, and bragged about bombings he'd orchestrated.

"I threw a grenade once on a Hells Angels' clubhouse roof." Clear juice dribbled down his chin. "It landed in the fucker's yard and blew up his rottweiler." He wiped his sticky fingers on a paper napkin and reached into his pocket. He produced something that resembled a pager, and my heart stopped. "Check this out." I knew instantly what it was.

"It's a bug detector." Monster held the device close to my chest. "The thing vibrates if it detects a wire."

"Nice." I smothered a smile, dipped a lobster claw into butter sauce, and felt light-headed. Thankfully, none of us had worn a wire that day.

Monster chuckled. "Fucking feds." He tucked the bug detector into his vest. "I *like* you." He laughed. "You're quiet, funny." He pressed his thumb to his temple. "You're smart." Then he pulled off his T-shirt with an Irish three-leaf clover and handed it to me. "Take it," he said, his flesh as pale as the underbelly of a fish. "You should have a souvenir." It meant something to him. The Outlaws' skeleton logo appeared on the front. They didn't make those shirts anymore. He thought it a great honor to give me the relic.

"The trick is not to mind it," I told Gringo.

"I mind it." Gringo's face reddened. We all did. The psychological warfare was worse than the physical. Each night at the clubhouse we reviewed the day's play, mentally checking off the conversations we'd had, the inflections and tones, the facial expressions. These were our maps. We studied them, memorized them, and learned to read them like white water. "Young" rivers had steep drops and waterfalls; "old" rivers coursed through flatlands; "middle-aged" rivers had a combination of both and were typically the most deadly.

That night I dreamed of rushing rapids, of light shallow water, of warning Vs in the ripples. *There's something down there*, I shouted into cold winds. But no one heard me. *River left*. I paddled furiously toward shore. *River left. Get out. Get out. Eddy the boat. Obstacle ahead.*

※

After that close call, I worried that I had become a liability to the team. M & M's impromptu strip search rattled me. It had been too close. And I had been helpless to defend against bullet spray. After four months, I begged my doctor to "take a second look" at my arm.

He scheduled another MRI. I waited anxiously in my paper robe for the results.

The doctor looked grim, his pasty cheeks drained of bloom. "I'm sorry," he began. "The first surgery did absolutely nothing." He suggested a "redo," that I simply rewind the last four months. I felt sick. The tendons in my shoulder had snapped like "rubber bands," he explained. If he cut just "two more inches" and reattached them, he might reduce the pain. *Might.* He warned that if this procedure failed, I would never regain mobility of my arm. I would lose everything. I would be an invalid, invalid. If I never punched again, never pulled a trigger, never rode a motorcycle . . . what would I be?

※

Guilt tore at me. I had risked my family, risked everything, for a chance to save them, for a chance to give them "normal." They trusted me. My wife did not deserve to be anonymous. I thought I could do it, penetrate a violent world, eradicate the beasts, and leave unscathed, leave the streets safer. After all, I had accomplished as much with the Vagos.

But being an Outlaw was entirely different. Not only was the gang infinitely more brutal and unpredictable, but I was different, too, and I had underestimated the toll my commitment to the work would have on my wife and son. In the program, she and I lived an artificially contained existence. Security was paramount, so much so that it made our lives sterile. We knew each other's schedules. We ate meals together and enjoyed full conversations. Undercover, that kind of routine wasn't possible. Even when I was home, I wasn't *home*. My thoughts drifted to the gang, to my dual persona. At night, if I slept at all, I had disturbing visions, pressure on my chest, loud bangs in my ear like exploding buckshot. I searched for my missing arm. Harsh wind blew through the gaping socket.

Post-traumatic stress—it floated through my subconscious. I thought I could control the visions. I thought I could drift effortlessly between worlds. But I couldn't. Instead, I escaped into the company of the other agents. We formed our own brotherhood bound by common trauma. And though I was nothing like them, I shared the same tension, the same isolation, the same goal. All of us prepared each day to sacrifice our lives for a greater cause. Over pizza, beer, and sports we unwound in the undercover house. The agents were witness to my life. My wife could not compete with my exhaustion. She understood that her "normal" had a different definition. And stress had degrees. Like the other agents, I lived my life "on duty."

Following my second surgery, I convalesced at home for a month. I had lost the use of my right arm. My days morphed into a monotonous stream of pain, pill popping, and half sleep. In an uncomfortable role reversal, my wife took care of me. We had a son I couldn't hold, diapers I couldn't change. Of all the roles I'd played, I hated this one. But I had no choice. I *had* to heal. I had left the program, and for now I didn't exist outside the Outlaws.

I had no salary, no sick leave. If I didn't get better, I wouldn't know how to live.

28

Gone Hunting

I wasn't better after my month off, but I still had to work. I drove Gringo's undercover car to the Easy Rider Bike Expo in Charlotte, North Carolina, to hunt the Enemy. An Outlaw named Tomcat, a former enforcer turned treasurer for the Maine chapter, rode with me. A transplant from the West Coast, we had much in common. As a former Marine and "hard-core drug dealer," a "coyote" who once smuggled human cargo across the border from Mexico, I actually understood Tomcat. We spoke the same language, knew the same places. He corroborated my backstory. And maybe that instilled his trust in me.

When we arrived at the expo, we parked in a back alley, on the lookout for wayward Hells Angels. M & M had conferred with the Outlaws' national boss, and leaders ordered members from Boston, Maine, and Virginia to "be prepared" for war. All of us were ordered to "shoot Hells Angels on sight."

But I knew that no Hells Angels would appear. The Outlaws ruled

Charlotte; Easy Rider was *their* event. Hells Angels steered clear of ambush. Still, the ATF, eager to capture recorded conversations of Outlaws plotting murder against their rival, concocted a ruse. An agent stationed in Charlotte contacted M & M, the Outlaws' enforcer, on the phone and alerted him to possible trouble: "Our sources say the Hells Angels plan to make an appearance at the Easy Rider show. . . . You can't stop them, it's a public venue. There'd better not be a brawl." *Of course there would be.* But the government hoped for reaction, outrage from the Outlaws, and the club's promise to shoot Hells Angels on sight if provoked. The Outlaws played right into the agents' hands as they set up human blockades and prepared to execute strays.

After six hours of nothing, I relaxed somewhat. Tomcat, maybe bored or restless, revealed that he had "done something really bad," that necessitated his having to change all his truck tires. My heartbeat increased. My hand shook as I reached inside my front pocket for my recorder and pushed the On switch. But the button snapped. Tomcat's dark eyes flashed in the dull afternoon sky. He stroked his small-caliber handgun in his lap and reflected that he enjoyed "maggot hunting," our name for Hells Angels. It was something that came "naturally" to him. I said nothing, afraid to move, to shift, worried that he might suddenly stop talking.

"I need to take a piss," he said and opened the door.

Meanwhile, I quietly snapped pictures of the gun he left on the seat with my cell phone and texted the images to the cover team. His need to urinate had disrupted the flow of conversation. Tomcat never elaborated on his really bad thing, and I had no way of reengaging him without arousing his suspicion. *A lost confession, a broken recorder, words drifting in the space.* Eventually I learned that he and Madman, the enforcer for the Maine chapter, had gunned down a Hells Angel in Maine on Milwaukee Jack's orders.

He "wanted revenge," Madman testified later in federal court. Weeks earlier, Hells Angels had beaten with ball-peen hammers two Outlaws at a gas station in Connecticut. "Milwaukee Jack told us to get two vests, however you have to get them. Or kill a Hells Angel." He told Madman to "take care of business." Madman and Tomcat had simply followed his orders.

They began hunting in Maine. Chilled, they stopped first for coffee at a café near a Hells Angels clubhouse. Madman, formerly a member of the Exiles, a Hells Angels support club, spotted an old "friend" driving by in his pickup truck. Madman and Tomcat followed the Hells Angel to his clubhouse, waited for him to open his door, and opened fire. Bullets shattered the Hells Angel's windshield, lodged in the side of his truck, and riddled the right side of his body.

Days later, Madman called JD. "I need a place to stay." He sounded frantic, breathless. With "all the attention in Maine," he needed to "leave town in a hurry." He and Tomcat arrived at our clubhouse close to midnight. JD ushered them inside. They sported new patches on their cuts: SS bolts. Madman paced our living room, skittish and pale, agitated by any sudden noise. Tomcat sat there coolly, staring straight ahead in stunned silence.

He lifted his shirt, traced fresh lightning bolts tattooed on his belly, and flashed me his new SS pin. "That Hells Angel wasn't the target," he whispered. We sat in the dark. Occasional headlights flashed over his face. "He was a crime of opportunity." Tomcat's pat explanation chilled me. I thought about the number of times I had idled my engine in our clubhouse driveway, afraid to open the car door. The Hells Angel's shooting had been so random, so quick. I worried about ambush, too, about being someone else's "opportunity."

"At least he didn't die." Tomcat shrugged as if that made the shooting okay. *No, but the Hells Angel would be on a ventilator for life.* Tomcat bunched up his face, looking like a child who had just cut the tail off a cat— not so bad, the animal still had legs and a head.

"Let's suppose that Maine thing *was* done by an Outlaw," he continued. "I'll tell you how it happened." I couldn't believe it. He was actually going to confess. "The HA looked at him funny."

"What do you mean?"

"Looked at him like, 'What the fuck you looking at, bro?' and then bam." Tomcat mimicked the Hells Angel's surprise and then the Outlaw's reaction as if he were staring at himself in the mirror trying on different expressions.

"I'm not afraid of the Hells Angels." He hugged his arms around his chest. "I'm afraid of the cops." He displayed the hilt of his gun tucked into his waistband.

"Shit, I'm afraid to mow my lawn. I take my gun with me when I take a piss."

I swallowed and pretended to be sympathetic. "They're not coming for you, bro."

"They're coming." Tomcat's eyes watered. "I can *feel* them." He described them like ghosts. "Ever try to shoot a ghost?"

※

"My gun jammed," Madman explained later in his federal trial. "Tomcat wanted to finish him off." He emptied his gun into the Hells Angel's truck and reloaded. But Madman objected, "I *wanted* my gun to jam. I pulled lightly on the trigger." Madman demonstrated for the jury. "Tomcat . . . he's the madman." Following the shooting, Madman tossed their guns over a bridge into a raging river. He gazed at the panel with large sleepy eyes, his head pronounced and unframed by a skullcap. In bold black ink across his throat he had tattooed MOM.

"You feel let down?" the prosecutor asked. For all of Madman's bravado, none of the Outlaws had visited him in prison.

"A little." Madman shrugged. Once a former wrestler, he shriveled on the stand.

"You feel used?"

"I followed orders."

"[Milwaukee Jack] told you to sell drugs?"

"He said times are tough. Brothers need to do what they need to do to get by."

"Even kill?"

Madman didn't respond, didn't disclose that Milwaukee Jack's orders to kill had been revised, that he was supposed to "just fuck [him] up."

≋

Murder was expensive. The Outlaws devised a scheme to increase club profits. L'il Dave, the Copper Region vice president, suggested we install illegal gambling machines in our Petersburg clubhouse; after all, the Lexington chapter had successfully recouped nearly $24,000 in profits over the last eight months. The Outlaws used the funds to pay club dues and outstanding bills. If we owned such machines, L'il Dave coaxed, we, too, could earn revenue for our chapter. It sounded like a good idea, but not for the reasons L'il Dave recited. We figured, with a gambling machine in our clubhouse, we could entice Outlaws to play right into our hands. That was the fascination of undercover work: Improvisation sometimes led to chance revelations, to exactly the criminal enterprise we hoped to label and ultimately convict the Outlaws.

The machines arrived the next day. They resembled video arcade games, but a simple switch converted the screens to poker and blackjack. The owners, stone-faced Mafia thugs, reviewed with us the operating rules: They expected to receive 40 percent of our profits. One wore diamond studs in his right lobe, a garish ring on his pinkie, and a thick gold necklace that surrounded his throat like rope. The other looked half formed, as if he had spurted from a tube into a fleshy blob and forgot to stretch. Smashed in and undefined, he had a lazy eye that made it impossible to look at him when he spoke. I added gambling to my job description and regularly fed the machines with government funds, mindful of entrapment. Soon, other Outlaws who visited our clubhouse took my cue.

And once a month the Mafia men returned to collect.

Meanwhile, M & M grumbled that he needed help with background investigations. He complained at a recent Church meeting about being "short staffed" and the paperwork was "mountainous." Hearing M & M's whines, I proposed to Gringo that he volunteer me for the position at the next bosses' meeting. Why not? It was a way in, a way to manipulate the game and make M & M think it was his idea. Gringo insisted to M & M that I would be "great, since I had paralegal experience." I slid into the opportunity and soon met with M & M regularly to review the club's records. I checked references on prospective members, identified addresses on applications, alerted M & M of fictitious or incomplete criminal histories. I made copies, one for the feds and the other for M &M. I provided synopses of my findings. M & M seemed pleased.

And with his paperwork in order, he could now turn to more pressing issues: killing Hells Angels. At first, he proposed that we randomly "burn houses around the Charlotte and North Carolina clubhouses" and smoke them out. The Hells Angels might plan to use them as fronts to launch attacks against the Outlaws. Snuff suggested we start with the Hells Angel's tattoo shop in Richmond, adding that killing the owner would be a good way for us to "earn our SS bolts." This was *war*, not crime. Snuff suggested we start with a high-powered rifle from the bed of a pickup truck and "blow the Hells Angel away while he smoked on his back porch."

He was tickled by his ingenuity, then he frowned. If the rifle was "too cumbersome," he could teach us how to make bombs. Mostly he wanted our commitment. "The murder should happen next week," he said, after he had a chance to obtain "professional-grade explosives." Snuff seemed winded by the conversation, and I realized then that I was looking at an old man. In his midfifties, Snuff aged like a dog, seven years at a stretch. He had been a criminal a long time, had already served twelve years in prison for initiating violent acts as a member of another motorcycle gang. Killing was breakfast conversation, as significant to him as discussing coffee brands.

"He expects us to kill him next week." I frowned.

M & M discussed a possible alibi with Gringo "just in case" things got shitty.

But a month later, M & M was "still working on the explosives issue."

✖

Meanwhile, Les shared how he'd assaulted a Hells Angel the week before in Rock Hill, South Carolina. The rival had "strayed too close" to the Outlaws' clubhouse; "no more free travel," he declared. No rival club had permission to "pass through" Outlaws territory without risking attack. Then he suggested any number of ways the agents and I could retaliate if we ever saw a stray: beatings, burnings, "even grenades."

Impatient with our lack of progress, Snuff suggested we conduct surveillance "to facilitate the assaults," find the enemy, and at the next regional bosses' meeting in Lexington, members produced maps that highlighted the Hells Angels clubhouses and homes. The marks resembled yellow blood spatter.

Murder, of course, was out of the question. We all knew that. We just needed a clever way to extricate ourselves from the plot without arousing suspicion, without blowing the investigation, without revealing our cover. We had to finesse the ending, position our players for the takedown, and thwart an all-out war.

29

Road's End

As I drove through neighborhoods in North Carolina searching for Hells Angels, I felt an impending sense of dread. What would I do if I saw one? I had orders to shoot on sight. And if anyone learned I didn't, I could be killed or stripped of my patch. I replayed what-if scenarios in my head, always prepared just in case. If the Outlaws attacked, I planned to participate, but with my fists, never a weapon. If an Outlaw offered me a gun, I would accept it but never shoot. If I saw a Hells Angel and I was alone, I would pretend I didn't see him.

A boy pedaled furiously across his lawn to me on a plastic big wheel, oblivious of the threat of violence. In any war there comes a point when the battle is over, when the soldiers are too weary to go on. We'd been working the gang for nearly two years; we'd patched in. We were Outlaws. We were done. We had gathered enough intelligence on the gang to put them away for years. We had confessions to attempted murders, to brutal assaults, to conspiracies to kill. But we could always hunt more. The more people who trusted us, the more intelligence we could gather. War was an addiction, but the barbed-wire fence surrounding my family was beginning to rust. It was time to go home.

I felt constantly sick and eerily lucky. All of us had dodged bullets, but exhaustion led to mistakes, and as tired and dragged down as we all felt, we knew it was only a matter of time before we slipped. Hunting was no longer something the Outlaws discussed; it was something they planned to do. We borrowed time. M & M would soon produce the "professional-grade" explosives. The Hells Angel who owned the tattoo shop would smoke one night on his back porch and notice fireflies flickering in the dark like sparks.

Snuff's proposed rifle loomed in my thoughts. We could stall him for only so long.

><

Three weeks before the government raids happened, I relocated my family. Like the Halloween town the Outlaws had rented, I quickly dissolved my makeshift set and chose another backdrop, a place where I could live steady. Steady was nice. Steady had its own heartbeat. I loaded our few possessions into the bed of a U-Haul and began the journey home. I told the Outlaws I was visiting my sick mother. Relief coursed through me. *I was almost there.*

Then Johnny died.

He crashed his motorcycle. His death tugged at me like a vibration. All Outlaws had to attend the funerals of members. If I didn't attend Johnny's, the whole investigation, everything we had worked so hard to achieve, might unravel prematurely. My wife seethed at the news. "There's a death every week," she observed. With all the talk of war and hunting, death by bike was the biggest threat to the Outlaws, to any motorcycle club. The highway stretched before me, dark and inviting. And I let her go one more time.

Gringo met me at the airport in his undercover Cadillac and we drove

to the South Carolina clubhouse where the Outlaws had preserved Johnny's body for viewing. His smashed face was pieced together like a rubber
mask. We gathered in the stuffy warehouse. Portable air-conditioning units
cooled Johnny's body, but the sweet stench of rot permeated the large room
like a cloying perfume. It seemed oddly fitting that he should wind up in a
box. Members saluted Johnny with beer; some openly wept. He still wore
his massive rings.

Tension rippled over the body as news of a Hells Angel sniping spread.

"The fucker shot Ho Jo in broad daylight." M & M frowned, looking
pissed, not sad. "The bullet pierced his oxygen tank. He died." His words
knocked around the space, sobering all who listened. They thought it
criminal to target a walking dead, an Outlaw already physically weak, his
life reduced to a tank and a motorized scooter. But debate heated over
"who shot first," as if that were the catalyst.

"We're in a *war*," one Outlaw explained to reporters later. "We're not a
gang. People always slap that thing on us. We're about brotherhood and
riding bikes."

One actually blamed the police for the long-standing gang feud. "They
want the Hells Angels and Outlaws to be at war, because if [we] get along,
they lose their intelligence."

"We're really private people," another Outlaw insisted. "No one in the
media is interested in the positive things done by the club, the fund-raisers
for burned children and toy stocking runs for the Salvation Army. . . . We
used to be renegades. . . . Now we're just normal."

≫≪

As the night wore on, members snored next to Johnny's body, oblivious of
the rot. The atmosphere morphed into a ghoulish tableau as the living
drank to be unconscious and the dead wished for the choice. All around
me, mirrors reflected lines of coke, bottles and cans spilled, pizza cartons
and half-eaten wings scattered on tables and carpet. I thought about Ho
Jo. He had been a decorated Vietnam veteran. He owned a tattoo shop,

minded his own business. Just like the Hells Angel down the street from us, the one Snuff ordered us to "smoke."

Ho Jo's death was payback for what happened in Maine.

❊

Tomcat plunked himself next to Johnny. "When I go, the cops are going with me." He sobered, looking pale and older than his years. Gray singed his temple. Stress ravaged him. "I have nightmares every night," he said, wiping condensation from his bottle. "I think about death all the time, my head split open like a pumpkin." He looked at me, and the coldness in his gaze chilled me. "Ever have those kinds of thoughts?"

I swallowed, shook my head.

Tomcat worried that Madman would talk. "He's been arrested, you know." I nodded. "I'm never getting caught." He finished his beer. In the shadowy dark he looked like Johnny's ghost. "When they come for me," he elaborated, "I'll open fire."

I didn't talk him out of it. I didn't believe him. Every criminal spoke of suicide by cop. I had. If Tomcat did execute his plan, he would catapult himself into legend; he would become the great "Outlaw cop killer," a label more prestigious than the SS bolts tattooed across his belly. He would achieve in death what he never managed in life: purpose. Tomcat dozed into his nightmare, his head resting on Johnny's glazed white arm. I switched off my recorder. In the haze, in the quiet, I processed Tomcat's exit, haunted by his promise. He would rather die an Outlaw than face a life behind bars, forced to relive his fractured past. Being a gangster was part of his blueprint, part of his identity. He accepted his scarred present, his life without future.

Johnny was lucky, he said. He died the way he lived, with no responsibility, no repercussion, a true Outlaw.

"He finished well."

❊

Johnny's funeral procession the next day resembled a presidential caval-
cade. Because my arm was in a sling, I led the pack of over three hundred
"marauding sociopaths" in my undercover SUV. Outlaws support clubs
roared alongside us. Crowds on the sidewalks parted for the procession;
police fanned around us like paparazzi, snapping photos, recording identities, absorbing the bearded faces, swastikas, and skulls. The Outlaws, still
in costume, played solemn. Acting was self-preservation. Most had to
know that the body in the box—calm faced and frighteningly ordinary—
could just as easily be them next week, next year. It was what I would have
become had I stayed a criminal. Family mixed with bikers and shed real
tears. The club had its own minister, who presided and blessed the body.
Every Outlaw signed a legal agreement when he joined, specifying whether
he wished to have a biker or "traditional" funeral. It was important to know
how they wanted to be remembered.

They were "Outlaws forever, forever Outlaws."

><

"You think he'll do it?" I shared Tomcat's suicide threat with JD only to
learn that Tomcat had also warned him.

"We have to prepare like he will."

On a quiet June morning just before dawn, federal agents, state police
troopers, and Old Orchard Beach police descended on a small house at
5 Sandy Circle. They crouched behind bushes, crunched along a gravel
path. The skies, heavy with impending rain, held a sense of foreboding.
A top window cracked open. A curtain fluttered in the breeze. The agents
wore bulletproof vests and full riot raid gear, and brought videotape and
an armored tank. Then gunfire shattered the stillness. Four ATF agents,
armed with rifles, returned fire. And in less than seven seconds, Tomcat's
life ended. Police found his body in the top bedroom, still clutching
his empty ten-shot .40 caliber semi-automatic pistol. Propped against
the wall, his rifle and shotgun waited beneath a banner that read GOD
FORGIVES, OUTLAWS DON'T. Tomcat's wife sobbed on the bed beside him,

spattered in his blood; across the hall, their young daughter blinked back tears.

"The whole scene was unsettling," a neighbor reported.

The word "unsettling" repeated in the media—definitive and empty.

Tomcat's death hit me especially hard. He represented what I might have become had I embraced that life. He had a family, too.

※

Meanwhile, on Milwaukee's south side, federal agents dressed in bullet-proof vests and full raid gear stormed the Outlaws' headquarters, an ominous black fortress boldly painted with skulls and pistons. They arrested twenty-seven of Milwaukee Jack's minions and associates and charged them in a sealed twelve-count indictment with operating a criminal enterprise that engaged in attempted murder, kidnapping, assault, robbery, extortion, witness intimidation, narcotics distribution, illegal gambling, and weapons violations. The government lauded the captures as "another aggressive attempt by the Department of Justice to dismantle" a gang "whose entire environment" revolved around violence." The Outlaws decried the arrests as nothing more than a "witch hunt to justify the money" expended on Operation Black Diamond.

The raids that spanned multiple states including Wisconsin, Maine, Montana, North Carolina, Tennessee, South Carolina, and Virginia produced an arsenal of illegal firearms—Mac-11s, Uzis, machine guns, assault rifles, sawed-off shotguns, small-caliber handguns, explosives—and large quantities of marijuana, cocaine, and oxycodone. With purported gangsters behind bars, the government prepared to litigate against a "violent enterprise" that ruled by "fear and intimidation" and "live[d], breathe[d], and celebrate[d] that violence."

But prosecutions against motorcycle gangs have notoriously led to deadly consequences for witnesses. The case of the *Milwaukee Sentinel* carrier, Larry Anstett, still smarted in people's memories. The teen blew up when he picked up a bomb disguised as a present. It had been placed on a car owned by a member of a rival motorcycle gang who had testified against the Outlaws. Six unsolved murders followed Anstett's bombing. Survivors of the explosion (both Outlaws and civilians) purported to have no knowledge of who placed the bomb on the car. Among those executed, an elderly couple and a wife and son found shot to death in their home.

In addition to murder, gangs, including the Outlaws, have litigated (and won) lawsuits against law enforcement for allegedly exercising "excessive force" and "overkill" when conducting raids. One account reported a "full-scale armed raid" on a biker gang's headquarters, replete with "snipers on rooftops, bulletproof vests and a tank" after a woman was found bleeding on the pavement outside the gang's clubhouse door. Police arrived with "all the boys, all the toys, and all the weaponry," and aimed "to create shock and awe, but all they achieved was to make a gang of hairy, scary outlaws look like sympathetic characters and the victims of excessive force."

"America is a wonderful place," one biker remarked to reporters after emerging victorious in his lawsuit. "Thanks to the police . . . every one of [us] has a new motorcycle and I've bought a very nice house in the country."

Milwaukee Jack sued, too, complaining of "mental anguish, anxiety, emotional distress, and loss of enjoyment of life" as a result of police harassment. Law enforcement arrested him after reports that he was laying in wait on his clubhouse rooftop armed with long rifles. His version: He was fixing a leaky roof. "Nineteen officers rushed the clubhouse without warrants, shoving guns in our faces." When reporters asked some of the Outlaws to explain the long rifle officers recovered from the rooftop, one remarked, "You know we don't talk."

><

Of the twenty-seven indicted, twenty-three entered guilty pleas. Four proceeded to trial in a federal Richmond court; two were acquitted, and the remaining two, despite the threat of retaliation, did testify for the government. Madman pled guilty to conspiracy charges and insisted he executed

Milwaukee Jack's orders when he shot the Hells Angel outside the club-house in Canaan, Maine.

"He's a wannabe national enforcer." A defense witness, an Outlaw named Barboza, dismissed Madman as a "rogue" who "liked to pump himself up." Barboza fidgeted on the stand, and looked to Jack for approval after he uttered each statement, as if he had been given a script in advance and was warned about improvisation. He conceded that some Outlaws had acted like apes, "thumping their chests, yelling and screaming," but as far as "organized crime," "never, no way."

Jack's public defender in closing argument dismissed Madman's accusations as "ridiculous"—there "was no organized war against the Hells Angels." Jack was a grandfather, a "working stiff," a "regular guy" who operated a small trucking company. He "doesn't smoke and has an occasional sip of Crown Royal." "A guy like that presents a good face for this group," his lawyer finished. She was partially right. Jack's sparse criminal history and "legitimate" salary gave him the appearance of a businessman, the perfect disguise for a gangster. Letters to the court described him as "hardworking," "dedicated," a man who "never quit before the job was finished." With a wife who'd overdosed and a son convicted of nine burglaries, Jack still considered himself a "family man" and someone who never kept his Outlaw status a secret. After a two-week trial and four days of deliberation, the jury of five women and seven men were hung.

Jack's attorney remarked that her client might be "the president of the Outlaws, but not the leader of a criminal conspiracy. Like any other organization, the club is not necessarily responsible for the actions of its members, much like corporations and law enforcement agencies." But that was precisely the government's point: Though the indictments charged individuals, it insisted that the members existed as Outlaws in order to expand their criminal empire.

Jurors believed as much when they convicted Les, the former Copper Region boss and current vice president of the Outlaws' South Carolina Rock

Hill chapter, of conspiracy to commit racketeering and to commit violence in aid of racketeering.

The government retried Jack, portraying him as the club's puppeteer. Prosecutors called him "the worst of the worst," a criminal who "spent decades dedicated to a criminal way of life," a man who needed to spend "decades in prison paying for his crimes." And jurors wised up; they convicted Jack of racketeering and committing violent crimes against the Hells Angels. U.S. District Court Judge Henry Hudson called Jack a "criminal architect" who designed "a culture of violence." He sentenced him to twenty years in prison.

And while the press insisted that his conviction struck "a crippling blow to [the] violent motorcycle gang," made Virginia a "safer place," and transformed the agents who "put their lives on the line" into heroes, we all still lived at full throttle, still wary of the day Jack would be released to rebuild.

We had reason to worry. Snuff's attorney, too, begged for leniency, said a "maximum sentence" would mean that her client would "never again see the light of day." When she wheeled Snuff to the podium, she hoped for sympathy. But he looked no less a monster in jail cotton. He pled guilty to conspiracy to violate federal racketeering laws. His worst repercussion: forfeiture of his motorcycle. His lawyer recited his many health issues: "emphysema, diabetes, chronic pain, kidney stones." "He could easily *die* in prison," she insisted. But the judge was unmoved. He pushed his readers higher on his nose, glared at Snuff's imposing body in the wheelchair, and waited for him to grovel.

"He's changed his life around," his lawyer tried again.

"That's unfortunate" and "a little too late," the judge groused. He directed his barbs at Snuff: "You went into this [endeavor] with your eyes wide open."

"I know I screwed up." Snuff shrugged. "Stick a fork in me, I'm finished."

The judge sentenced him to five years in federal prison.

In the end, most, like Snuff, pled for deliverance. They begged for mercy and concession. They insisted they hunted maggots, not people, not humans with conscience. None showed remorse. Instead they boasted of consistency and flaunted the most important "tool" of a gangster—the ability "to kill [their] conscience." As "opportunists," they made deals, time in exchange for voyeurism, for a glimpse into their world, for a chance to stop their growth. They flipped on each other like a crafty outlay of dominoes, each the other's own worst enemy.

"The best witnesses are gang members," the police explained. "Most have shifting loyalties, scores to settle, lasting grudges, and scorned friends." *It doesn't take much.*

As the members toppled, one by one, and went off to prison to live out lonely existences behind bars, the agents, too, resumed solo acts. Bobby returned to Iraq; Gringo and JD recycled into new undercover assignments in undisclosed areas of the country. And I quietly disappeared, comforted by the knowledge that I had helped to "suffocate a criminal octopus" whose hold over the East Coast had released a violent ink so debilitating it nearly crippled the communities suctioned in its tentacles. But like every sea creature, it was only a matter of time before it reproduced, mutated, revived, and spread new malignant cells.

Aftermath

❧

OPERATION 22 GREEN

The following defendants were convicted of murder, manslaughter, assault with a deadly weapon, and/or narcotics-related charges—all felonies—either by plea or a jury trial.

BANDIT (Adam Lannon). Assault with a deadly weapon; one year in jail and one strike.

BUBBA (Kenneth Willoughby). Assault with a deadly weapon and distribution and manufacture of a controlled substance; two years and one strike.

ELMO (Scott Hawthorne). Assault with a deadly weapon and distribution of marijuana.

ERIC (Eric Zwarkowski). Assault with a deadly weapon.

JOE (Josiah Apduhan). Assault with a deadly weapon.

KNUCKLES (Keith Ennis). Assault with a deadly weapon and distribution of methamphetamine; four years in state prison.

POWDER (Lawrence Shefchick Jr.). Two counts possession to distribute dangerous weapons. Five years' probation; two strikes.

PSYCHO (Scott Sikoff). Assault with a deadly weapon and distribution of marijuana; one year and one strike.

RHINO (Ryan Matteson). Voluntary manslaughter and attempted burglary; one year and one strike.

RUST (Rodney Rust). Assault with a deadly weapon; one year and one strike.

TERRIBLE (Terry Sherwood). Distribution and manufacture of a controlled substance; consecutive five years in state prison, ten in federal.

TWIST (Daniel Lee Foreman). Murder, life sentence.

VINNY (Vincent Mariano). Distribution of marijuana; one year and one strike.

WALTER (Walter Merritt). Assault with a deadly weapon.

MURDERED

TRUCK (Tim Quarders).

OPERATION BLACK DIAMOND

The following defendants were convicted of RICO-related crimes (conspiracy to engage in racketeering activities and to engage in violence in aid of racketeering) by plea or a jury trial, and were sentenced to federal prison.

ALIBI (Christopher Timbers). Thirty-seven, Outlaw in the Manassas/Shenandoah Valley chapter of the Copper Region. Convicted at trial; seven and a half years.

JOSEPH ALLMAN. Forty-six, Outlaw in the Red region, previously president and enforcer in the Maine chapter. Fifteen months.

BRETT (Brett Longendyke). Thirty-two, Outlaw in the Copper Region and served as the Manassas/Shenandoah Valley chapter enforcer. Pled guilty; four years.

BULL (John Banthem). Forty-six, president of a new prospective Outlaws chapter in Montana. Pled guilty; twenty-four months.

CHRIS (Chris Gagner). Thirty-seven, Outlaw in the Copper Region and president and treasurer of the Asheville, North Carolina, chapter. Twelve months.

HARRY (Harry Rhyne McCall). Fifty-three, Outlaw in the Copper Region, Lexington, North Carolina, chapter. Convicted at trial; thirteen and a half years.

JASON (Mark Jason Fiel). Thirty-seven, former Outlaw in the Copper Region and former leader in the Manassas/Shenandoah Valley chapter. Sentenced to 114 months or 9.5 years.

LES (Leslie Werth). Forty-seven, Outlaw and vice president of the Rock Hill, South Carolina, chapter; previously boss of the Copper Region. Convicted at trial; twenty-two months.

LITTLE DAVID (David Lowry). Forty-fine, Outlaw Copper Region boss. Cooperated with the government and pled guilty to reduced charges; nine years.

MADMAN (Michael Pedini). Thirty-nine, Outlaw in the Red Region and former enforcer in the Northern Maine chapter. Pled guilty to conspiracy charges; sixty-three months in federal prison.

M & M (Michael Mariaca). Fifty, former president of the Outlaws' Rock Hill, South Carolina, chapter and Copper Region enforcer. Cooperated with the government and pled guilty to reduced charges; nine years.

MILWAUKEE JACK (Jack Rosga). Fifty-three, national boss of the Outlaws organization and member of the Gold Region, Milwaukee, Wisconsin, chapter. Convicted at a second trial; twenty years.

MICHAEL SMITH. Fifty-one, Outlaw in the Copper Region and president of the Hickory, North Carolina, chapter. Forty-two months.

SNUFF (Steven Mark Fiel). Fifty-nine, Outlaw in the Copper Region and former leader in the Manassas/Shenandoah Valley chapter. Pled guilty; five years.

TAZ (Thomas Benvie). Forty-one, Outlaw in the Red Region and president of the Maine chapter. Fifteen months.

VERN (James Townsend). Forty-four, president of the Outlaws' Lexington, North Carolina, chapter. Two months.

KILLED

TOMCAT (Thomas Mayne). Fifty-nine, Outlaw in the Red Region and former regional treasurer and enforcer. He was gunned down.

CONDUCTING ILLEGAL GAMBLING BUSINESS

L'IL DAVE (Harold Herndon). Forty-eight, former vice president of the Lexington, North Carolina, Outlaws chapter. Pled guilty; sixteen months.

ROBBERY

IVAN (Mark Lester). Fifty-five, Outlaw in the Knoxville, Tennessee, chapter and served as the boss of the Grey Region. Twenty-seven months.

DRUG CHARGES AND POSSESSION OF A FIREARM

BRIAN (Brian McDermott). Fifty, Outlaw in the Copper Region's Hickory, North Carolina, chapter. Pled guilty to distribution of methamphetamine and possession of firearms in furtherance of a drug crime; eight years.

ACQUITTED

LYTNIN (Mark Spradling). Fifty-two, former treasurer of the Outlaws' Copper Region.

REBEL (William Davey). Forty-six, Outlaw in the Copper Region and formerly the enforcer of the Asheville, North Carolina, chapter.